COLORADO
POSTAL
HISTORY:

the post offices.

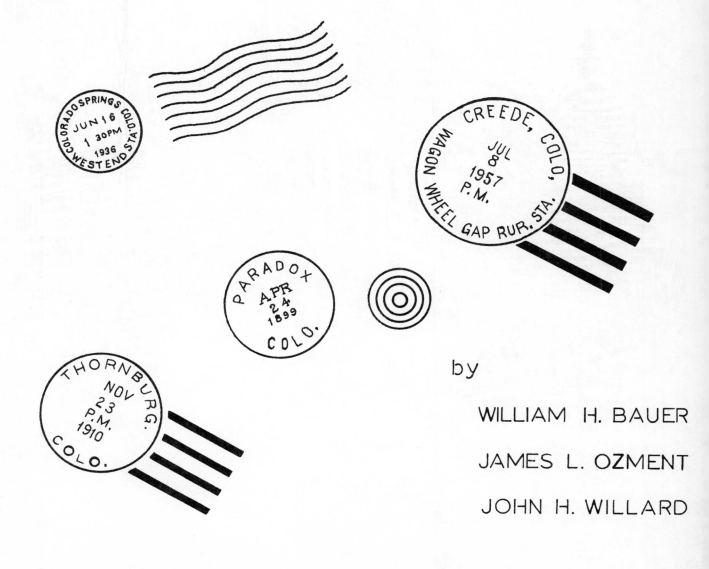

by

WILLIAM H. BAUER

JAMES L. OZMENT

JOHN H. WILLARD

TABLE OF CONTENTS

ILLUSTRATIONS OF COLORADO COVERS

POSTAL HISTORY OF COLORADO

INTRODUCTION

In spite of a rich potential for postal history research, Colorado remains a near void in philatelic literature. Almost all of the previously published material consists of short articles that deal with a single office or a restricted period of time. To date only two studies have appeared that prepare the way for a detailed investigation of the postal history of the region that is now the state of Colorado. In 1957 Sheldon Dike published a list of the post offices established during the Territorial Period (1861-1876), and in 1970 W. H. Bauer prepared a summary listing of the recorded changes in Colorado Post Office names from 1859 to 1970. Currently David L. Jarrett is researching an in depth study of the Territorial Post Offices, including postmasters and postal markings. However, the Territorial Period is only a small portion of Colorado history and although 350 post offices were established during that 18 year span nearly 2,200 additional offices have existed for varying lengths of time since Colorado achieved statehood in 1876.

The first post office to be established in Colorado is still a point of contention. From Post Office Department records it appears that in late December 1858 an office was authorized for "Auroria", Nebraska Territory (Bauer 1970) with Samuel S. Curtis as the postmaster. It can be proved that Mr. Curtis was in "Denver" on Christmas Day 1858, but the location of Auroria is uncertain. The most likely site is on the Cache La Poudre River near La Porte, at what was later "Colona". On January 18, 1859 post offices were authorized for Auraria and Montana in Kansas Territory, and for St. Vrain in Nebraska Territory. However, the earliest recorded "Colorado" covers are from Coraville which was not authorized until Mar 22, 1859. Thus, although not the first authorized, Coraville may well have been the first post office to actually begin operating within what is now Colorado.

The initial period of settlement in Colorado began with the 1859 Gold Rush, and throughout the remainder of the 19th Century each subsequent mining boom opened new areas of the state, and led to a flurry of postal development. During the last decade of the 19th Century and the first quarter of the 20th Century, the emphasis shifted to agriculture, and a much larger area of the state entered a period of expanding population. Since 1930 the extent of the postal system in Colorado has steadily declined, with far more discontinuances than openings. In recent years only an occasional new post office has been established and the trend is to conversion of the smaller post offices to Rurual Branches and eventual discontinuation.

Throughout the period of growth nearly every new mining camp, or cross-roads general store felt a need for its "own" post office and most achieved official status quite early in their life cycle. However, many passed into history in a matter of months, or at most a few years.

The history of many offices is complicated by their mobility. Post offices were moved from one camp or cross-roads to another with great regularity, often depending on the availability of an individual qualified and willing to serve as postmaster. With this mobility, and the casual attitude of the U. S. Post Office Department with regards to the names of the post offices, it becomes difficult to trace or establish the continuity of many small offices. Hence, a review of the post offices needs to encompass a detailed analysis of the names and locations, both in space and time, of all named settlements within the area. At present the principal need is for a basic listing of the post offices that have existed in Colorado, and this publication is an attempt to achieve that aim and thus to provide a framework for more detailed subsequent studies.

The authors have, as an eventual goal, the production of an encyclopedic listing of all settlements within Colorado, briefly identifying their location and raison d' etre. Such a study would be integrated through postal history to detail the development of the written communications network within Colorado. This would include tabulations of the postmasters, a study of the postal markings, and a review of the mail routes, both stage and rail. Some of this information has already been accumulated, but considerably more is needed, and the authors hope that this book will generate additional interest in Colorado postal history and encourage others to contribute their knowledge to our project.

SOURCES OF INFORMATION

The prime source for the information contained in this book is the Post Office Department "Records of Postmaster Appointments" for the Territory and State of Colorado. This is avilable on microfilm from the National Archieves for the period from 1859 to about 1931. Later records are also available, but may have to be examined at the Post Office Department in Washington. These "Records of Appointment" provide the dates of establishment and discontinuance, the changes in office name, and the postmasters and the dates of their appointments. For the period subsequent to 1931, reference has been made to the monthly, quarterly, and annual reports of the Post Office Department. These were published on a monthly basis until June 1944, and on a quarterly basis until April 1953. Since then, only the annual report has been issued (other than the weekly "Postal Bulletin"). Although these periodic reports list the establishments, discontinuaces, and changes in name, they do not report the effective dates.

Beginning in 1874 the Post Office Department has issued an annual "Postal Guide" (between 1937 and 1955 it was a bi-annual publication) which presents three basic listings: alphabetic, alphabetic by state, and alphabetic by state and county. The guides for most of the years since 1876 have been examined and used as a cross-check of the post offices listed on the microfilmed records. This cross-check did reveal some errors, for example an office in Jefferson County, Ohio was erroneously recorded under Jefferson County, Colorado. The major importance of using the guides is to question whether several offices operated during the full time span indicated by the records of appointment, and in some cases whether an office ever operated at all.

Prior to 1874 similar listings appeared as a "Post Office Directory" or as a "List of Post Offices and Postmasters". Copies of these publications are scarce and only the years 1869-1870 have been available for reference.

Several additional sources have been used to fill gaps in the records described above. Issues of the weekly "Postal Bulletin", published since 1967, have been reviewed, and prior to publication of a second volume we hope to have access to a more complete file of that journal. There are other private atlases which list or identify the post offices existing at various times, but these have not been of much assistance. The personal knowledge of the authors has pointed to many problems and helped to resolve others. Material from the Authors' personal collections, particularly "last day" covers have been used to fill some of the gaps in the post-1931 records.

One Source that has not been utilized for this book is the published newspapers of Colorado. They could be of considerable assistance in regards to the 19th century postal history of Colorado, but such a review would be a formidable task, since these early papers are scattered in libraries throughout the United States.

PROBLEMS AND LIMITATIONS

Some the problems encountered in preparing this book are inherent in the sources used. The "Records of Appointment" were recorded by hand in a variety of scripts and inks of many densities. This results, now, in portions of the microfilm being difficult to read and in uncertainty as to the exact spelling of some office names or of the dates of establishment and discontinuance. The cross-check, using the annual guides, has, we hope, resolved the problems in spelling and did point to some of the mis-readings of dates. However, the guides also contain a few spelling errors, and undoubtedly errors in dates remain to be recognized.

The dates of establishment, discontinuance, and re-establishment listed in Section A are the dates recorded by the Post Office Department.

They should not be considered as absolute limits for the period of existence of the office. It took time to provide supplies to a new post office and most probably operation did not begin until days, weeks, or even months after the official date of establishment. It is possible that some began operation prior to their official date. An individual, having applied for a post office, and believing its granting a mere formality, could have made arrangements with a cooperative established office for a stock of stamps and the dispatch of mail. Actual events might have denied him the office or assigned it a different name. Such a situation would explain the reported existence of manuscript cancels from "Black Pine" and "Cholerow" and others which do not appear in the Post Office Department records.

Dates of discontinuance may be even more uncertain. A post office could cease operating with the departure or death of the postmaster, and it may have been much later, after failure to find a replacement, that the office was officially reported closed.

For many post offices, there were short periods of discontinued status. The Fort Collins Post Office was supposedly closed from October 19, 1865 to May 12, 1866; however, a clear April 3, 1866 cancellation exists. It could be an error in setting the date, or the discontinuance might not have been effected.

The lack of exact information for the post 1931 period has been previously mentioned. Fortunately the decline in post office changes during this time reduces the problem to what we feel is an acceptable level so as not to prevent publication at this time. This problem would be resolved with access to the proper records.

A major problem does exist in interpreting the records, particularly in regards to the changes in post office names and to a lesser extent the continuity of many offices. This can be summarized by saying that the Post Office Department was more concerned with administrative continuity than with the physical position of a post office. Thus, many of the changes in name truly include the closing of an office in one settlement and the opening of a new facility at another settlement, even though the same postmaster served at both locations. In some instances the "re-establishment" of a post office was at a site well removed from the original location, but no mention of this fact appears in the Records of Appointments. It is to resolve these situations that the study of all settlement names and locations are necessary.

An excellent example of the complexity of this problem is the relationship of the offices of Baldwin, Mount Carbon and Cameville in Gunnison County. Reference to the town list (Section A) will show that there were two Baldwins, that Mount Carbon was discontinued and re-established, and that the name of Mount Carbon was changed to Baldwin. The original Baldwin was located on a northerly fork of Ohio Creek and served a large coal mine on the north flank of Mount Carbon. A post office was established there on

September 17, 1883 and discontinued on March 31, 1902. The settlement of
Mount Carbon was on Ohio Creek, on the south flank of the mountain. The
Mount Carbon Post Office was first established on August 26, 1884, discon-
tinued on July 28, 1891, re-established on March 16, 1901, and on June 26,
1909 the name was changed to Baldwin. This change in name occurred after
the coal company had shifted its operation to the Ohio Creek side of Mount
Carbon in order to gain easier access to the coal seam. An early 20th century map of the region brings out another point. It identifies the Mount
Carbon office with its change to Baldwin, but also locates a "Mount Carbon
P. O." some distance further up Ohio Creek. This was most probably the
Mount Carbon of 1884-1891, and the re-establishment in 1901 was not at
the previous location. No mention of this appears in the Records of Appointments. The situation is further complicated by the fact that Cameville, located at the junction of Ohio Creek and the North Fork was orig-
inally known as "Baldwin" although its post office never bore that name.

        The discussion of Mount Carbon brings to attention another
problem inherent in the records. The records are in five segments: 1861-
1863, 1864-1878, 1879-1891, 1892-1901, and 1902-1929. If an office was
discontinued and later re-established within one of these periods, the
"re-establishment" is almost always clearly indicated and the continuity
of the name is established. But, this is not always true of the continuity
of location, such as with Mount Carbon. However, if the re-establishment
was during a later period, there is usually no indication as to whether
this was an entirely new office or a reopening of an older facility. The
situation becomes even less clear if a subdivision of the county occurred
in the meantime, and the office is listed under two different counties.

        There is considerable work to be done in the area of "physical
location". Basically there are four types of problems to be solved: 1)
was the re-establishment of an office at the same general location as the
previous operation?; 2) does a change in name indicate a new name for the
same facility or the movement of the office to another settlement?; 3)
did post offices with the same name, but of different periods represent
the re-establishment of a previous office or the creation of a new facility?;
4) which, if any post offices underwent major shifts in location that are
not indicated in the Records of Appointment?

        With these possibilities it is not unlikely that the reader will
discover an entry that conflicts with his personal knowledge. In preparing
this book a number of maps and reports have been studied, and many ambiguous
situations have been resolved. Many problems, both obvious and unrecognized
are undoubtedly still present in the listings. Reference to additional maps
and government records will help. However, the reader can be of great assistance by referring to the authors any personal knowledge which will correct an error or clarify a relationship. We welcome correspondence with
other collectors of Colorado postal history, or with students of Colorado
history.

ACKNOWLEDGEMENTS

The authors wish to express their thanks for the knowledge, suggestions, and encouragement provided by W. C. Aichele, R. W. Helbock, D. L. Jarrett, R. L. Newburn, Jr., L. N. Persson, E. C. Peyton, D. Stone and C. Tuthill. Particular appreciation is due Arthur Rupert for his valuable assistance in identifying the Rural Stations and Branches of Colorado. Charles Waltz and Richard S. Johnston of the Denver Region U. S. Post Office, willingly supplied from the Post Office Department files information on the stations, branches, and rural establishments which is unavailable from any other source.

Thanks are also due Sheldon Dike for his preliminary work and to the late Robert Baughman whose format for the listing of Kansas Post Offices has been adapted for this book.

We wish to again make a concerted plea for assistance in continuing this research project. In particular we are in need of maps or published information (newspapers, books, or articles) that can resolve the many existing problems. The location of readily accessible files of the Postal Bulletins or of specific issues of the Postal Guide and its predecessor would be greatly appreciated.

Hotel DENVER

GLENWOOD SPRINGS
COLORADO

DOYLEVILLE
NOV
28
...M.
1967
81225

JIM OZMENT
109 IDAHO - APT. #9W
PUEBLO, COLO. 81005

8

A DECADE OF ACHIEVEMENT

JOHN H. WILLARD
1025 MONROE ST.
DENVER, COLO. 80206

After 5 days, return to

RED MOUNTAIN, Ouray Co., COLO.

Mrs. Kate Miller,
No 1216 Larimer St.,
Denver,
Colo.

RETURN IN FIVE DAYS TO

The Otto Kuehne Preserving Co.
TOPEKA, KANSAS
Denver, Colo.
MANUFACTURERS OF

Farmers & Traders Natl. Bank

La Grande   Ore.

S E C T I O N   A

THE POST OFFICES OF COLORADO

LISTED ALPHABETICALLY BY OFFICE

This report, is to the best of our knowledge, a complete listing of the officially recognized post offices that exist, did exist, or might have existed within what is now the state of Colorado. The names that are listed herein are those names that were adopted by the Post Office Department, and are not necessarily the same names that were generally accepted by the citizens - then or now.

July 1, 1971 is the termination date for this report. Changes in status of existing post offices, or new post offices established after July 1, 1971 are not included in this volume.

The list is organized alphabetically, however, the I B M alphabetic scheme is used, whereby a "blank" or "space" precedes all letters in determining the sequence. Thus Marshall Pass precedes Marshallpark, La Veta precedes Laboca, etc. This scheme was used in the hope that the information we have and will assemble, can eventually be computerized for study. The format is as follows:

Column 1, in capital letters, is the name of the post office.

Column 2, is the county, or counties within whose political boundaries the office has existed. The counties are listed vertically in their order of succession of authority (Refer to Section C for the dates of the county changes). At this time no attempt has been made to identify the present county within which the site if an early discontinued post office is now located.

Column 3, provides the date of establishment, or re-establishment for each office.

Column 4, lists the dates of discontinuance. Repeated periods of operation, for the same office, are listed vertically in chronological order in columns three and four. A blank line in this column, with no note of explanation, indicates that the post office was on active status as of Jul 1, 1971.

For dates primarily in the post 1931 period, only a partial date is provided. This indicates the monthly, quarterly, or annual report in which the change was reported. These dates will vary from the actual date by as little as a few days, or as much as several months. During the period 1939-1955 where only the bi-annual guides were available for reference, a "?" has been entered in the date column and reference is made to the year of the annual in which the office is either first or last listed. There are a few partial dates in the pre-1931 period and these represent omissions of the complete date from the Records of Appointment. Given time and access to the Postal Bulletins and other government records the unknown dates can be found.

Column 5 contains remarks pertinent to the history of the office. Primarily this is to clarify changes in name or location, but also includes notes concerning offices which although authorized were later rescinded, or are known to have never been in operation. The remarks column is also used to indicate changes in status to branch, station, or rural branch and to call attention to major inconsistencies between the dates reported by the annual guides and those recorded in the Records of Appointment.

OFFICE	COUNTY	ESTABLISHED	DISCONTINUED	REMARKS
ABARR	Yuma	Feb 26,1923	Jan 1948	
ABBEY	Pueblo	May 29,1891	Dec 31,1914	Same place as Muddy Creek.
ABBEYVILLE	Gunnison	Nov 20,1882	Dec 3,1884	Formerly named Hillerton.
ABBOTT	Arapahoe Adams Washington	Aug 6,1887	Apr 15,1926	
ABERDEEN	Gunnison	Feb 15,1890	Jun 16,1891	
ABEYTA	Las Animas	Dec 19,1914	Dec 19,1914	Rescinded. Also known as San Isidro.
ABEYTON	Las Animas	Mar 7,1884	Aug 20,1890	
ACEQUIA	Douglas	Jan 30,1874 Apr 22,1887	Jun 9,1881 Jul 14,1900	
ACKMEN	Montezuma	Nov 5,1917	Jun 1941	Known earlier as Pleasant View then Sandstone.
ADAMS	Larimer	Sep 10,1885 (not listed in 1898,1899 Postal Guides.)	Oct 19,1899	P. O. moved from Bush.
ADAMS CITY	Adams	Sep 26,1923	1964	Converted to branch of Commerce City.
ADELAIDE	Lake	Sep 27,1878	May 12,1879	
ADELAIDE	Fremont	Nov 15,1894	Nov 15,1901	
ADENA	Morgan	Nov 8,1910	Oct 1949	
ADRIAN	Summit	Apr 12,1882	Aug 31,1882	
AGATE	Pueblo	Apr 7,1880	Apr 15,1881	
AGATE	Elbert	Apr 24,1882		Formerly named Gebhard.
AGUILAR	Las Animas	Dec 16,1890		
AIRPORT	Pueblo	Dec 1,1953	Aug 31,1955	Established as a rural station of Pueblo.
AKRON	Weld Washington	Jan 30,1883		

OFFICE	COUNTY	ESTABLISHED	DISCONTINUED	REMARKS
ALAMO	Huerfano	Feb 21,1923	Sep 30,1938	P. O. moved to Butte Valley.
ALAMOSA	Conejos Alamosa	Mar 12,1878		
ALBANO	El Paso	Oct 27,1904	Nov 30,1912	
ALBANY	Bent Prowers	Jul 21,1887 Jun 23,1902	May 1,1891 Sep 30,1905	
ALCOTT	Arapahoe Denver	May 18,1896	Jun 30,1904	Formerly Berkeley. Converted to station of Denver.
ALCREEK	Las Animas	Jul 28,1916	Apr 1935	
ALDA	Delta	May 2,1913	Dec 15,1914	
ALDER	Saguache	Aug 29,1881 Nov 11,1911	Aug 31,1910 Nov 30,1927	Also known as Round Hill.
ALDER CREEK	Ouray	Dec 31,1878	Sep 6,1880	
ALEXANDER	Lake	Aug 1,1879	Oct 2,1879	
ALEXANDER	Otero	Mar 20,1900	Mar 31,1900	P. O. formerly named Fowler. Renamed Fowler. Originally named Oxford.
ALFALFA	Las Animas	Apr 19,1881 Jan 7,1885 Jan 31,1900	Sep 18,1882 Dec 26,1889 Dec 15,1923	Formerly named Raton.
ALFALFA	Weld	Feb 19,1892	Oct 29,1892	
ALFORD	Larimer	Jun 28,1882	Feb 15,1909	
ALICANTE	Lake	Jun 15,1881	Apr 22,1887	P. O. moved to Climax.
ALICE	Clear Creek	Aug 20,1898 Oct 16,1900 Dec 1936	Jun 20,1899 Oct 10,1925 Jan 1939	Rescinded Ghost Town
ALKALI	Bent	Jun 24,1874	Jun 14,1875	
ALKALI	Dolores	May 6,1916	?	Rescinded ?
ALLEN	Gunnison	Aug 1,1881 (Listing in Postal Guides not changed until 1895.)	Mar 11,1892	P. O. moved to Gateview. Name later changed to Madera.

OFFICE	COUNTY	ESTABLISHED	DISCONTINUED	REMARKS
ALLENSPARK	Boulder	Aug 18,1896 May 5,1906	Nov 30,1905	
ALLISON	La Plata	Aug 22,1904 (Last listed in 1953 Postal Guide.)	Nov 30,1954	Known earlier as Vallejo.
ALMA	Park	Mar 7,1873		
ALMONT	Gunnison	Mar 6,1882 Apr 21,1904 Apr 28,1910 Jul 21,1913	May 3,1893 Oct 31,1908 Jan 31,1913	Originally known as Fisher's Ranch.
ALNWICK	El Paso	Aug 11,1887	Oct 26,1893	
ALPINE	Lake Chaffee	Oct 26,1874	Jun 30,1904	Ghost Town
ALTMAN	El Paso Teller	Jan 28,1894 Mar 21,1895	Feb 20,1895 May 20,1911	P. O. moved to Macon.
ALTONA	Boulder	Oct 2,1879	Jul 15,1916	P. O. moved from Ni Wot.
ALVA	Arapahoe	Aug 6,1887	Sep 18,1888	Changed to Idalia
ALVIN	Yuma	Sep 12,1910	Feb 28,1929	
AMERICAN RANCH	Weld	Feb 9, 1863 May 1, 1865	Dec 12,1864 Nov 25,1867	Stage Station.
AMES	Ouray San Miguel	Dec 20,1880 Oct 24,1881 Oct 6,1900	Apr 15,1881 Aug 6,1900 Jun 3,1922	P. O. moved to Ophir. ("New" Ophir)
AMETHYST	Saguache Mineral	Jan 25,1892	Feb 2,1909	Name changed to Creede.
AMHERST	Logan Phillips	Feb 18,1888 Apr 18,1907	Aug 18,1899	
AMITY	Prowers	Jul 18,1898	Apr 1937	
AMO	El Paso	Apr 14,1899 Apr 28,1905	Jul 30,1904 Jul 31,1916	
AMY	Lincoln	Feb 2,1909	Mar 31,1937	

OFFICE	COUNTY	ESTABLISHED	DISCONTINUED	REMARKS
ANACONDA	El Paso	Dec 7,1893	Mar 31,1909	Formerly named Barry.
	Teller	Feb 15,1911	Nov 15,1917	Ghost Town.
ANDERSONVILLE	Pueblo	Dec 1,1868	Aug 19,1869	
ANDRIX	Las Animas	Feb 16,1920	Jan 1953	
ANGORA	Otero	Jun 18,1891	Jul 7,1894	
ANGORA	Rio Blanco	Oct 24,1896	Sep 30,1912	
ANIMAS	La Plata	Jul 10,1886	Sep 29,1900	Formerly named Animas City.
ANIMAS CITY	La Plata	May 24,1877	Aug 19,1885	Re-named Animas.
ANIMAS FORKS	La Plata	Feb 8,1875	Feb 26,1889	
	San Juan	Oct 21,1889	Nov 14,1891	
		Jul 25,1904	Nov 30,1915	Ghost Town.
ANITA	Fremont	Jun 30,1892 (not listed in Postal Guides.)	May 10,1894	
ANTELOPE SPRINGS	Hinsdale Mineral	May 5,1876	May 30,1903	
ANTELOPE SPRINGS	Morgan	Mar 27,1911	Aug 15,1917	
ANTERO	Chaffee	Oct 5,1895 (never operational ?)	Apr 3,1896	
ANTHRACITE	Gunnison	Nov 14,1884	Dec 30,1896	
ANTHRACITE	Routt	Feb 11,1905	Jul 17,1906	
ANTLERS	Garfield	Jul 1,1891	May 31,1906	Formerly named Ferguson.
		Feb 26,1908	Apr 1954	R. R. Station named Ives.
ANTON	Washington	Jul 18,1916 Aug 1934 (not listed in 1923 Guide.)	Oct 15,1928	
ANTONITO	Conejos	Jan 24,1881		Formerly named San Antonio
APACHE	Huerfano	May 31,1878	Nov 10,1882	P. O. moved to Huerfano

OFFICE	COUNTY	ESTABLISHED	DISCONTINUED	REMARKS
APACHE	Huerfano	Sep 10,1894 Jun 21,1898 Apr 28,1923	May 6,1898 Feb 28,1923 Aug 31,1925	In Huerfano County there were two locations named Apache.
APEX	Gilpin	Nov 12,1894 (not listed in 1915,1916 Postal Guides.)	Apr 30,1932	
APISHAPA	Las Animas	Aug 26,1867 Nov 11,1872 Aug 7,1876 Mar 21,1882 Apr 1,1896 Aug 1,1910	Jul 23,1868 May 24,1875 Feb 10,1882 Mar 18,1896 Nov 30,1909 Sep 27,1911	Formerly named San Antonia Changed to Augusta
ARAPAHOE	Kansas Terr. Arapahoe Cheyenne	Jan 17,1860 May 5,1906	Oct 12,1861	Essentially same location as in territorial times.
ARASTRA	San Juan	Jun 15,1895 (not listed in 1910,1911 Postal Guides.)	Mar 31,1919	
ARBOLES	Conejos Archuleta	Dec 13,1882 Apr 13,1899	Apr 4,1899	
ARBOURVILLE	Chaffee	Sep 12,1879	Aug 15,1881	Changed to Conrow
ARCHERS	Jefferson	Sep 10,1888	Jul 25,1893	
ARDEN	Bent	Jun 22,1888	Nov 5,1888	
ARENA	Cheyenne	May 2,1910	Apr 30,1923	
AREQUA	El Paso	Jul 9,1894	Sep 1,1894	Rescinded.
ARGENTA	Gunnison	Jul 2,1880	Aug 23,1880	Name changed to Tomichi.
ARGENTINE	Summit	Jan 31,1881 Nov 18,1901	Oct 22,1883 Feb 28,1907	Formerly Conger
ARGO	Arapahoe Denver	Apr 11,1881 Jun 11,1890 May 18,1904	Mar 21,1890 Jan 15,1904 Sep 15,1911	
ARICKAREE	Arapahoe Adams Washington	Jun 9,1888 Mar 23,1900	Oct 31,1898 Jun 23,1961	

OFFICE	COUNTY	ESTABLISHED	DISCONTINUED	REMARKS
ARKANSAS	Chaffee	Jun 16,1880	Mar 28,1881	Name changed to Salida.
ARKANSAS JUNCTION	Lake	May 2,1890 Aug 23,1912	Sep 30,1910 Aug 10,1918	
ARKINS	Larimer	Feb 26,1887	Mar 31,1906	
ARLAND	Pueblo	Jan 7,1895	Jul 15,1895	Rescinded
ARLENE	Yuma	Oct 30,1916	Aug 31,1918	
ARLINGTON	Mesa	May 25,1883	Aug 12,1884	Formerly Jones
ARLINGTON	Bent Kiowa	Aug 16,1887		
ARLOA	Montezuma	Mar 12,1903	Apr 15,1914	Also known as Glencoe.
ARMEL	Yuma	Oct 17,1903	1958	
ARMOUR	Pueblo	May 6,1886	Feb 3,1892	
ARMSTRONG	Logan	Oct 30,1911	Jun 15,1917	
ARNOLD	Logan	Jan 26,1897 (not listed in Postal Guides.)	Mar 30,1900	Changed to Willard
ARNOLD	Yuma	Nov 17,1913	Sep 15,1914	
AROYA	Cheyenne	Sep 17,1889	1965	
ARRIBA	Elbert Lincoln	Feb 4,1889		
ARRIOLA	Montezuma	Dec 18,1894 Jun 20,1908	Jun 15,1904 Sep 1933	
ARROW	Grand	Mar 21,1905	Mar 15,1915	
ARROYA	Elbert	Jan 16,1877 May 7, 1879	Feb 11,1878 Jan 17,1881	
ARTESIA	Moffat	Jul 1946	1966	Name changed to Dinosaur
ARTMAN	Pueblo	Aug 31,1892	Feb 14,1901	
ARVADA	Jefferson	Feb 16,1871		

OFFICE	COUNTY	ESTABLISHED	DISCONTINUED	REMARKS
ASH	Ouray	Oct 11,1899	Dec 31,1905	
ASHCROFT	Gunnison Pitkin	Aug 12,1880 Jan 3,1882	Aug 5,1881 Nov 30,1912	Name changed to Chloride. Re-named Ashcroft.
ASHLAND	Kit Carson	Jan 14,1890	May 15,1909	
ASPEN	Gunnison Pitkin	Jun 7,1880		
ASPEN-GERBAZ	Pitkin	Dec 4,1967		Established as a rural branch of Aspen.
ASPEN JUNCTION	Eagle	Feb 13,1890	Jun 19,1895	Name changed to Basalt.
ASSOCIATION CAMP	Larimer	May 29,1916		Converted April 30, 1966 to rural branch of Fort Collins.
ATCHEE	Garfield	Sep 26,1905 Sep 27,1910 Sep 27,1920	Jan 2,1907 Jul 15,1920 Apr 30,1940	
ATLANTA	Las Animas Baca	Dec 13,1887	Aug 31,1899	(first listed in 1890 Postal Guide.)
ATHENS	Arapahoe	Jul 20,1892	May 13,1896	
ATWELL	Las Animas	Jan 29,1915	Aug 31,1920	
ATWOOD	Weld Logan	Aug 10,1885		
AUGUSTA	Custer	May 5,1890	Apr 15,1902	
AUGUSTA	Las Animas	Sep 27,1911	May 15,1928	Formerly named Apishapa. Originally named San Antonia.
AULT	Weld	Mar 29,1898		
AURARIA	Kansas Terr.	Jan 18,1859	Feb 11,1860	Name and place changed to Denver City.
AURORA	Ouray	May 10,1880	Feb 19,1884	Known later as Dallas Divide.
AURORA	Adams Arapahoe Adams	Jan 15,1908 Apr 28,1962**	Dec 1939*	*Converted to branch of Denver (1939-1962) **Re-established in Adams County.

OFFICE	COUNTY	ESTABLISHED	DISCONTINUED	REMARKS
AURORIA	Nebraska Terr. (The location of this office, within the present boundaries of Colorado, has not been confirmed, but is believed correct.)	Dec 11,1858	Apr 27,1860	Changed to Colona
AUSTIN	Garfield	Jul 21,1890	Jun 6,1896	
AUSTIN	Delta	May 19,1905		
AVALO	Weld	Jul 1,1898	Jun 1936	
AVENDALE	Elbert Kit Carson	Feb 5,1889	Sep 12,1890	
AVOCA	Arapahoe	Jun 10,1889	Oct 27,1891	
AVON	Eagle	Nov 26,1900		
AVONDALE	Pueblo	Mar 22,1892		
AXIAL	Routt Garfield (?) Routt Moffat	Mar 6,1883 Nov 9,1886 Mar 4,1890	Apr 9,1886 Apr 3,1888 1958	
AYER	Otero	Oct 18,1911	Sep 1941	
AYLMER	Las Animas	Dec 14,1899 Mar 23,1900	Feb 2,1900 Sep 18,1906	Rescinded Changed to Bowen
AYR	Bent Prowers	Jul 25,1888	Aug 8,1891	
BADGER	Arapahoe	Jan 1,1890 Apr 20,1894 (not listed in 1892 Postal Guide.)	Sep 4,1893 Jul 20,1894	
BADITO	Huerfano Las Animas Huerfano	Sep 12,1865	Nov 15,1910	Formerly Little Orphan
BAILEY	Park	Nov 20,1878		P. O. moved from Deer Valley
BAKER	Baca	Feb 27,1915	Jun 30,1921	

OFFICE	COUNTY	ESTABLISHED	DISCONTINUED	REMARKS
BALARAT	Boulder	Sep 12,1879 Jan 31,1887	Oct 20,1881 May 13,1887	
BALD MOUNTAIN	Gilpin	Dec 16,1869	Oct 15,1921	Formerly named Nevada.
BALDWIN	Gunnison	Sep 17,1883	Mar 31,1902	
BALDWIN	Gunnison	Jan 26,1909	Jun 1949	Name changed from Mount Carbon
BALFOUR	Park	Feb 6,1894	Jan 31,1907	
BALTIMORE	Gilpin	Aug 28,1896 Mar 3,1898	Dec 12,1896 Oct 26,1904	P. O. moved to Tolland. Ghost Town.
BALTZER	Kit Carson	Jun 4,1907	Dec 14,1907	
BALZAC	Garfield	May 23,1891	Mar 31,1903	
BARBEE	Routt	Jan 13,1906	Aug 14,1909	
BARDEEN	El Paso	Mar 7,1917	May 31,1924	
BARDINE	Gunnison	Mar 11,1903	Oct 15,1908	
BAREHILLS	Fremont	Apr 28,1896	Jun 29,1901	
BARELA	Las Animas	Jul 28,1874 Mar 19,1887 Apr 9,1902	May 21,1886 Oct 19,1896 Sep 30,1931	Formerly Glenham
BARLOW	Garfield	Jun 25,1883	Mar 28,1884	Changed to Glenwood Springs.
BARNES	Montrose	Nov 15,1901	Apr 15,1903	
BARNESVILLE	Weld	Jun 9,1910	Oct 1935	
BARNUM	Saguache Gunnison	Mar 10,1876	Jun 7,1881	
BARNUM	Arapahoe	Feb 5,1892	Jun 30,1901	
BARR	Arapahoe Adams	Mar 15,1883	Oct 17,1914	Name changed to Barr Lake.
BARR LAKE	Adams	Oct 17,1914	Oct 1952	Formerly named Barr.
BARRY	El Paso	Mar 1,1892	Dec 7,1893	Changed to Anaconda.

OFFICE	COUNTY	ESTABLISHED	DISCONTINUED	REMARKS
BARTLETT	Baca	Sep 5,1928	Apr 1938	
BARTON	Prowers	Mar 29,1895	Oct 15,1917	P. O. moved from Zuck. Place was also known as Byron Station and Adana.
BASALT	Eagle	Jun 19,1895		Place formerly named Aspen Junction.
BASHOR	Adams	Mar 5,1909	Jul 31,1918	
BASSETTS MILLS	El Paso	Jun 15,1869 May 26,1872	Jan 4,1872 Sep 13,1872	P. O. moved to Southwater
BASSICK	Custer	May 19,1917	Dec 31,1920	
BATH	Chaffee	Jul 25,1893 Nov 15,1901 Apr 18,1904	Feb 20,1894 Sep 9,1903 Jul 28,1904	Rescinded
BATTLE CREEK	Routt	Mar 3,1911	Mar 1938	
BAYFIELD	La Plata	Feb 25,1899		P. O. moved from Los Pinos.
BEACON	Las Animas	Aug 11,1910	Nov 15,1913	Formerly Green Canon.
BEAR CANON	Douglas	Apr 7,1863	Aug 29,1867	
BEAR CANYON	Douglas	Apr 8,1869	Aug 4,1879	Same location as Bear Canon.
BEAR RIVER	Routt	Nov 10,1914 Jun 29,1925	Jun 30,1925 Oct 1940	
BEARCREEK	Montezuma	Mar 11,1899 Apr 13,1907	Mar 31,1900 Dec 14,1918	
BEATY	Dolores	Aug 20,1902	Jan 2,1903	
BEAVER	Fremont Pueblo	Apr 11,1902	Apr 30,1910	Formerly named Beaver Creek. Originally named Toof.
BEAVER BROOK	Jefferson	Apr 19,1875 Feb 18,1889	Apr 28,1886 May 31,1892	
BEAVER CREEK	Fremont Pueblo (?)	Oct 3,1862	Jan 6,1874	
BEAVER CREEK	Fremont	Jan 8,1883	Apr 11,1902	Formerly named Toof. Name changed to Beaver.

OFFICE	COUNTY	ESTABLISHED	DISCONTINUED	REMARKS
BEAVER CREEK	Arapahoe	Feb 9,1915	Feb 15,1916	
BEAVERTON	Kit Carson	Oct 17,1910	Nov 30,1915	
BEDROCK	Montrose	Nov 8,1883 Oct 12,1911	Sep 15,1903	
BEE	Bent	Aug 16,1887 Oct 15,1887	Sep 20,1887 Oct 27,1887*	Changed to Sheridan Lake: Change rescinded. *Changed to Sheridan Lake.
BEECHER	Arapahoe Adams Yuma	Aug 12,1902 Aug 31,1905	Feb 28,1905 Nov 3,1905	
BEECHER ISLAND	Yuma	Feb 25,1925	1958	Formerly Glory
BELFORD	Hinsdale	Dec 10,1879	Nov 21,1881	
BELFORD	Clear Creek	Mar 7,1884	Aug 11,1884	
BELOIT	Elbert Kit Carson	Mar 27,1888	Sep 29,1893	
BELLE MONTE	Boulder	Jan 3,1866	Aug 31,1866	
BELLEVILLE	Jefferson	Mar 7,1881	Jul 27,1881	
BELLVUE	Larimer	Jun 24,1884		
BENKO	Elbert	Sep 18,1915	Mar 31,1917	
BENNET	Arapahoe Adams	Mar 16,1877	Jun 1,1907	Spelling changed to Bennett.
BENNET SPRINGS	Douglas	Dec 20,1862	Sep 12,1865	
BENNETT	Adams	Jun 1,1907		Formerly spelled Bennet.
BENT CANYON	Las Animas	Mar 28,1872	Jun 30,1902	
BENTS FORT	Huerfano Las Animas Pueblo Bent	Jun 4,1863	Dec 2,1873	
BERKELEY	Arapahoe	Oct 24,1890	May 18,1896	P. O. moved to Alcott. Now within Denver.

OFFICE	COUNTY	ESTABLISHED	DISCONTINUED	REMARKS
BERNICE	Costilla	Feb 26,1901	May 16,1902	
BERNARD	Mesa	Jan 27,1896	May 31,1905	
BERRY	Kit Carson	Apr 13,1911	Apr 15,1912	
BERTHOUD	Larimer	Apr 4,1878		Formerly Little Thompson.
BERWIND	Las Animas	Mar 10,1892	May 30,1931	
BESHOAR	Las Animas	Jan 25,1901	Jun 30,1903	
BETHESDA	Douglas	Mar 28,1902	Sep 15,1909	
BETHUNE	Elbert	Jan 19,1889	May 15,1905	
	Kit Carson	Sep 17,1906		
BEUCK	Elbert	Mar 23,1918	May 1,1918	Formerly spelled Buick; Change rescinded.
BEULAH	Pueblo	Oct 25,1876		Formerly named Mace's Hole.
BIEDELL	Saguache	Jun 25,1883	Apr 28,1884	P. O. moved to Carnero.
BIG ELK	Boulder	Jun 3,1915	Sep 15,1917	
BIG SANDY	El Paso	Dec 13,1876	Nov 6,1877	
		Jan 17,1882	Nov 24,1888	P. O. moved to Calhan.
BIG THOMPSON	Larimer	Nov 12,1862	Jan 10,1878	Changed to Loveland.
BIGHORN	Larimer	Mar 3,1898	Feb 15,1900	
BIJOU BASIN	Douglas	Apr 8,1869	Mar 7,1882	
	El Paso	Aug 2,1882	Aug 26,1884	
	Elbert	Jan 28,1885	Mar 30,1907	
	El Paso	(Listed under both El Paso		
	Elbert	and Elbert counties in the		
	El Paso	1886 Postal Guide)		
BIJOU VIEW	Morgan	Jun 10,1921	Nov 16,1925	Formerly spelled Bijouview.
BIJOUVIEW	Morgan	Apr 3,1914	Jun 10,1921	Spelling changed to Bijou View.
BIRD	Arapahoe	Aug 4,1880	?	
		Oct 4,1880	Nov 22,1880	

OFFICE	COUNTY	ESTABLISHED	DISCONTINUED	REMARKS
BIRMINGHAM	Huerfano	May 25,1883	Sep 19,1894	
BISMARK	Saguache	Feb 7,1872	Oct 10,1879	
BISON	Routt	Feb 18,1898	?	Never in operation.
BITTNER	Gunnison	Sep 7,1905	Dec 7,1904*	*Apparent error in records.
BLACK FOREST	El Paso	Apr 16,1960		Established as a rural branch of Colorado Springs.
BLACK HAWK	Gilpin	Feb 8,1871	Jan 30,1895	Formerly named Black Hawk Point. Spelling changed to Blackhawk.
BLACK HAWK	Gilpin	Jul 1950		Formerly spelled Blackhawk.
BLACK HAWK POINT	Gilpin	Dec 6,1862	Feb 8,1871	Name changed to Black Hawk.
BLACK MOUNTAIN	Park	Jun 20,1899	Oct 14,1911	Formerly Devine
BLACK WOLF	Weld	Mar 9,1885	Oct 30,1885	
BLACKBURN	Custer	Aug 1,1881	May 11,1889	
BLACKHAWK	Gilpin	Jan 30,1895	Jul 1950	Formerly spelled Black Hawk. Renamed Black Hawk.
BLACKWELL	Bent	Jul 7,1881 Jan 5,1882 Mar 24,1884	Oct 31,1881 Dec 31,1883 May 11,1886	Name changed to Lamar.
BLAINE	Eagle	Jul 7,1884	Feb 1,1886	
BLAINE	Baca	Aug 4,1900	Sep 15,1939	
BLAINVALE	Rio Grande	Jun 29,1882 Feb 4,1884	Aug 31,1882 Sep 10,1884	P. O. moved to Loyton.
BLANCA	Costilla	Oct 5,1894 Apr 17,1898 Dec 28,1900 Oct 28,1908	Jul 31,1895 Aug 31,1900 Feb 15,1902	
BLAND	Elbert	May 2,1883	Feb 15,1921	
BLOOM	Otero	Apr 18,1899 Apr 19,1913	Dec 11,1899 May 31,1938	Rescinded. P. O. moved from Delhi. Formerly named Iron Spring.

OFFICE	COUNTY	ESTABLISHED	DISCONTINUED	REMARKS
BLUE MOUNTAIN	Moffat	Jan 17,1950	1955	P. O. moved from Skull Creek.
BLUMENAU	Custer	Jan 16,1879 Aug 8,1879	Jul 16,1879 Oct 9,1890	Formerly Colfax
BOAZ	Fremont El Paso	Mar 7,1895	Oct 31,1898	
BOILER	Larimer	Sep 3,1914	Sep 15,1915	
BOLTON	Arapahoe	May 1,1900	Sep 9,1901	P. O. moved to Clugh in Cheyenne County, Kansas.
BONANZA	Saguache	Aug 12,1880 May 24,1895 Jun 27,1921	Apr 27,1895 May 31,1921 Jun 1938	Not effected.
BONCARBO	Las Animas	Nov 15,1917		
BOND	Lake	Jul 16,1886	Oct 25,1888	
BOND	Eagle	Jan 1936		
BONITO	Saguache	Mar 7,1881	Aug 28,1883	
BONNY	Kit Carson	Jun 3,1915	Feb 29,1924	
BOONE	Pueblo	Dec 5,1891		Formerly named Booneville.
BOONEVILLE	Pueblo	Jan 2,1863	Dec 5,1891	Name changed to Boone.
BORDENVILLE	Park	Sep 29,1879	Nov 28,1884	
BOREAS	Summit	Jan 2,1896	Jan 31,1905	Ghost Town.
BOSTON	Las Animas Baca	Apr 14,1887	Jun 16,1893	
BOULDER	Nebraska Terr. Boulder	Apr 22,1859		
BOULDER CITY	Nebraska Terr. (This designation appears in 'Chase-Cabeen' but has not been seen elsewhere. It is apparently an early designation of "Boulder."			
BOVINA	Elbert Lincoln	Jan 8,1899	1955	

OFFICE	COUNTY	ESTABLISHED	DISCONTINUED	REMARKS
BOWEN	Dolores Rio Grande	May 2,1883	Sep 30,1901	
BOWEN	Las Animas	Sep 18,1906	Jan 15,1929	Formerly Aylmer
BOWENTON	Rio Grande	Aug 10,1881	Aug 21,1884	
BOWERMAN	Gunnison	Oct 28,1903	May 27,1910	P. O. moved to Waunita Hot Springs. Ghost Town.
BOWIE	Delta	Feb 5,1907	1967	
BOWMAN	Gunnison	Jun 7,1880	Apr 28,1882	
BOWSER	Elbert	Jun 9,1888	Oct 10,1888	Changed to Flagler
BOX ELDER	Larimer	Jun 2,1876 Apr 29,1884	Dec 26,1877 Oct 30,1894	P. O. moved to Bristol. Spelling changed to Boxelder.
BOXELDER	Larimer	Oct 30,1894 May 16,1924	Jun 15,1923 Nov 19,1924	Spelling changed to Box Elder.
BOYERO	Lincoln	Mar 3,1902		
BRADDOCK	Summit	Jan 18,1884	Dec 27,1890	P. O. moved from Preston. Originally named Delaware City.
BRADFORD	Huerfano	Nov 27,1889	Aug 21,1895	
BRANDON	Bent Kiowa	May 19,1888 May 28,1908	May 3,1893	Converted Feb 28,1963 to a rural branch of Eads.
BRANSON	Las Animas	Jul 30,1918		Formerly Coloflats
BRAZIL	Las Animas	May 14,1895 Feb 20,1911	Aug 31,1899 May 31,1912	
BRECKENRIDGE	Utah Terr. Summit	Jan 18,1860		
BREEN	La Plata	Jul 19,1901 (Last listed in 1953 Postal Guide.)	?	Name of Post Office at the Fort Lewis Indian School
BREWSTER	Fremont	Oct 9,1899 Apr 21,1914	Dec 15,1900 Sep 30,1916	

OFFICE	COUNTY	ESTABLISHED	DISCONTINUED	REMARKS
BRIGGSDALE	Weld	Aug 1,1910		
BRIGHTSIDE	Jefferson	Nov 13,1900 Feb 4,1902	Dec 31,1901 Nov 29,1902	
BRIGHTON	Arapshoe Adams	Aug 4,1879		Formerly named Hughes.
BRISTOL	Larimer	Dec 26,1877	Dec 2,1890	P. O. moved from Box Elder.
BRISTOL	Prowers	Jul 1,1908		
BRODHEAD	Las Animas	Aug 14,1902 Jul 19,1915	Apr 15,1913 May 1939	
BRONQUIST	Pueblo	Aug 30,1917	Jun 30,1925	
BROOK FOREST	Jefferson	Oct 11,1921	Apr 1949	
BROOKFIELD	Las Animas Baca	Aug 30,1887	Jul 15,1902	
BROOKSIDE	Fremont	May 21,1888 Dec 18,1908	Oct 15,1905 Mar 15,1909	
BROOKSTON	Routt	Mar 25,1914	Apr 15,1930	
BROOKVALE	Clear Creek	Jul 24,1876 Mar 22,1883 Jun 14,1889	Jan 3,1883 Sep 16,1885 May 1942	
BROOMFIELD	Boulder	Sep 26,1884		
BROWN	Montrose	Apr 2,1883 Jun 2,1892	Oct 1,1891 Jun 4,1896*	P. O. moved to Menoken; change rescinded. *Name changed to Olathe.
BROWN CANON	Chaffee	Mar 9,1904	Jun 30,1908	Formerly Browns Canon and Kraft.
BROWNS CANON	Chaffee	May 8,1888	Jul 25,1893	Formerly named Kraft. Later, changed to Brown Canon.
BROWNSVILLE	Clear Creek	Apr 7,1871	Dec 1,1875	Name changed to Silver Plume. ½ mile difference in locations.
BROWNSVILLE	Jefferson	Jan 3,1879	Oct 5,1883	
BROYLES	Conejos	Sep 29,1905	Oct 31,1908	

OFFICE	COUNTY	ESTABLISHED	DISCONTINUED	REMARKS
BRUNKER	Washington	Dec 28,1907	Jan 31,1917	
BRUSH	Weld Morgan	Sep 19,1882		
BRYANT	Logan Phillips Yuma	Mar 27,1888	Mar 31,1916	
BUCKHORN	Larimer	Aug 2,1878	Aug 18,1888	
BUCKINGHAM	Weld	Dec 21,1888 Apr 8,1910	Jan 8,1890 1967	
BUCKSKIN	Park	Dec 21,1865	Jan 24,1873	Town named Buckskin Joe. Formerly named Laurette. Ghost Town.
BUCKSKIN JOE	Fremont	Jun 1,1961	Mar 31,1966	Established as a rural station of Canon City.
BUENA VISTA	Chaffee	Sep 18,1879		P. O. moved from Mahonville.
BUFFALO	Weld	Jun 24,1874	Feb 21,1883	Changed to Merino.
BUFFALO CREEK	Jefferson	Aug 16,1878		Converted Sep 14,1963 to a rural branch of Pine.
BUFFALO SPRINGS	Park	May 28,1875	May 15,1912	
BUFFER	Summit	Dec 5,1917	Oct 15,1921	
BUFORD	Rio Blanco	Mar 19,1890 Dec 6,1921	Jun 30,1919 1962	
BUICK	Elbert	Sep 19,1916 May 1,1918	Mar 23,1918 Aug 15,1925	Name changed to Beuck. Change rescinded. Name changed to Godfrey.
BULGER	Larimer	Oct 4,1909	Jul 31,1912	
BULKLEY	San Miguel	Mar 7,1895	Mar 29,1895	
BUNCE	Boulder	Oct 12,1895	May 31,1901	
BUNELL	Adams	Feb 14,1919	Nov 2,1921	Formerly Camp Speer. P. O. moved to Fitzsimmons. Located outside military reserve.

OFFICE	COUNTY	ESTABLISHED	DISCONTINUED	REMARKS
BURDETT	Washington	Apr 4,1888	Jun 1937	
BURLINGTON	Boulder	Nov 6,1862	Apr 4,1873	P. O. moved to Longmont. (½ mile)
BURLINGTON	Elbert Kit Carson	Apr 29,1887		
BURNS	Eagle	May 14,1895		
BURNT MILL	Pueblo	Oct 7,1911	Sep 30,1921	Formerly named Kinkel.
BURROWS PARK	Hinsdale	Sep 26,1876	Sep 28,1882	P. O. moved to White Cross.
BURT	El Paso	Mar 24,1910	Aug 15,1916	
BUSH	Larimer	Oct 11,1882	Sep 10,1885	P. O. moved to Adams.
BUSK	Lake	Dec 15,1890	Mar 2,1894	
BUSTER	Las Animas Baca	Jul 28,1916	Jul 30,1927	
BUTLER	Larimer Jackson	Jun 16,1890	Nov 30,1911	
BUTTE VALLEY	Huerfano	Jul 6,1869 May 20,1878	Feb 26,1878 Aug 26,1878	This Butte Valley was later re-named Mustang.
BUTTE VALLEY	Huerfano	Oct 1,1938	Oct 1949	P. O. moved from Alamo.
BUTTES	El Paso	Jan 24,1895	Apr 15,1922	Formerly named El Paso.
BYERS	Arapahoe	Feb 27,1873		
CABLE	Lincoln	Jul 19,1893	Jan 30,1895	Changed to Genoa.
CACHARAS	Huerfano	Dec 8,1870	Sep 20,1872	Name changed to Cucharas.
CADDOA	Bent	Nov 7,1881 Jun 12,1884	Jun 9,1884 1958	
CAHONE	Dolores	May 21,1916 Jun 12,1920	Nov 20,1917	
CAISSON	Moffat	Sep 3,1920	Feb 1938	
CALCITE	Fremont	Jun 29,1904	Apr 30,1930	

OFFICE	COUNTY	ESTABLISHED	DISCONTINUED	REMARKS
CALCIUM	Pitkin	Mar 10,1888	Mar 31,1890	Changed to Thomasville
CALHAN	El Paso	Nov 24,1888		P. O. moved from Big Sandy.
CALUMET	Chaffee	Jan 24,1882	Feb 9,1885	
CALVERT	Logan	Dec 22,1887	Aug 8,1888	Changed to Fleming.
CAMARGO	Custer	Apr 19,1881	Nov 31,1881	
CAMEO	Mesa	Dec 14,1907	Feb 28,1969	
CAMERON	Teller	Apr 10,1901	Aug 31,1909	Formerly Touraine
CAMEVILLE	Gunnison Montrose	Nov 7,1882	Aug 20,1890	
CAMFIELD	Weld	Apr 18,1910	Feb 15,1921	
CAMP GENTER	Gunnison	Feb 12,1925	Jan 15,1930	Ghost Town.
CAMP SHUMWAY	Huerfano	Apr 13,1911 (Still listed as McGuire in the 1911 and 1912 Postal Guides.)	Jul 1,1924	P. O. moved from McGuire. Changed to Gordon.
CAMP SPEER	Adams	Dec 5,1918	Feb 14,1919	P. O. moved to Bunell
CAMPBIRD	Ouray	Apr 28,1898	Mar 15,1918	
CAMPO	Baca	Apr 10,1913		
CANADIAN	Grand Larimer	Mar 6,1883	Jul 3,1891	
CANFIELD	Boulder	Mar 28,1878	Jun 15,1906	
CANON CITY	Kansas Terr. Fremont	Dec 8,1860 Dec 15,1904	Jul 30,1904	Name changed to Canyon City, change rescinded.
CANYON CITY	Fremont	Jul 30,1904	Dec 15,1904	Formerly named Canon City. Re-named Canon City.
CAPITOL CITY	Hinsdale	May 18,1877	Oct 30,1920	
CAPPS	Huerfano	Sep 26,1894	Aug 15,1901	Formerly named Scissors. Originally named Quebec.

OFFICE	COUNTY	ESTABLISHED	DISCONTINUED	REMARKS
CAPULIN	Conejos	Aug 10,1881 Sep 21,1923	Jul 14,1922	
CARBONATE	Garfield	Apr 13,1883	Nov 15,1886	
CARBONATEVILLE	Summit	Feb 2,1879	Jan 27,1881	
CARBONDALE	Garfield	Jan 6,1887 May 14,1887	Feb 14,1887	Known locally as Yellow Dog.
CARDIFF	Garfield	Aug 1,1889	Jul 31,1918	Ghost Town.
CARDINAL	Boulder	Jul 13,1905 Sep 27,1911 Jan 28,1915	Oct 15,1910 Feb 28,1913 Oct 15,1919	
CAREY	Pitkin	Aug 21,1883	Jan 7,1884	
CAREY	Kit Carson	Dec 12,1910	Dec 30,1916	
CARIBOU	Boulder	Jan 31,1871	Mar 31,1917	Same P. O. - Two townsites. The first Caribou burned.
CARLISLE	Elbert Kit Carson	Jul 21,1887	Jun 9,1890	
CARLTON	Prowers	Jan 14,1891	1960	Earlier named Conroe.
CARMEL	Chaffee	Jun 15,1881	Oct 26,1882	
CARNERO	Saguache	Jun 16,1870 Mar 8,1880	Jul 11,1876 Mar 18,1884	P. O. moved to Green
CARNERO	Saguache	Apr 28,1884 Dec 7,1894	Nov 30,1886 Aug 31,1911	P. O. moved from Beidell.
CARPENTER	Mesa	Jun 11,1890	Aug 3,1891	
CARR	Weld	Mar 26,1872 Oct 17,1884	Nov 19,1878	
CARR CROSSING	Lincoln	Mar 25,1915	Apr 15,1930	
CARRACAS	Archuleta	Mar 3,1909	Jan 31,1911	
CARRISO	Las Animas Baca	Jun 2,1887 Oct 30,1890 Apr 17,1894	Dec 26,1889 Mar 3,1891 Jul 11,1895	See Carrizo and Corrizo

OFFICE	COUNTY	ESTABLISHED	DISCONTINUED	REMARKS
CARRISO SPRINGS	Las Animas Baca	Aug 27,1888	May 17,1890	Loc. about 6 mi. N. of Carrizo
CARRIZO	Baca	Sep 21,1907	Nov 27,1907	Rescinded. Known earlier as townsite.
		Dec 14,1907	Jan 31,1916	Formerly spelled Corrizo and Carriso.
CARSON	Huerfano	Sep 23,1868	Oct 23,1868	
		Jun 15,1869	Dec 7,1873	
CARSON	Hinsdale	Sep 16,1889	Oct 15,1903	
CARSONHART	Las Animas	Nov 15,1917	?	Rescinded
CARY	Arapahoe	Apr 23,1888	Feb 28,1890	
CARY RANCH	Routt	Mar 25,1914	Nov 29,1930	
CASCADE	La Plata	Jun 14,1880	Apr 22,1881	
		May 11,1881	Jul 24,1882	
CASCADE	El Paso	Aug 16,1887		
CASE	Douglas	Aug 7,1897	Jun 24,1913	Changed to Irving.
CASH CREEK	Lake	Aug 2,1862	Feb 27,1871	
CASHIN	Montrose	Sep 14,1898	Apr 30,1904	This was the Post Office at a copper mine.
		Jan 4,1905	Apr 29,1905	
CASSELS	Park	Jun 19,1899	Sep 30,1929	
CASTELAR	La Plata	May 9,1905	Jun 30,1912	
CASTLE	Eagle	Feb 18,1885	Sep 3,1891	Name changed to Eagle.
CASTLE ROCK	Douglas	Apr 5,1871	May 18,1874	P. O. moved to Douglas.
CASTLE ROCK	Douglas	May 18,1874		This P. O. formerly named New Memphis.
CASTLETON	Gunnison	Dec 8,1882	Oct 11,1894	
CATHEDRAL	Hinsdale	Jul 18,1898	Sep 30,1921	
CATHERIN	Corejos	Sep 25,1888	Oct 18,1890	

OFFICE	COUNTY	ESTABLISHED	DISCONTINUED	REMARKS
CATHERIN	Garfield	Oct 18,1892	Feb 15,1902	
CATLIN	Bent Otero	Nov 6,1879	Nov 4,1895	Name changed to Manzanola.
CEBOLLA	Gunnison	Mar 20,1894	Oct 1935	
CEDAR	San Miguel	Apr 7,1892 Nov 2,1923	Jan 15,1921 Dec 1943	
CEDAR BROOK	Montrose	Oct 19,1904 Dec 8,1910 Mar 7,1917	Jul 31,1906 Oct 31,1912 Jan 15,1924	
CEDARHURST	Las Animas	Aug 27,1903	Mar 31,1913	
CEDAREDGE	Delta	Dec 5,1894		
CEDARWOOD	Pueblo	Mar 22,1912	Apr 1943	
CENICERO	Conejos	Apr 13,1894	Mar 14,1902	Changed to Lobatos.
CENTER	Saguache	Jul 1,1899		Formerly named Centerview.
CENTERVIEW	Saguache	Apr 22,1898	Jul 1,1899	Name changed to Center
CENTREVILLE	Lake Chaffee	Apr 22,1868	Apr 30,1930	
CENTRAL CITY	Gilpin	Oct 8,1869		Formerly Mountain City
CHAFFEE	Chaffee	Jun 6,1879	May 14,1883	Name changed to Monarch.
CHALK CREEK	Chaffee	Aug 29,1879	Sep 8,1880	Changed to Nathrop
CHAMA	Costilla	May 3,1907 (Not listed in 1917 Postal Guide.)		
CHAMBERS	Larimer	Sep 21,1880	Aug 17,1886	
CHAMBERS LAKE	Larimer	Sep 21,1926 (Not listed in Postal Guides.)	?	
CHANCE	Gunnison	Nov 24,1894	Dec 14,1901	Ghost Town.
CHANDLER	Fremont	Aug 4,1890	Dec 1942	

OFFICE	COUNTY	ESTABLISHED	DISCONTINUED	REMARKS
CHANEY	Gunnison	Aug 25,1892 (Not listed in Postal Guides.)	May 10,1894	
CHAPEL	Las Animas	Dec 6,1894	Jan 3,1895	Changed to Graycreek
CHAPELTON	Weld	Jan 11,1917	Jun 15,1922	
CHAPIN	Kit Carson	Feb 15,1890	Nov 10,1894	
CHAPMAN	Garfield	May 19,1884	Apr 23,1888	Name changed to New Castle.
CHASE	Park	Jul 15,1892	Oct 31,1911	Railroad station named Weller.
CHATTANOOGA	San Juan	Apr 4,1883	Jun 4,1894	
CHEDSEY	Jackson	May 12,1917	Jun 15,1918	
CHEESMAN	Jefferson	Mar 5,1900	Oct 31,1904	Construction Camp.
CHEMUNG	Cheyenne	Dec 22,1906	Aug 15,1910	
CHENEYCENTER	Prowers	Feb 24,1917	Aug 1936	
CHENOA	Weld Logan	Nov 19,1886	Nov 19,1895	
CHENOWETH	Elbert	Jan 16,1897	Sep 29,1900	
CHERAW	Otero	Aug 13,1910		
CHEROKEE CITY	Weld	Nov 25,1862	Nov 25,1863	Name changed to Latham.
CHEROKEE PARK	Larimer	Feb 14,1913 Dec 26,1922	Feb 15,1919 Jun 1933	Formerly Saint Cloud.
CHERRELYN	Arapahoe	Jun 6,1894	Feb 29,1916	Located within Englewood. Replaced by Station 41 of Denver.
CHERRY	Douglas	Apr 7,1900	Aug 31,1920	
CHERRY CREEK	Arapahoe	Jul 26,1869 (Last listed in 1886 Postal Guide.)	?	
CHEYENNE WELLS	Douglas	Feb 10,1869	Apr 11,1870	
CHEYENNE WELLS	Bent Cheyenne	May 8,1876 Oct 2,1895	Aug 21,1895	

OFFICE	COUNTY	ESTABLISHED	DISCONTINUED	REMARKS
CHICOSA	Las Animas	May 19,1890 Aug 2,1896 Apr 7,1905 (First listed in 1897 Postal Guide.)	Jun 30,1894 Mar 31,1904 Aug 15,1910	
CHIHUAHUA	Summit	Jan 23,1880	May 9,1892	Ghost Town.
CHILCOTT	Pueblo	Mar 24,1884	Oct 21,1890	
CHILDS PARK	Hinsdale	May 9,1912	Feb 28,1919	
CHIMNEY ROCK	Archuleta	Oct 1950		Formerly named Dyke. Converted Apr 7,1967 to a rural branch of Pagosa Springs.
CHIPETA	Gunnison	Oct 21,1881	Sep 15,1882	Changed to Naturita.
CHIPETA	Delta	Jun 14,1895	Sep 7,1895	
CHIPETA	Pitkin	Apr 20,1899	Oct 17,1899	
CHIPITA PARK	El Paso	Apr 1935		Converted Jun 31,1967 to a rural branch of Cascade. Summer P. O. 6/1 to 9/30
CHIVINGTON	Bent Kiowa	Oct 24,1887		
CHLORIDE	Gunnison Pitkin	Aug 5,1881	Jan 3,1882	Formerly named Ashcroft. Re-named Ashcroft.
CHROMO	Archuleta	Oct 30,1885		
CIMARRON	Montrose	Aug 28,1883		
CLANDA	Las Animas	Feb 11,1920	Dec 31,1926	
CLAREMONT	Elbert Kit Carson	Sep 11,1888	Mar 24,1906	Name changed to Stratton.
CLARENCE	Gunnison	Feb 4,1892	Mar 2,1892	P. O. moved to Marble. Marble and Clarence were adjoining townsites.
CLARK	Routt	Sep 16,1889		
CLARKSON	Grand	Jul 28,1892	Dec 8,1898	

OFFICE	COUNTY	ESTABLISHED	DISCONTINUED	REMARKS
CLARKVILLE	Yuma	Jun 1938	Jul 1954	
CLAUD	Elbert	Oct 30,1882	Apr 3,1888	
CLAYTONIA	Saguache	Mar 11,1881	Mar 10,1892	
CLEARWATER	Weld	Sep 10,1862	Jan 20,1864	P. O. moved from Julesburgh I. Moved to Julesburgh II.
CLEMMONS	Elbert	Oct 23,1882	Oct 31,1898	Re-named Schley.
CLEORA	Lake Chaffee	Dec 5,1876	Mar 7,1882	
CLERMONT	Elbert	Mar 25,1881	Jul 23,1883	See Claremont.
CLEVELAND	Summit Eagle	Mar 21,1883	Aug 14,1884	
CLEVELAND	Custer	Feb 5,1885	May 13,1886	
CLIFF	Jefferson	Jan 24,1889 May 4,1896	Nov 2,1894 Apr 5,1923	Name changed to Cliffdale.
CLIFFDALE	Jefferson	Apr 5,1923	Jun 1933	Formerly named Cliff.
CLIFFORD	Lincoln	Apr 11,1908	Feb 28,1918	Also known as Mirage.
CLIFTON	Mesa	Aug 18,1900		
CLIMAX	Lake Summit Lake	Apr 22,1887 Dec 5,1917	Apr 12,1898	P. O. moved from Alicante
CLINTON	Custer	Aug 4,1879	Oct 13,1881	
CLONMELL	Fremont	Jul 18,1898	Feb 7,1901	Changed to Cramer
CLOUDCREST	Jefferson	Apr 15,1916	Oct 15,1918	
CLOVER	Mesa	Feb 1,1895 Feb 28,1898	Nov 8,1895 Sep 30,1902	
CLOVER	Huerfano	Dec 12,1912	Aug 31,1922	
CLYDE	Las Animas	Feb 18,1889	Mar 28,1890	
CLYDE	Teller	Oct 12,1899 Sep 3,1901	Sep 15,1900 Sep 30,1909	Formerly Seward

OFFICE	COUNTY	ESTABLISHED	DISCONTINUED	REMARKS
CLYDE	Baca	Oct 25,1913 (Not listed in Postal Guides.)	Jun 15,1920	
COAL CREEK	Boulder	Apr 9,1864	Oct 29,1873	
COAL CREEK	Fremont	Nov 4,1873	May 31,1894	Changed to Coalcreek.
COAL CREEK	Fremont	1964		Formerly Coalcreek.
COAL PARK	Boulder	May 5,1890	May 13,1895	Spelling changed to Coalpark.
COALBASIN	Pitkin	Dec 14,1901	Sep 15,1909	Ghost Town.
COALBY	Delta	Apr 11,1906	Aug 15,1912	
COALCREEK	Fremont	May 31,1894	1964	Formerly Coal Creek. Renamed Coal Creek.
COALDALE	Fremont	Feb 16,1891		Formerly Hendricks. Originally Hayden Creek.
COALMONT	Jackson	Mar 11,1912		
COALPARK	Boulder	May 13,1895	Oct 5,1896	Formerly spelled Coal Park.
COALRIDGE	Garfield	Aug 6,1889 Oct 23,1893*	Oct 6,1892 Oct 26,1893	Changed to Vulcan *Re-named Coalridge
COALVIEW	Routt	Dec 12,1916	Nov 30,1921	Formerly Junction City
COCHEM	Chaffee	Jun 5,1897	May 8,1899	
COCHETOPA	Saguache	Feb 23,1877 May 21,1892	Jul 27,1885 Oct 31,1911	P. O. moved from Los Pinos. P. O. moved from Cuenin.
COCKRELL	Conejos	Oct 15,1879	Dec 22,1892	
COKEDALE	Las Animas	Dec 26,1906		
COLE	Kit Carson	Mar 7,1907	May 31,1919	
COLEMAN	Weld	Apr 10,1915	Mar 31,1919	
COLFAX	Douglas	Jul 14,1862	Oct 21,1863	
COLFAX	Fremont Custer	May 2,1870	Jan 16,1879	Name changed to Blumenau.

OFFICE	COUNTY	ESTABLISHED	DISCONTINUED	REMARKS
COLLBRAN	Mesa	Jan 9,1892		
COLLEGE VIEW	Arapahoe	Aug 7,1946	May 31,1948	Established as a rural station of Denver.
COLOFLATS	Las Animas	Aug 19,1915	Jul 30,1918	Changed to Branson.
COLONA	Nebraska Terr.	Apr 27,1860	Feb 11,1861	Formerly Auroria.
	(The location of this office within the present boundaries of Colorado has not been confirmed.)			
COLONA	Ouray	Oct 19,1891	Apr 1943	
COLORADO CITY	Kansas Terr.	Mar 24,1860	Jun 30,1917	Replaced by West End Station of Colorado Springs.
COLORADO CITY	Pueblo	Sep 1,1964		Established as a rural branch of Pueblo
COLORADO SIERRA	Gilpin	Aug 16,1966		Established as a non-personnel rural branch of Golden
COLORADO SPRINGS	El Paso	Dec 1,1871		
COLOROW	Grand	May 24,1882	May 20,1903	Also known locally as Coloraw.
COLUMBINE	Routt	Jun 5,1896	1967	
COLUMBUS	Chaffee	Apr 10,1882	Aug 11,1884	
COLUMBUS	La Plata	Nov 15,1894 Jun 22,1898	Jul 30,1897 Apr 30,1903	
COMANCHE	Adams	Jul 6,1911	Oct 31,1923	
COMMERCE CITY	Adams	1963		Formerly named Derby.
COMO	Park	Jul 23,1879		Converted Aug 31,1963 to a rural branch of Fairplay.
CONCRETE	Fremont	May 28,1908	May 31,1921	
CONDON	Arapahoe	Jun 7,1888	May 23,1892	P. O. moved to Vernon. Also known as Congdon.
CONEJOS	Conejos	Feb 25,1862		

OFFICE	COUNTY	ESTABLISHED	DISCONTINUED	REMARKS
CONGER	Summit	Jul 8,1880	Jan 3,1881	Changed to Argentine
CONGER	Routt	Mar 27,1894	Jul 15,1895	Name changed to Pallas.
CONGRESS	San Juan	Apr 2,1883	Jan 7,1884	
CONIFER	Jefferson	Nov 16,1894 Oct 1,1961	Feb 28,1929	Formerly named Hutchison. P. O. moved from Pine.
CONRAD	Park	Jul 7,1897	Oct 14,1905	
CONROW	Chaffee	Aug 15,1881	Nov 9,1882	Formerly Arbourville
CONSOLIDATED	Huerfano	Sep 1,1905	Oct 26,1905	Rescinded.
CONTENT	La Plata	Sep 21,1901	Oct 15,1913	
COOPER	Summit	Jun 15,1881	Sep 28,1882	Changed to Taylor
COOPER	Eagle	Jul 31,1886	Feb 6,1890	Formerly Taylor. Changed to Tennessee Pass.
COPE	Arapahoe Adams Washington	Jul 16,1889		Formerly Gray.
COPPER	Mesa	May 9,1898	Mar 2,1899	Changed to Ionia
COPPER ROCK	Boulder	Jun 30,1892 Feb 18,1915	Jun 30,1903 Dec 15,1915	
COPPER SPUR	Eagle	Oct 1,1929	1956	Formerly named Coppertown.
COPPERDALE	Jefferson	Mar 22,1882	Jan 30,1883	
COPPERFIELD	Fremont	Jun 18,1907	Dec 31,1910	
COPPERTON	Eagle	Mar 17,1917	Aug 11,1917	
COPPERTOWN	Eagle	Dec 8,1922	Oct 1,1929	Name changed to Copper Spur.
CORAVILLE	Kansas Terr.	Mar 22,1859	Jun 25,1859	
CORAVILLE	Boulder	Aug 19,1887	Nov 21,1888	
CORCORAN	Arapahoe	Sep 11,1889	Apr 19,1894	
CORDOVA	Las Animas	May 19,1881	Sep 9,1889	Place named East Weston. P. O. moved to Weston.

OFFICE	COUNTY	ESTABLISHED	DISCONTINUED	REMARKS
CORINTH	Las Animas	Mar 18,1887	Aug 12,1887	Changed to Minneapolis.
CORNELL	San Miguel	Mar 11,1903	Jul 10,1903	Rescinded.
CORNISH	Weld	Nov 24,1914	1967	
CORNWALL	Rio Grande	Oct 31,1879	Nov 20,1882	P. O. moved to Jasper.
CORONA	Weld	Apr 14,1874	Dec 20,1878	Formerly Green City.
	Morgan	Nov 10,1882	Dec 2,1896	Name changed to Wiggins.
CORRIZO	Baca	Dec 13,1899	Dec 14,1907	Spelling changed to Carrizo.
CORTEZ	La Plata	Jun 21,1887		
	Montezuma			
CORTRITE	Park	Nov 22,1889 (Spelled Contrite in 1891 Postal Guide.)	Mar 29,1892	
CORY	Delta	Mar 12,1895		
CORYELL	Costilla	Aug 29,1887	Jan 8,1890	Changed to Stanley
COSDEN	Gunnison	Aug 28,1883	Feb 4,1885	
COSTILLA	Costilla	Dec 13,1862	*	*Moved to Taos County, New Mexico, Oct 21,1872.
COTOPAXI	Fremont	May 25,1880		
COTSWORTH	Weld	Sep 28,1882	Jan 17,1883	
COTTON CREEK	Saguache	Aug 9,1875	Feb 13,1895	Name changed to Mirage.
COTTONWOOD SPRINGS	Chaffee	Jul 28,1879 Mar 5,1890	Nov 23,1885 Nov 11,1895	
COULTER	Grand	Aug 14,1884	Oct 14,1905	
COUSIN SPRINGS	Pueblo	Oct 8,1914	Nov 30,1920	
COVENTRY	Montrose	Dec 26,1894	Dec 15,1917	
COWANS	Lincoln	Nov 2,1915	Jul 31,1929	
COWDREY	Larimer	Dec 21,1901	Jan 15,1907	

OFFICE	COUNTY	ESTABLISHED	DISCONTINUED	REMARKS
COWDREY	Jackson	Apr 5,1915		
COX	Gunnison	Apr 25,1903	Feb 15,1905	
CRAGMOR	El Paso	Feb 5,1927	Feb 1936	
CRAGS	Boulder	Mar 4,1911	Sep 15,1913	
CRAIG	Routt Moffat	Aug 28,1889		Formerly named Yampa.
CRAMER	Fremont	Feb 7,1901	Jun 30,1904	Formerly Clonmell
CRAWFORD	Delta	Apr 14,1883		
CREEDE	Saguache Mineral	Jul 1,1891	Nov 28,1908	Formerly named Willow. P. O. moved to North Creede.
CREEDE	Mineral	Feb 9,1909		P. O. formerly named Amethyst.
CRESCENT	Larimer	Apr 7,1880	Nov 22,1880	
CRESCENT	Grand	Feb 14,1889	Apr 16,1894	
CRESCENT	Boulder	Feb 5,1907 Jun 23,1920 Oct 16,1959	Feb 15,1918 Nov 15,1922	Re-established as a rural branch of Golden.
CREST	Weld	Mar 8,1909	Jun 30,1923	
CRESTED BUTTE	Gunnison	May 26,1879		
CRESTONE	Saguache	Nov 16,1880		Also known as Creston.
CRESWELL	Jefferson	Oct 7,1870	Feb 15,1908	
CRIPPLE CREEK	El Paso Teller	Jun 20,1892		Formerly Fremont.
CRISMAN	Boulder	Jul 20,1876 Jan 4,1898	Jun 15,1894 May 31,1918	
CRISTONIE	Saguache	Feb 7,1872	Oct 29,1873	Crestone (?)
CRITCHELL	Jefferson	Jun 19,1899 (Last listed in the 1943 Postal Guide.)	?	

OFFICE	COUNTY	ESTABLISHED	DISCONTINUED	REMARKS
CROCKER	Fremont (?)	Feb 18,1880	Oct 31,1881	
	Summit	Jun 16,1882	Sep 13,1882	
CROOK	Weld	May 26,1882		
	Logan			
CROOKSTOWN	Saguache	May 25,1904	Feb 28,1906	Also Crooksville and Crookston.
	Gunnison			
CROOKSVILLE	Gunnison	Jun 3,1878	Dec 15,1885	Also Crookstown and Crookston.
CROSS MOUNTAIN	Moffat	Jul 16,1919	Dec 1943	
CROSSON	Jefferson	Aug 14,1879	Aug 25,1885	Same place as Crossons.
CROSSONS	Jefferson	Jun 2,1920	Jan 1932	Same place as Crosson.
CROW	Pueblo	Oct 30,1885	May 4,1891	
		Sep 2,1896	Nov 30,1907	
CROWLEY	Crowley	Dec 18,1914		
CROWS ROOST	El Paso	Nov 4,1913	Jul 31,1916	Ranch Post Office.
CRYSTAL	Gunnison	Jul 28,1882	Oct 31,1909	Town named Crystal City. Ghost Town.
CRYSTAL LAKE	Jefferson	Jun 28,1892	Nov 2,1894	
CRYSTOLA	Teller	Nov 24,1911	Dec 31,1913	Formerly named Langdon.
CUATRO	Las Animas	Dec 21,1903	Aug 6,1907	A coal camp properly spelled Quatro.
CUCHARA	Huerfano			P. O. moved from Cuchara Camps. Converted Jul 1,1959 to a rural station of La Veta
CUCHARA CAMPS	Huerfano	Jan 20,1916	1957	P. O. moved to Cuchara.
CUCHARAS	Huerfano	Sep 20,1872	Jul 12,1877	Formerly spelled Cacharas.
		Jul 26,1877	Jan 15,1921	
CUENIN	Saguache	Feb 4,1884	May 21,1892	P. O. moved to Cochetopa.
CUMBRES	Conejos	Nov 25,1889	Sep 6,1893	
		Feb 8,1895	Aug 31,1901	
		Dec 13,1906	Jul 13,1918	
		Nov 1,1923	Apr 1937	

OFFICE	COUNTY	ESTABLISHED	DISCONTINUED	REMARKS
CURRAN	Gunnison	Aug 8,1880	Sep 10,1880	
CURRANT	Fremont	Oct 2,1894	Feb 28,1901	Formerly named Currant Creek.
CURRANT CREEK	Fremont	Aug 29,1870	Oct 2,1894	Name changed to Currant.
CURTIS	Washington	Apr 27,1888	Apr 30,1901	
CURTIS	El Paso	Oct 15,1901	Mar 15,1915	
CYANIDE	Fremont	Oct 23,1895	May 31,1907	
DACONO	Weld	Dec 21,1907		
DAFFODIL	Jefferson Douglas	Apr 11,1896	Feb 19,1908	Town name was Trumbull. P. O. moved to Deckers.
DAILEY	Garfield	Sep 6,1900	Dec 14,1903	
DAILEY	Logan	Jun 28,1915	1962	
DAKAN	Douglas	Dec 30,1896	Aug 2,1898	
DAKE	Park	May 23,1883	Oct 8,1892	
DALEROSE	Las Animas	Jun 21,1916	Apr 1943	
DALLAS	Ouray	Feb 11,1884	Oct 31,1899	Named Dallas City. P. O. moved from Lawrence. Ghost Town.
DALLAS DIVIDE	San Miguel Ouray San Miguel	Mar 24,1894	Jul 23,1909	P. O. moved to Noel. Formerly named Aurora.
DALLASVILLE	Ouray	Dec 21,1877	Jul 9,1879	
DAMASCUS	Lincoln	Jun 6,1914	Feb 15,1917	
DANIELS	Jefferson	Apr 8,1948	Dec 15,1949	Established as a rural branch of Golden. Changed to Edgemont Rural Branch.
DAVIDSON	Boulder	Dec 4,1873 Jun 29,1876 Jun 27,1877	Apr 17,1876 Apr 4,1877 Oct 15,1878	
DAVIES	Pitkin	Jan 7,1895	Oct 11,1895	
DAVIS	Las Animas	Aug 6,1878	Apr 23,1879	

OFFICE	COUNTY	ESTABLISHED	DISCONTINUED	REMARKS
DAWKINS	Pueblo	Feb 5,1885	Feb 21,1907	P. O. moved to Pinon. ½ mile.
DAWSON	Jefferson	Jun 9,1890 (Not listed in Postal Guides.)	Jun 31,1894	
DAWSON	Routt	Nov 27,1917	Nov 15,1919	
DAYTON	Lake	Oct 16,1866	Nov 30,1868	P. O. moved to Granite. (See Twin Lakes.)
DAYTON	Bent	Jun 1,1887	Dec 8,1887	
DAYTON	Gunnison	Jan 26,1897 Jan 13,1905	Mar 31,1904 Oct 31,1911	
DE BEQUE	Mesa	Mar 23,1888* May 27,1902#	Apr 28,1894+	P. O. moved from Ravens. *Formerly Ravensbeque +Changed to Debeque #Re-named De Beque
DE NOVA	Washington	Mar 20,1916 (Last listed in 1953 Postal Guide.)	?	Formerly Dillingham
DEAN Las	Las Animas	Apr 4,1900	Jun 15,1913	
DEANE	Douglas	Dec 19,1879	Oct 16,1884	P. O. moved from Platte Canon. Name changed to Deansbury.
DEANSBURY	Douglas	Jun 23,1890	Feb 3,1892	Formerly named Deane. Name changed to Strontia Springs.
DEBEQUE	Mesa	Apr 28,1894	May 27,1902	P. O. originally moved from Ravens. Formerly spelled De Beque. Re-named De Beque.
DEBS	Hinsdale	Sep 10,1915	Jan 31,1925	
DECATUR	Summit	Oct 3,1879	Jan 28,1885	Ghost Town
DECATUR	Las Animas Baca	Jul 25,1888	Aug 8,1891	
DECKERS	Douglas	Feb 19,1908	Dec 1933	Daffodil post office, moved from the town of Trumbull.
DEEP CHANNEL	Moffat	Jun 28,1922	Aug 31,1926	

OFFICE	COUNTY	ESTABLISHED	DISCONTINUED	REMARKS
DEEPCREEK	Routt	Jan 30,1900	Feb 1936	
DEER TRAIL	Arapahoe	Jun 3,1875 Oct 1950	May 17,1894	Spelling changed to Deertrail.
DEER VALLEY	Park	Aug 25,1871	Nov 20,1878	P. O. moved to Bailey.
DEERCREEK	Jefferson	Aug 24,1896	Dec 15,1899	
DEERTRAIL	Arapahoe	May 17,1894	Oct 1950	Formerly spelled Deer Trail. Re-named Deer Trail.
DEL MINE	San Juan	Jun 22,1883	May 19,1884	
DEL NORTE	Conejos Rio Grande	Jan 28,1873		P. O. moved from Loma.
DEL RIO	Conejos	Sep 1942	Apr 1946	
DELAGUA	Las Animas	Apr 30,1903	May 31,1954	
DELAWARE CITY	Summit	Nov 13,1861 Sep 10,1863	Jul 15,1863 Jul 13,1875	Changed to Preston.
DELAWARE FLATS	Kansas Terr.	?	?	Listed in "Chase-Cabeen". No other record.
DELCARBON	Huerfano	Nov 20,1915	Dec 31,1953	
DELHI	Las Animas	Mar 16,1908 Dec 26,1919	Apr 19,1913	P. O. moved to Bloom. P. O. moved from Edwest
DELPHI	Boulder	Oct 31,1895	Apr 18,1898	Changed to Wallstreet
DELTA	Gunnison Delta	Jan 5,1882		
DENVER	Arapahoe Denver	Feb 13,1866		Originally Auraria Formerly Denver City
DENVER CITY	Kansas Terr. Arapahoe	Feb 11,1860	Feb 13,1866	Formerly named Auraria. Name changed to Denver.
DENVER JUNCTION	Weld	Jan 7,1885	May 26,1886	P. O. moved from Julesburgh II. P. O. renamed Julesburg (present day).

OFFICE	COUNTY	ESTABLISHED	DISCONTINUED	REMARKS
DENVER MILLS	Arapahoe Denver	Jan 20,1892 Apr 17,1908	Feb 29,1908 Sep 30,1918	Formerly named Sheffield.
DEORA	Baca	Apr 21,1920		
DERBLAY	Arapahoe	Jul 13,1892	Dec 22,1892	Formerly named Washburn. Re-named Washburn.
DERBY	Eagle	Aug 16,1888	Sep 16,1889	
DERBY	Adams	Jan 27,1910	1963	Name changed to Commerce City.
DEUEL	Weld Morgan	Feb 15,1883	Jul 18,1907	P. O. moved from Morgan. Name changed to Weldona.
DEVINE	Park	Feb 17,1898	Jun 20,1899	Changed to Black Mountain.
DEXTER	Grand	Sep 25,1896	May 20,1911	
DICKEY	Summit	Feb 19,1892	Sep 13,1893	
DICKS	Las Animas	Jun 29,1926	Nov 1935	
DICKSON	Huerfano	Jan 30,1879	Jan 7,1885	
DILLINGHAM	Washington	Jan 24,1911 Apr 29,1916	Mar 20,1916 Jul 1,1920	P. O. moved to De Nova
DILLON	Summit	Oct 24,1879 Jun 28,1881	Jan 5,1881	Town has been moved to present location.
DINAN	San Miguel	Oct 9,1929	?	Rescinded
DINOSAUR	Moffat	1966		Formerly named Artesia.
DISAPPOINTMENT	Dolores	Apr 19,1919	Jun 30,1920	
DISTON	Kiowa	Jun 29,1908	Aug 15,1908	Rescinded
DIVIDE	Lake Chaffee	Jun 24,1874	Aug 19,1885	
DIVIDE	El Paso Teller	Jul 26,1889		
DIX	La Plata	Apr 8,1890 Jun 6,1895 Jul 20,1907	May 14,1895 Sep 29,1900 Dec 14,1907	

OFFICE	COUNTY	ESTABLISHED	DISCONTINUED	REMARKS
DODD	Morgan	Apr 7,1904	Dec 31,1907	
DODGEVILLE	Kit Carson	Sep 14,1907	Dec 14,1907	Rescinded
DODSONVILLE	Las Animas	Dec 10,1873	Apr 17,1876	Changed to Linwood
DOLOMITE	Chaffee	Oct 11,1886	Aug 27,1890	Changed to Higgins
DOLORES	La Plata Montezuma	Apr 5,1878		
DOME ROCK	Jefferson	Jul 12,1880	Jan 5,1881	
		Feb 21,1883	May 11,1886	
		Jun 25,1907	Apr 4,1911	P. O. Name changed to Longview
DOMINGUEZ	Delta	Aug 17,1907	Oct 31,1913	
DORA	Custer	Jul 11,1879	Oct 31,1883	Ghost Town. Now submerged.
DORA	Chaffee	Jan 10,1906	Nov 31,1906	
DORAN	Park	Nov 1,1901	Jan 2,1907	
DORCHESTER	Gunnison	Aug 2,1900	Jul 31,1912	
DOTSERO	Eagle	Jun 29,1883	Apr 12,1895	
		Aug 14,1895	Sep 30,1905	
		Aug 1933	Apr 1948	
DOUGLAS	Douglas	May 18,1874	Dec 12,1884	P. O. moved from Castle Rock.
DOVE CREEK	Dolores	Jan 16,1915		
DOVER	Weld	Dec 16,1905	Apr 30,1931	
DOWNER	Boulder	Aug 9,1904	Apr 15,1915	Place was named Monarch.
DOWNING	Las Animas	Nov 3,1886	Sep 14,1896	
DOYLEVILLE	Gunnison	Oct 24,1881	Apr 9,1882	Name changed to Gilman.
		Mar 24,1883	Apr 4,1969	Re-named Doyleville.
DRAGOO	El Paso	Apr 19,1915	Aug 15,1916	
DRAKE	Gunnison	Sep 13,1881	Oct 5,1882	
DRAKE	Larimer	Dec 14,1905		

OFFICE	COUNTY	ESTABLISHED	DISCONTINUED	REMARKS
DRENNAN	El Paso	?	Oct 1,1951	Established as a rural station of Colorado Springs.
DREW	Gunnison	Feb 7,1884 Nov 2,1885	Jul 21,1885 Mar 29,1886	
DRISCOLL	Fremont	May 2,1896	May 27,1896	Rescinded
DRUCE	Las Animas	Aug 31,1916	May 2,1922	
DRYER	Jackson	Aug 3,1916	Oct 31,1917	
DRYGULCH	Routt	Jul 2,1896 (Not listed in Postal Guides.)	Jun 2,1898	
DUBLIN BAY	Morgan	Jul 18,1916 (Not listed in Postal Guides.)	?	
DUBOIS	Gunnison	Jan 9,1894	Feb 28,1910	
DUER	Prowers	Mar 25,1916	May 31,1920	
DUDLEY	Park	Oct 31,1872	Oct 22,1880	P. O. moved from Montgomery City. Ghost Town.
DUFF	Arapahoe	May 1,1884 Jun 23,1892	Nov 2,1891 Jul 28,1896	Also known as Magnolia.
DUKE	Pueblo	May 5,1908	Aug 4,1908	
DUMONT	Clear Creek	May 17,1880		Formerly named Mill City.
DUNCAN	Saguache	Nov 21,1892	Sep 15,1900	
DUNCAN	Las Animas	Jul 8,1901	Aug 17,1916	Changed to Gotera
DUNE	Saguache	Apr 24,1891 (Not listed in Postal Guides.)	Jun 10,1895	
DUNKLEY	Routt	Dec 16,1892	Jan 1943	
DUNTON	Dolores	Aug 9,1892 Mar 19,1896	Nov 8,1895 ?	Discontinued. Date unknown.
DUPONT	Adams	Jun 19,1926		

OFFICE	COUNTY	ESTABLISHED	DISCONTINUED	REMARKS
DURANGO	La Plata	Nov 19,1880		
DYKE	Archuleta	Apr 10,1901	Sep 30,1910	
		Dec 20,1910	Jul 15,1913	
		Mar 17,1917	Oct 1950	Changed to Chimney Rock
EADS	Bent Kiowa	Nov 18,1887		
EAGLE	Summit	Oct 4,1880	Mar 6,1882	
EAGLE	Eagle	Sep 3,1891		Formerly named Castle.
EAGLE ROCK	Boulder	Jun 22,1876	Jun 20,1877	
		(Listed as 'Eagle Creek' in the 1876 Postal Guide.)		
EAGLITE	Mesa	Dec 3,1885	Aug 26,1901	Name changed to Plateau City.
EARL	Las Animas	Jul 31,1895	Aug 3,1897	
		Nov 19,1900	Dec 15,1923	
		(Not listed in 1915 Postal Guide.)		
EARLY SPRING	Garfield	Apr 20,1883	Jul 20,1883	
EAST ARGENTINE	Clear Creek	Aug 26,1867	Nov 15,1867	
EAST PORTAL	Gilpin	Oct 12,1923	Jan 31,1928	
		Mar 1933	Sep 1934	
		May 1937	Jan 29,1962	
EAST TINCUP	Jefferson	Jun 1,1960	Sep 1,1963	Established as a rural station of Golden.
EASTDALE	Costilla	Apr 27,1895	Jul 15,1909	
EASTLAKE	Adams	Jun 8,1912		
EASTON	El Paso	May 6,1872	Jul 2,1873	
		Jun 24,1874	Sep 28,1883	Name changed to Eastonville.
EASTONVILLE	El Paso	Sep 28,1883	Jun 1932	Formerly named Easton. Ghost Town.
EATON	Weld	Sep 28,1883		Formerly named Eatonton.
EATONTON	Weld	Sep 25,1882	Sep 28,1883	Name changed to Eaton.

OFFICE	COUNTY	ESTABLISHED	DISCONTINUED	REMARKS
ECKERT	Delta	Oct 27,1891 (First listed in the 1893 Postal Guide.)		
ECKLEY	Weld Washington Yuma	Nov 15,1883 Aug 14,1885	Jun 16,1884	
EDDY	Routt	Mar 19,1890	Aug 31,1913	
EDEN	Pueblo	Jan 14,1890	Mar 31,1914	
EDENVIEW	Las Animas	Feb 20,1919	Aug 31,1920	
EDGEMONT	Jefferson	Dec 15,1949		Formerly Daniels Rural Branch. Rural Branch of Golden.
EDGERTON	El Paso	Jun 16,1870 Sep 6,1895	Jun 7,1895 Aug 28,1902	P. O. moved to Pikeview.
EDGEWATER	Jefferson	Mar 1,1892	Aug 1937	Converted to a branch of Denver.
EDITH	Routt	Feb 21,1883	Jul 9,1885	
EDITH	Archuleta	Oct 28,1895	Oct 31,1917	Listed under Rio Arriba County, New Mexico from May 5,1904 to Feb 5,1909.
EDLER	Baca	Feb 16,1916	Jan 1948	
EDLOWE	El Paso Teller	Jun 9,1896	Jun 16,1899	
EDWARDS	Eagle	Jul 10,1883		
EDWEST	Las Animas	Nov 14,1916	Dec 26,1919	P. O. moved to Delhi.
EGERIA	Routt	Apr 2,1883	Mar 15,1900	
EGGERS	Larimer	Apr 23,1926	May 1944	
EGNAR	Dolores San Miguel	May 28,1917		
EL MORO	Las Animas	Apr 17,1876 Jul 1,1880	Jun 30,1880 Jan 1896	Spelling changed to Elmoro.
EL PASO	El Paso	Oct 21,1862	Jul 11,1893	Name changed to Buttes.

OFFICE	COUNTY	ESTABLISHED	DISCONTINUED	REMARKS
EL RANCHO	Jefferson	Jul 1,1956		Established as a rural branch of Golden.
ELBA	Washington	May 9,1910	1958	
ELBERT	Elbert	Mar 12,1875 Jun 27,1882	Jul 27,1880	P. O. moved from Gomers Mills.
ELCO	La Plata	Jul 28,1905	May 31,1914	
ELDORA	Boulder	Feb 13,1897		Converted May 19,1967 to a rural branch of Nederland. Summer P. O. 6/1 to 9/30.
ELDORADO SPRINGS	Boulder	May 1,1930		P. O. formerly named Hawthorne.
ELDRED	Fremont	Sep 9,1892	Dec 15,1907	
ELEPHANT	Clear Creek	Jun 28,1881	Nov 7,1881	
ELGIN	Gunnison	Oct 11,1882	Sep 10,1885	P. O. moved to Waunita.
ELIZABETH	Elbert	Apr 24,1882		
ELK CREEK	Jefferson	Mar 23,1864	Apr 18,1865	
ELK SPRINGS	Moffat	Jun 9,1924 Jul 1948	Apr 1944	Converted May 6,1966 to a rural branch of Craig.
ELKDALE	Grand	Jun 17,1920	Sep 30,1925	
ELKHEAD	Routt	Jun 2,1884 Jan 4,1910 Nov 10,1919	Jan 28,1885 Nov 15,1917 Sep 15,1924	
ELKHEAD	Moffat	Jan 17,1927	Jan 31,1929	
ELKHORN	Larimer	Jun 5,1879 Apr 14,1900	Feb 6,1890 Oct 31,1917	
ELKO	Gunnison	Aug 15,1881	Sep 24,1884	
ELKTON	Gunnison	Jul 14,1881	Nov 15,1882	
ELKTON	El Paso Teller	Apr 2,1895	Nov 15,1926	Ghost Town.

OFFICE	COUNTY	ESTABLISHED	DISCONTINUED	REMARKS
ELLA	Bent	May 14,1873	Feb 2,1876	
ELLICOTT	El Paso	Apr 29,1895	Jul 31,1916	
ELMORO	Las Animas	Jan 1896 Jan 20,1911	Dec 15,1910 Oct 1933	Formerly spelled El Moro.
ELPHIS	Kit Carson	Dec 8,1916	Dec 31,1923	
ELSMERE	El Paso	Nov 18,1889	Feb 4,1890	
ELWOOD	Rio Grande	Sep 18,1882 Oct 2,1895	Oct 5,1883 Aug 16,1899	
ELYRIA	Arapahoe Denver	Feb 15,1895	Jan 15,1904	P. O. moved from Lyman. Located within Denver.
EMBARGO	Saguache	Sep 25,1903	Mar 15,1905	
EMERSON	Logan Phillips	Mar 27,1888	Sep 20,1890	
EMERY	La Plata	Feb 5,1892	Nov 11,1897	
EMMA	Summit Gunnison (?)	Sep 27,1881	Nov 10,1882	
EMMA	Garfield Eagle Pitkin	Nov 23,1883 Jul 21,1931 (Last listed in the 1947 Postal Guide.)	Jul 3,1920 ?	
EMPIRE	Clear Creek	May 7,1886		Formerly named Empire City.
EMPIRE CITY	Clear Creek	Jun 28,1861	May 7,1886	Name changed to Empire.
ENGLE	Las Animas	Mar 31,1882 Jan 12,1883	Sep 12,1882 Apr 15,1913	Town named Engleville.
ENGLEBURG	Las Animas	Jun 6,1918	Oct 31,1923	
ENGLEWOOD	Arapahoe	Oct 24,1903 Sep 15,1930	Nov 30,1913	Branch of Denver, 1913-1930
ENTERPRISE	Jefferson	Oct 3,1879	Mar 11,1881	Name changed to Platte Canon.
EPHRAIM	Conejos	Jul 5,1881	Jun 2,1888	P. O. moved to Sanford.

52

OFFICE	COUNTY	ESTABLISHED	DISCONTINUED	REMARKS
ERIE	Weld	Jan 24,1871		
ESCALANTE	Routt	Sep 18,1889	Aug 31,1893	
ESCALANTE	Mesa	Sep 9,1903	Dec 5,1903	Rescinded
ESCALANTE FORKS	Mesa	Oct 16,1916	1958	
ESKDALE	Adams	Jul 11,1911	Sep 1933	
ESPINOZA	Conejos	Feb 4,1905	Oct 1933	
ESTABROOK	Park	Aug 9,1880 May 28,1895	Apr 22,1895 Dec 1937	
ESTELENE	Baca	Apr 8,1910	Aug 10,1927	
ESTES PARK	Larimer	Jun 2,1876		
EUREKA	La Plata San Juan	Aug 9,1875	May 1942	
EULA	Routt	Jun 23,1900	Apr 15,1902	
EVA	Montrose	Jun 14,1889	Nov 20,1889	
EVANS	Weld	May 16,1870		P. O. moved from Latham which was originally Cherokee City.
EVERGREEN	Jefferson	Jul 17,1876		
EVERRETT	Lake	Mar 31,1881	Dec 15,1887	
EVERSMAN	Boulder	Sep 7,1899	Aug 31,1900	
EXCELSIOR	Pueblo	Feb 16,1866 Feb 19,1867	Dec 19,1866 Apr 24,1871	
EXCELSIOR	Mesa	Feb 18,1899	Oct 16,1890	
EXCHEQUER	Saguache	Jul 22,1881	Jun 6,1883	
FAIR PLAY	Park	Aug 2,1862	Oct 1,1924	Spelling changed to Fairplay.
FAIRFAX	Grand	Jan 14,1884	Jul 9,1885	
FAIRMOUNT	Otero	Jan 19,1900	Feb 7,1906	Name changed to Swink.

OFFICE	COUNTY	ESTABLISHED	DISCONTINUED	REMARKS
FAIRPLAY	Park	Oct 1,1924		Formerly spelled Fair Play.
FAIRVIEW	Custer	Oct 24,1882 Oct 15,1907	Aug 31,1893 Aug 15,1913	
FAIRVILLE	Park	Sep 13,1878 Nov 7,1879	Jan 28,1879 Feb 23,1882	Name changed to Slaghts, later to Shawnee.
FAIRY	Fremont	May 18,1881	Sep 28,1881	
FALCON	El Paso	Oct 10,1888	Oct 1942	
FALFA	La Plata	Nov 19,1924 (Last listed in the 1953 Postal Guide.)	Nov 30,1954	Formerly named Griffith.
FALL CREEK	San Miguel	Aug 1933	Dec 1943	
FARISITA	Huerfano	Apr 24,1923		
FARLEY	Kit Carson	Mar 31,1908	Oct 15,1908	
FARNHAM	Summit	Dec 2,1881	Nov 2,1895	
FARR	Huerfano	Dec 3,1907	Jul 1946	
FARWELL	Pitkin	Jul 14,1881	Jul 3,1882	
FARWELL	Garfield	Apr 25,1888	Sep 18,1888	
FARWELL	Rio Blanco	Feb 5,1892 (Not listed in Postal Guides.)	May 10,1894	
FERBERITE	Boulder	May 27,1916	Oct 15,1918	
FERGUS	Bent Kiowa	Jun 7,1888	Sep 2,1890	Originally named Hawkins.
FERGUSON	Garfield	Apr 16,1883	Jul 1,1891	Name changed to Antlers. Railroad station was known as Ives.
FIDLER	Fremont	Jun 17,1881	Oct 26,1882	
FIRESTONE	Weld	Aug 30,1907		
FIRSTVIEW	Cheyenne	Jun 25,1907	Nov 24,1961	

OFFICE	COUNTY	ESTABLISHED	DISCONTINUED	REMARKS
FISHER	Chaffee	Sep 12,1889	Aug 15,1890	
FISHER	Pueblo	Feb 11,1895	Jul 31,1908	
FITZSIMMONS	Adams	Nov 2,1921	Apr 30,1923	Originally Camp Speer. Formerly Bunell. Converted to a branch of Denver.
FLAGLER	Elbert Kit Carson	Oct 12,1888		Formerly Bowser
FLAT TOP	Washington	Jan 30,1915	Jan 15,1921	
FLEMING	Logan	Aug 8,1888 Sep 16,1904	May 31,1904	Formerly Calvert
FLEMMINGS RANCH	Weld	Mar 23,1863	Sep 1,1875	Stage Station
FLORA	Sedgwick	Nov 4,1889	Jul 30,1894	
FLORENCE	Fremont	May 8,1873		
FLORESTA	Gunnison	Jan 16,1897	Nov 15,1919	
FLORIDA	La Plata	Aug 8,1877	Mar 31,1881	
FLORISSANT	Park El Paso Teller	Nov 20,1872		
FLOYD HILL	Clear Creek	Sep 9,1912	Aug 1937	
FLUES	Las Animas	Aug 26,1915	Aug 1933	
FOCUS	Custer	May 5,1921	Oct 30,1926	
FOLSOM	Ouray	Aug 17,1880	Dec 13,1880	P. O. formerly located at Telluride. P. O. returned to Telluride.
FONDIS	Elbert	Nov 25,1895	Jul 1954	
FOOTHILLS	Pueblo	Aug 10,1921	Feb 5,1927	
FORBES	Las Animas	Feb 13,1889 Mar 24,1905	Jul 20,1896 Jan 15,1929	

OFFICE	COUNTY	ESTABLISHED	DISCONTINUED	REMARKS
FORBES JUNCTION	Las Animas	Oct 25,1906	Jul 30,1910	
FORD	Fremont	Jan 4,1881	Sep 10,1885	Name changed to Texas Creek. (P. O. moved across river.)
FORD	Yuma	Jun 4,1909	Mar 31,1917	Changed to Wages.
FORDER	Lincoln	Mar 5,1901	Oct 1944	
FORESTDALE	Custer	Oct 1,1914	Apr 30,1926	
FORKS	Larimer	Apr 5,1898 Dec 3,1904	Oct 14,1903 Jun 15,1905	
FORKS CREEK	Jefferson	Apr 5,1878	Jun 4,1895	Spelling changed to Forkscreek.
FORKSCREEK	Jefferson	Jun 4,1895	Jun 10,1927	Formerly spelled Forks Creek. A ghost but not a town.
FORMBY	Montezuma	May 11,1895	Feb 14,1901	
FORT COLLINS	Larimer	Jun 27,1865 Dec 5,1866	Oct 19,1865	
FORT GARLAND	Costilla	Feb 25,1862		
FORT JUNCTION	Weld (?) Gilpin	Feb 5,1866	Mar 19,1867	
FORT LEWIS	La Plata	Oct 5,1880	Oct 10,1891	P. O. moved to Hesperus. Outside Military Reservation.
FORT LOGAN	Arapahoe	May 3,1889		
FORT LUPTON	Nebraska Terr. Weld	Jan 14,1861	Jan 18,1869	Name changed to Weld. Located 1 mile north of present Ft. Lupton.
FORT LUPTON	Weld	Jan 18,1869 May 9,1873	Apr 17,1873	
FORT LYON	Huerfano Las Animas Pueblo Bent	Aug 2,1862	Dec 26,1889	Formerly named Fort Wise. Located north of Prowers.
FORT LYON	Bent	Oct 25,1919 (Listed as U.S. Fort Lyon in 1921 Postal Guide.)		1919-1922, rural station of Las Animas.

OFFICE	COUNTY	ESTABLISHED	DISCONTINUED	REMARKS
FORT MOORE	Gilpin (?) Weld	Jan 15,1866	Jan 22,1868	
FORT MORGAN	Weld	Jul 16,1866	Jun 26,1868	P. O. moved from Junction House.
FORT MORGAN	Weld Morgan	May 28,1884		
FORT REYNOLDS	Pueblo	Jun 15,1869	Feb 25,1870	
FORT SEDGWICK	Weld	May 3,1866	Apr 8,1869	P. O. moved from Julesburgh. Re-established at Julesburgh.
FORT WISE	Kansas Terr. Huerfano	Mar 5,1860	Aug 2,1862	Name changed to "old" Fort Lyon.
FORTIFICATION	Routt	Jan 15,1883	Aug 27,1885	
FORTIFICATION	Moffat	Apr 18,1919	Jun 30,1922	
FOSSTON	Weld	Apr 5,1910	Aug 1941	
FOUNTAIN	El Paso	Aug 8,1864		
FOUNTAIN VALLEY SCHOOL	El Paso	May 18,1957		Established as a rural station of Colorado Springs.
FOURET	Las Animas	Sep 14,1919		Never operated
FOURMILE	Routt	Mar 16,1895	Jul 24,1899	
FOWLER	Otero	Sep 6,1890 Mar 31,1900	Mar 20,1900	P. O. formerly named Oxford. Name changed to Alexander. P. O. change rescinded.
FOX	Arapahoe Adams Yuma	May 17,1890	Dec 15,1912	
FOXTON	Jefferson	Jan 21,1909		
FRANCES	Boulder	Oct 26,1898	Jan 15,1907	
FRANCEVILLE	El Paso	Nov 2,1881	May 14,1894	
FRANCEVILLE JUNCTION	El Paso	Mar 12,1892	Nov 15,1899	

OFFICE	COUNTY	ESTABLISHED	DISCONTINUED	REMARKS
FRANKTOWN	Douglas	Sep 8,1862		Formerly Russellville
FRASER	Grand	Jul 26,1876		
FRAWLEY	Summit	Jul 29,1916	Jul 31,1918	
FREDERICK	Weld	Dec 21,1907		
FREDONIA	Bent	May 27,1892	Sep 29,1900	
FREE GOLD	Chaffee	Apr 12,1880	Apr 6,1881	
FREEDOM	Conejos	May 14,1901	Apr 15,1905	Formerly Morgan
FREELAND	Clear Creek	Jan 16,1879	Sep 15,1908	
FREMONT	El Paso	Jul 29,1891 Feb 4,1892	Dec 9,1891 Jun 20,1892	Changed to Morland. Re-named Fremont. Changed to Cripple Creek.
FREMONT	Washington	Oct 28,1908	Feb 15,1914	
FREMONTS ORCHARD	Weld	Aug 28,1863 Oct 26,1874	Apr 9,1864 Mar 2,1877	South bank of Platte River opposite the present town of Orchard
FRIEND	Arapahoe	Jun 21,1887	Jul 31,1901	
FRISCO	Summit	Aug 29,1879		
FROST	Arapahoe	Jul 15,1899	Aug 15,1901	
FROSTS RANCH	Douglas	Feb 8,1871	Feb 12,1872	Formerly Virginia. Changed to Rock Ridge.
FRUITA	Mesa	Mar 4,1884		Formerly Mesa.
FRUITVALE	Mesa	Jul 1,1948	Aug 24,1950	Established as a rural station of Grand Junction.
FULFORD	Eagle	Feb 5,1892	May 15,1910	
FULTON	Arapahoe	Mar 27,1866	Aug 22,1867	
GARBERT	Ouray	Apr 22,1898	Oct 14,1903	
GALATEA	Bent Kiowa	Dec 22,1887	Oct 1948	

OFFICE	COUNTY	ESTABLISHED	DISCONTINUED	REMARKS
GALENA	Fremont	Feb 16,1877 Aug 25,1879	Jun 8,1877 Nov 4,1885	Ghost Town.
GALETON	Weld	Sep 16,1910		Formerly Zita.
GARCIA	Costilla	Feb 6,1915		Converted Jul 3,1964 to a rural branch of San Luis.
GARDNER	Huerfano	Dec 15,1871		Formerly Huerfano Canyon
GARFIELD	Chaffee	Jul 8,1880 Jan 11,1905 Sep 9,1911	Nov 9,1889 Feb 28,1911	Formerly named Junction City. Converted Dec 30,1963 to a rural branch of Salida.
GARIBALDI	Saguache	Jun 13,1870	Jan 19,1872	Changed to Villa Grove.
GARLAND	Costilla	Jul 24,1877	Jun 27,1878	Railroad construction camp.
GARNETT	Costilla Alamosa	Mar 3,1888	Sep 30,1921	
GARO	Park	Jun 29,1880 (Last listed in 1953 Postal Guide.)	Feb 28,1955	
GARRISON	Costilla	Jan 26,1891	Jul 17,1896	Changed to Hooper
GARY	Morgan	Feb 7,1899	Jul 1954	
GASKILL	Grand	Oct 22,1880	Nov 11,1886	Ghost Town.
GATEVIEW	Gunnison	Mar 11,1892 (Listing in Postal Guides not changed until 1895.)	Nov 7,1895	Formerly Allen
GATEWAY	Mesa	Apr 25,1903 Jul 16,1904	Jul 29,1903	
GAULT	Weld	Jul 13,1900	Oct 31,1916	
GAVIN	Mesa	Sep 26,1916	Jul 31,1917	
GEARY	Weld	May 21,1888 (Not listed in Postal Guides.)	Jun 30,1894	
GEBHARD	Elbert	Apr 8,1881	Apr 24,1882	Changed to Agate.

OFFICE	COUNTY	ESTABLISHED	DISCONTINUED	REMARKS
GEM	Bent	Aug 30,1907	May 31,1913	
GENOA	Lincoln	Jan 30,1895	Jun 29,1895	P. O. moved from Cable.
		Mar 31,1903		
GEORGETOWN	Clear Creek	Jun 19,1866		
GERBAZDALE	Pitkin	Jun 14,1918	Aug 10,1918	Formerly named Watson.
GIBSON	Saguache	Dec 1,1911	Aug 14,1923	Formerly Wabash.
GILCREST	Weld	May 17,1907		
GILL	Weld	Dec 27,1910		
GILLESPIE	Jefferson	May 24,1890	Jun 20,1894	
GILLETT	El Paso	Aug 29,1894	Jun 15,1908	
	Teller	Feb 2,1909	Mar 15,1913	Ghost Town.
GILLETTE	Las Animas	Jul 2,1888	Oct 20,1888	
GILMAN	Jefferson	Dec 17,1874	Aug 8,1876	
GILMAN	Gunnison	Apr 9,1882	Feb 5,1883	Formerly named Doyleville. Renamed Doyleville.
GILMAN	Eagle	Nov 3,1886		
GILPIN	Gilpin	Apr 7,1897	Sep 29,1917	
GILSONITE	Mesa	May 18,1957		Established as a rural branch of Fruita.
GIRARD	Lincoln	Mar 22,1912	Nov 30,1917	
GLACIER	Gunnison	Apr 20,1914	Nov 30,1915	
GLACIER LAKE	Boulder	Mar 3,1906	Aug 15,1908	Ghost Resort.
GLADE PARK	Mesa	Nov 11,1910		
GLADEL	San Miguel	Dec 14,1922	May 31,1929	
GLADSTONE	San Juan	Jan 24,1878	Nov 6,1879	
		Jun 25,1883	Dec 17,1887	
		Jun 17,1898	Jan 15,1912	Ghost Town.

OFFICE	COUNTY	ESTABLISHED	DISCONTINUED	REMARKS
GLADWYN	Archuleta	Aug 2,1885	Apr 14,1890	
GLEN	Washington	Jun 25,1905	May 31,1920	
GLEN GROVE	Douglas	Nov 29,1869	Jul 24,1877	
GLEN HAVEN	Larimer	May 28,1917 May 26,1922 May 18,1926 (First listed in 1918 Postal Guide.)	Jul 31,1919 Jul 31,1924	
GLENDALE	Fremont	Dec 28,1877	May 8,1909	Name changed to Penrose.
GLENDEVEY	Larimer	May 19,1902		Converted 1964 to a rural branch of Jelm, Wyoming. Transferred to rural branch of Walden in 1965.
GLENEATH	El Paso	Oct 22,1910	Jul 31,1916	
GLENEYRE	Larimer	Jun 16,1895	Apr 30,1912	
GLENHAM	Las Animas	May 19,1873	Jul 28,1874	Changed to Barela
GLENN	El Paso	Sep 23,1896 Jun 15,1903	Jul 31,1901 Dec 5,1903	
GLENTIVAR	Park	Apr 13,1921 Dec 1935 (Last listed in 1953 Postal Guide.)	Nov 30,1929 ?	
GLENWOOD SPRINGS	Garfield	Mar 28,1884		Formerly Harlow
GLOBEVILLE	Arapahoe	Mar 4,1890	Jun 16,1900	Converted to station of Denver
GLORY	Yuma	Nov 13,1924	Feb 1,1925	Name changed to Beecher Island.
GODFREY	Elbert	Jan 29,1908	Apr 11,1908	Rescinded. Place also named Buick.
GOFF	Elbert Kit Carson	Apr 23,1888	Jun 15,1910	

OFFICE	COUNTY	ESTABLISHED	DISCONTINUED	REMARKS
GOLCONDA	Montezuma	Apr 26,1894	Jul 1,1895	
GOLD DIRT	Boulder Gilpin	Aug 13,1861	Oct 11,1867	Ghost Town.
GOLD HILL	Boulder	Jan 13,1863 Dec 26,1879	Apr 17,1866 Jun 4,1895	P. O. moved from Left Hand. Spelling changed to Goldhill.
GOLD PARK	Summit Eagle	Mar 31,1881	Oct 5,1883	Ghost Town.
GOLDDALE	Douglas	Jun 29,1882	Feb 2,1885	
GOLDEN	Jefferson	Jun 27,1876		Formerly named Golden City.
GOLDEN CITY	Kansas Terr. Jefferson	Apr 6,1860	Jun 27,1876	Name changed to Golden.
GOLDEN GATE	Kansas Terr. Jefferson	Sep 6,1860	Aug 19,1863	
GOLDFIELD	El Paso Teller	May 5,1895	Aug 1932	
GOLDHILL	Boulder	Jun 4,1895 May 25,1923	May 31,1920 Oct 1952	Formerly spelled Gold Hill.
GOLDROCK	El Paso	Apr 14,1896	Aug 31,1896	Rescinded.
GOMERS MILLS	Douglas (?) Elbert	Jun 13,1870 Aug 22,1876	Mar 15,1876 Jun 27,1882	Changed to Elbert.
GOODPASTURE	Pueblo	May 25,1895	May 31,1923	
GOODRICH	Morgan	Dec 14,1908		
GORDON	Huerfano	Jul 1,1924	Jan 1938	Formerly Camp Shumway. Originally McGuire.
GORHAM	Boulder	Aug 31,1899 Aug 5,1901	Jan 31,1901 Jan 1942	Formerly Langford.
GOTERA	Las Animas	Aug 17,1916	Jan 23,1922	Formerly Duncan. Changed to Lone Oak.
GOTHIC	Gunnison	Aug 5,1879 Jun 20,1907	Jun 22,1896 Jan 31,1914	

OFFICE	COUNTY	ESTABLISHED	DISCONTINUED	REMARKS
GOULD	Jackson	May 1937		Formerly Peneold
GOVE	Custer	Dec 6,1883	Oct 9,1883	
GOWANDA	Weld	Aug 3,1915	Nov 15,1930	
GRACELAND	Elbert	Apr 20,1908	Sep 30,1911	
GRADENS	Montezuma	Jul 7,1896	Nov 30,1903	
GRAFT	Baca	Aug 12,1916	Feb 1935	
GRAHAM	Weld	Apr 1,1911	Feb 28,1918	
GRANADA	Bent Prowers	Jul 10,1873		
GRANBY	Grand	Oct 26,1905		
GRAND JUNCTION	Gunnison Delta (?) Mesa	May 26,1882		Formerly Ute
GRAND LAKE	Grand	Jan 10,1879 Apr 1938	Jan 30,1895	Spelling changed to Grandlake. Spelling reverted to Grand Lake.
GRAND MESA	Delta	Jun 23,1927	Aug 31,1958	
GRAND VALLEY	Garfield	Aug 19,1904		Formerly named Parachute.
GRANDLAKE	Grand	Jan 30,1895	Apr 1938	Formerly spelled Grand Lake. Spelling reverted to Grand Lake.
GRANEROS	Pueblo	Aug 17,1889	Apr 15,1925	
GRANGER	El Paso	Jan 12,1883	Dec 13,1888	
GRANGER	Rio Grande	Oct 14,1902	Jan 12,1903	Rescinded
GRANI.	Lake Chaffee	Nov 30,1868		Converted Mar 25,1966 to a rural branch of Salida.
GRANITE VALE	Park	Dec 19,1861	Jan 31,1870	
GRANT	Park	May 16,1871 Jan 14,1925 Jan 1948	Oct 13,1918 Rescinded	P. O. formerly named Olava. Town was named Grant.
GRAPE	Fremont	Jun 4,1883	Jan 13,1887	Also known as Soda Springs.

OFFICE	COUNTY	ESTABLISHED	DISCONTINUED	REMARKS
GRASSY HILL	San Juan	Jan 30,1879	Jul 15,1880	
GRAY	Arapahoe	Apr 23,1888	Jul 16,1889	Changed to Cope
GRAYCREEK	Las Animas	Jan 3,1895	Aug 31,1921	Formerly Chapel
GRAYLIN	Logan	Sep 26,1910	Dec 15,1917	
GRAYMONT	Clear Creek	May 19,1884	Oct 16,1884	
GRAYS RANCH	Huerfano	Sep 1,1863	Feb 6,1866	P. O. moved to Trinidad.
GREAT DIVIDE	Moffat	Jan 30,1917	Oct 1954	
GREELEY	Weld	Apr 21,1870		
GREEN	Saguache	Mar 18,1884	Sep 30,1884	P. O. moved from Carnero.
GREEN	El Paso	Sep 20,1894	Jun 25,1901	Formerly named Green Mountain Falls. Re-named Green Mountain Falls.
GREEN CANON	Las Animas	Feb 4,1909	Aug 11,1910	Changed to Beacon.
GREEN CITY	Weld	Jun 15,1871	Apr 14,1874	Changed to Corona
GREEN KNOLL	Lincoln	Mar 31,1917	Sep 1933	
GREEN MOUNTAIN FALLS	El Paso	Aug 28,1888 Jun 25,1901	Sep 28,1894	Changed to Green. Re-named Green Mountain Falls.
GREENHORN	Huerfano Pueblo	Dec 10,1866 Oct 16,1897 (Not listed in 1910 Postal Guide.)	Jun 5,1896 Dec 15,1911	
GREENLAND	Douglas	Jun 3,1873	1959	
GREENWOOD	Fremont Custer	Feb 16,1872	Jun 29,1918	
GRESHAM	Garfield	Jun 20,1883	Dec 1,1884	
GRESHAM	Boulder	Jul 17,1895	Nov 30,1912	
GREYSTONE	Moffat	Jun 20,1921		
GRIFFITH	La Plata	Dec 2,1909	Nov 19,1924	Name changed to Falfa.
GRIMALDI	Pueblo	Aug 22,1913	Nov 30,1920	

OFFICE	COUNTY	ESTABLISHED	DISCONTINUED	REMARKS
GRINELL	Las Animas	Dec 18,1878	Jul 10,1883	Formerly San Jose
GROMMET	La Plata	May 3,1904	Jan 13,1908	Changed to Oxford
GROTTO	Jefferson	Mar 7,1881	Mar 21,1882	
GROUSEMONT	Park	Feb 4,1918	Jan 15,1919	Formerly named Kaiserheim.
GROVER	Weld	Mar 3,1885		
GUFFEY	Park	May 23,1896		Formerly named Freshwater. P. O. moved from Idaville.
GULCH	Boulder	Jun 20,1892	Jan 7,1893	
GULCH	Pitkin	Apr 19,1895	Dec 15,1916	P. O. formerly named Spring Gulch. Name for settlement remained Spring Gulch.
GULNARE	Las Animas	Dec 16,1890		
GUNNISON	Lake Gunnison	Oct 2,1876		
GURNEY	Yuma	Sep 17,1907	Sep 15,1923	Formerly in Cheyenne county Kansas. Dates are for the period in Colorado.
GUSTON	Ouray	Jan 26,1892	Nov 16,1898	
GWILLIMSVILLE	El Paso	Apr 18,1878 Apr 29,1887	Aug 27,1886 Sep 25,1890	
GYPSUM	Eagle	Jun 14,1883		
HAHNS PEARK	Routt	May 3,1877	Dec 1941	
HALE	Arapahoe Adams Yuma	May 17,1890 Oct 30,1900	Feb 16,1894	
HALFWAY	El Paso	Aug 21,1903	May 31,1917	Ghost Resort.
HALL VALLEY	Park	Aug 10,1874 Dec 27,1876	Nov 27,1876 Nov 5,1894	Name changed to Hallvale.
HALLVALE	Park	Nov 5,1894	Mar 4,1898	Formerly named Hall Valley.

OFFICE	COUNTY	ESTABLISHED	DISCONTINUED	REMARKS
HAMILTON	Kansas Terr. Park	Jul 26,1860	Nov 10,1881	Ghost Town
HAMILTON	Routt Moffat	Jul 7,1896 Sep 2,1920	Aug 15,1917	
HAMMOND	Park	Apr 10,1896	May 15,1903	
HANCOCK	Chaffee	Sep 10,1880 Nov 14,1903	Jun 24,1887 Dec 31,1904	
HANOVER	Kit Carson	Jul 7,1908	Oct 29,1908	Rescinded.
HANOVER	El Paso	Jun 10,1913	Apr 30,1921	
HAPPYVILLE	Yuma	Jul 26,1910	Feb 28,1922	
HARBOURDALE	Bent	Sep 20,1915	Jun 15,1925	
HARDIN	Weld	Nov 2,1881 Dec 6,1894 (Last listed in 1953 Postal Guide.)	Apr 7,1894 ?	Formerly named Platte Valley.
HARDSCRABBLE	Routt	Feb 12,1925	Nov 15,1925	
HARGISVILLE	Elbert	May 20,1908	Nov 15,1915	No town. Location was a country store.
HARLOW	Mesa	May 17,1890	Apr 7,1891	
HARMAN	Arapahoe Denver	Aug 16,1887	Jan 15,1904	
HARRIS	Arapahoe Adams	Apr 21,1890	Jun 5,1908	Changed to Westminster.
HARRISBURG	Arapahoe Adams Washington	Feb 19,1887 Jan 19,1889 Oct 29,1908 (Last listed in 1953 Postal Guide.)	Sep 21,1888 Aug 31,1906 ?	P. O. moved to Lindon.
HARRISON	Routt	Mar 27,1901	Jan 15,1908	
HARTMAN	Prowers	Mar 2,1908		

OFFICE	COUNTY	ESTABLISHED	DISCONTINUED	REMARKS
HARTSEL	Park	Mar 16,1875		
HARTSTRONG	Yuma	May 31,1921	Jan 31,1940	
HASKILL	San Miguel	Feb 10,1888	Feb 28,1907	
HASTINGS	Las Animas	Sep 12,1889	Feb 15,1939	
HASTY	Bent	Dec 7,1910		
HASWELL	Kiowa	Mar 31,1903 ?	Jan 1956	Date re-established unknown.
HATTON	Fremont	Jun 12,1882	Aug 10,1887	
HAUMANN	Saguache	Jan 9,1882	Aug 25,1885	
HAVERLY	Gunnison	Aug 30,1880	Nov 22,1880	
HAWORTH	Grand Larimer	Aug 26,1884 Jun 17,1905	Mar 17,1898 May 31,1906	
HAWTHORNE	Boulder	Sep 12,1906	May 1,1930	Name changed to Eldorado Springs.
HAWXHURST	Gunnison Mesa	Aug 25,1882	Mar 3,1892	
HAXTUM	Logan Phillips	Apr 25,1888	Jan 17,1922	Name changed to Haxtun.
HAXTUN	Phillips	Jan 17,1922		Formerly named Haxtum.
HAYBRO	Routt	Mar 15,1918 (Last listed in 1951 Postal Guide.)	?	Formerly named Junction City.
HAYDEN	Grand Routt	Nov 15,1875 Nov 22,1880 Oct 24,1881	Sep 30,1880 Aug 1,1881	
HAYDEN CREEK	Fremont	May 4,1878	Feb 10,1880	Changed to Palmer
HAYMAN	Park	Aug 13,1904	Aug 10,1918	
HAYNES RANCH	Pueblo	Jul 31,1861	Mar 3,1863	
HAYWOOD	Summit	Aug 14,1879	Oct 2,1882	

OFFICE	COUNTY	ESTABLISHED	DISCONTINUED	REMARKS
HAZELTINE	Arapahoe Adams	Jan 7,1893	Jan 15,1907	Formerly named Washburn.
HEATHTON	Fremont	Dec 28,1906	May 15,1908	
HEBRON	Grand Larimer Jackson	Jul 11,1884	Feb 15,1922	
HECLA	Garfield	Apr 29,1891 (Not listed in Postal Guides.)	Jun 11,1895	
HEENEY	Summit	Aug 1939		Converted May 15,1960 to a rural station of Kremmling. Summer P. O. 6/16 to 10/15
HEIBERGER	Mesa	Oct 30,1908	Feb 14,1925	
HELENA	Lake Chaffee	Oct 16,1866	Mar 10,1880	
HENDERSON	Weld	May 7,1883	Sep 10,1885	Name changed to Sedgwick.
HENDERSON	Arapahoe Adams	Mar 1,1894		Formerly named Island Station.
HENDRICKS	Fremont	Jan 31,1887	Feb 16,1891	Formerly Palmer. Originally Hayden Creek. Changed to Coaldale.
HENRY	Lake	Jun 3,1880	Jan 20,1882	
HENRY	Rio Grande	Apr 16,1884	Feb 18,1886	Formerly named Lariat. Name changed to Monte Vista.
HENRY	Conejos	Nov 29,1889 Jun 11,1895	May 11,1892 Feb 21,1896	
HENRY	Washington	Dec 26,1907	Nov 15,1917	
HENSON	Hinsdale	May 17,1883	Apr 22,1884	
HENSON	Hinsdale	Nov 12,1892	Nov 30,1913	
HERARD	Saguache	Nov 13,1905	Dec 15,1912	
HEREFORD	Weld	Dec 21,1888 (Not listed in Postal Guides.)	Jun 30,1894	

OFFICE	COUNTY	ESTABLISHED	DISCONTINUED	REMARKS
HEREFORD	Weld	May 8,1909		
HERMES	Yuma	Sep 11,1908 (Listed under Kit Carson county in the 1916 and 1917 Postal Guides.)	Nov 15,1919	
HERMIT	Hinsdale	Jul 6,1904	Sep 15,1920	
HERMITAGE	Grand	May 17,1878 Apr 22,1879	Dec 18,1878 Jan 10,1884	
HERMITAGE	Dolores	Oct 17,1904	Jun 29,1907	
HERMOSA	La Plata	Jul 27,1876 Mar 10,1896 Dec 23,1896	Dec 21,1895 Nov 10,1896 Sep 29,1900	
HERMOSILLA	Huerfano Pueblo	Mar 21,1867 May 16,1870	Jan 25,1870 Jan 15,1872	
HERNDON	Jefferson	Feb 25,1884	Aug 1,1884	
HESPERUS	La Plata	Oct 10,1891		P. O. moved from Port Lewis. Outside Military Reservation.
HESSIE	Boulder	Mar 19,1898	Jun 30,1902	
HESTER	Otero Crowley	Jun 16,1905	Nov 30,1912	
HEWIT	La Plata	Jul 14,1882 Jun 25,1883	Jan 5,1883 Jul 9,1885	
HEYWOOD	Chaffee	Jun 20,1884 (Listed as Haywood in 1885 Postal Guide.)	Feb 15,1888	Formerly named Hortense.
HEZRON	Huerfano	Jan 20,1902	Feb 14,1912	
HICKMAN	Fremont	Dec 10,1866 Jul 17,1867	May 29,1867 Sep 20,1869	
HICKS	Las Animas	Apr 4,1895	Feb 15,1918	Hicks P. O. was at one time located at Powell, south of Hicks.
HIDEWAY PARK	Grand	? (First listed in 1951 Postal Guide.)		

OFFICE	COUNTY	ESTABLISHED	DISCONTINUED	REMARKS
HIGBEE	Bent Otero	Apr 25,1872	Feb 28,1925	
HIGGINS	Chaffee	Aug 27,1890 Mar 3,1893	Nov 21,1892 Apr 22,1895	Formerly Dolomite. Changed to Newett.
HIGGINS	Las Animas	Dec 26,1911	Jun 15,1914	
HIGHLAND LAKE	Weld	Jan 29,1910	Aug 9,1913	Spelling changed from Highlandlake.
HIGHLAND MARY	San Juan	Mar 26,1878	Jun 29,1885	
HIGHLANDLAKE	Weld	Nov 8,1883	Jan 29,1910	Spelling changed to Highland Lake.
HIGHLANDS	Arapahoe	Oct 15,1884	Nov 13,1897	Formerly named Highlandtown. Later re-established as a station of Denver.
HIGHLANDTOWN	Arapahoe	Jun 29,1883	Oct 15,1884	Changed to Highlands.
HIGHMORE	Garfield	Mar 21,1889	Oct 15,1931	
HIGHO	Larimer Jackson	Jun 14,1889 Apr 14,1900	Jan 31,1900 Aug 15,1930	
HIGHPARK	El Paso Teller	Jul 2,1896 Jan 17,1902 Sep 3,1914	Jun 3,1899 Apr 30,1913 May 31,1917	
HILL TOP	Douglas	Feb 17,1890 (Day and month not re-corded)	1896	Spelling changed to Hilltop. Known earlier as Bellevue.
HILLERTON	Gunnison	May 26,1879	Nov 20,1882	Name changed to Abbeyville
HILLROSE	Morgan	Nov 26,1900		
HILLSBORO	Weld	Apr 12,1891 Feb 14,1896	Jun 29,1894 Nov 14,1903	Formerly spelled Hillsborough.
HILLSBOROUGH	Weld	Jun 15,1871	Apr 12,1891	Spelling changed to Hillsboro.
HILLSDALE	Fremont	Feb 18,1880	Aug 2,1880	

OFFICE	COUNTY	ESTABLISHED	DISCONTINUED	REMARKS
HILLSIDE	Fremont	Jan 24,1884		P. O. moved from Texas. Converted Dec. 4, 1964 to a rural branch of Canon City. Transferred to rural branch of Salida Jul 25,1970.
HILLTOP	Douglas	* 1896 (* Day and month not recorded.)	Feb 1944	Formerly spelled Hill Top.
HILTONVILLE	Weld	Oct 10,1873	Sep 24,1875	P. O. moved to Wheatland.
HIRST	Costilla	Jun 19,1899	Jul 31,1901	
HOBART	Teller	Feb 6,1900	Feb 15,1902	
HOEHNE	Las Animas	Nov 2,1886		P. O. moved from Pulaski.
HOGG	Montezuma	Mar 12,1903	Mar 15,1906	
HOLBROOK	Otero	Jun 6,1906	Feb 27,1907	Rescinded.
HOLDEN	Pueblo	Jan 15,1892	Jun 13,1893	
HOLLAND	Park	Feb 24,1874	Dec 23,1874	
HOLLY	Bent Prowers	Nov 26,1880		
HOLTWOLD	Elbert El Paso	Jan 16,1889 Apr 22,1910	Apr 15,1902 Feb 28,1917	
HOLY CROSS	Summit Eagle	Jan 23,1882 Dec 7,1904	Feb 8,1899 Aug 7,1905	Named Holy Cross City. Ghost Town
HOLYOKE	Logan Phillips	Nov 9,1887		
HOME	Larimer	Feb 7,1882	Apr 1946	
HOMELAKE	Rio Grande	Feb 11,1919		Converted Dec 4,1965 to a rural station of Monte Vista.
HONNOLD	Routt	Apr 26,1890	Apr 30,1904	
HOOPER	Costilla Alamosa	Jul 17,1896		Formerly Garrison
HOOPUP	Las Animas	Feb 26,1919 Sep 27,1920	Jul 31,1920 Nov 1937	

OFFICE	COUNTY	ESTABLISHED	DISCONTINUED	REMARKS
HOPE	Lake	Nov 3,1885	Nov 24,1890	Changed to Snowden
HOPE	Mesa	Apr 22,1896	Mar 3,1900	
HORACE	El Paso	Jun 5,1896	Mar 8,1899	
HORSE SHOE	Park	Aug 23,1880	Jul 8,1886	Spelling later changed to one word.
HORSEFLY	Montrose	May 1,1886 Jun 1,1912	Feb 18,1888 Dec 31,1915	
HORSESHOE	Park	Apr 4,1890	Jul 2,1894	Formerly spelled two words.
HORTENSE	Lake Chaffee	May 11,1877	Jun 20,1884	Name changed to Heywood. Also spelled Haywood.
HORTENSE	Chaffee	May 24,1901	Sep 14,1907	
HOT SPRINGS	Ouray	May 4,1877	Aug 28,1879	
HOT SULPHUR SPRINGS	Grand	Sep 10,1874 Feb 15,1912	Jun 26,1894	Name changed to Sulphur Springs. Re-named Hot Sulphur Springs.
HOTCHKISS	Gunnison Delta	Oct 3,1882		
HOUCK	Huerfano	Feb 13,1883	May 31,1883	
HOWARD	Fremont	Jul 26,1882		Formerly named Pleasant Valley.
HOWARDSVILLE	La Plata San Juan	Jun 24,1874 Jan 18,1923	Sep 30,1922 Nov 1939	
HOWBERT	Park	Dec 22,1887	Aug 1933	
HOWEVILLE	Gunnison	Jun 26,1879 Dec 28,1900	Mar 11,1880 May 14,1904	Name changed to Jacks Cabin.
HOWLAND	Lake	Aug 8,1879	Sep 19,1882	
HOYT	Elbert	Mar 27,1888	Nov 10,1888	
HOYT	Morgan	Jun 9,1906		
HUDSON	Weld	Mar 27,1883		

OFFICE	COUNTY	ESTABLISHED	DISCONTINUED	REMARKS
HUERFANO	Huerfano	Feb 25,1862	Jan 20,1879	P. O. moved to Undercliffe.
	Pueblo	Nov 10,1882	Feb 5,1883	P. O. moved from Apache.
		May 9,1883	Feb 15,1884	
		Apr 27,1900	Apr 15,1929	P. O. formerly named Ute, at the town of Huerfano.
HUERFANO CANON	Huerfano	Apr 5,1878	Jul 21,1887	
		Jan 18,1888	Oct 16,1890	Changed to Talpa
HUERFANO CANYON	Huerfano	Apr 13,1871	Oct 3,1871	Changed to Gardner
		Dec 1,1871	Dec 15,1871	
HUGGINS	Routt	Mar 23,1906	Sep 15,1908	Formerly Pallas. Later re-established as Pallas.
HUGHES	Arapahoe	Apr 13,1871	Aug 4,1879	Name changed to Brighton.
HUGHES	Yuma	Apr 11,1913	Oct 1954	
HUGO	Douglas Elbert Lincoln	Dec 1,1871		
HUKILL	Clear Creek	May 12,1879	May 10,1880	
HUMBAR	Las Animas	Aug 6,1887	Oct 27,1887	Changed to Troy
HUMMEL	Chaffee	Oct 3,1882	Jan 26,1882	
HUNTSVILLE	Kansas Terr.	Mar 24,1860	Jul 9,1861	
	Douglas	Jan 22,1862	Aug 29,1867	
		Apr 8,1869	Dec 13,1871	Changed to Larkspur
HUSTED	El Paso	Oct 1,1878	Nov 7,1895	
		Jul 30,1896	Oct 15,1920	Formerly Southwater
HUTCHINSON	Jefferson	Apr 27,1865	Sep 25,1869	
		Feb 19,1872	Jan 3,1894	
		Jun 15,1881	Nov 16,1894	Name changed to Conifer.
HYDE	Weld	Aug 1,1882	Nov 21,1883	
	Yuma	May 28,1884	Apr 16,1898	
	Washington	Nov 21,1907	May 15,1909	
		Aug 18,1911	Oct 15,1918	
		Aug 2,1920	Feb 1940	
HYDRATE	Routt	Jun 17,1920	Oct 1937	

OFFICE	COUNTY	ESTABLISHED	DISCONTINUED	REMARKS
HYDRAULIC	Montrose	Jul 25,1888 Oct 1,1901	May 24,1893 May 31,1905	
HYGIENE	Boulder	Jun 25,1883		
HYNES	La Plata	May 19,1884	Feb 4,1885	
IBEX	Lake	Mar 7,1896 Mar 8,1898	Aug 31,1896 Apr 15,1905	
IDAHO	Clear Creek	Mar 22,1862	Apr 7,1876	Changed to Idaho Springs Also spelled Idaho<u>E</u>
IDAHO SPRINGS	Clear Creek	Apr 7,1876		Formerly Idaho
IDALIA	Arapahoe Adams Yuma	Sep 18,1888		Formerly Alva
IDAVILLE	Park	Apr 12,1895	May 23,1896	Changed to Guffey
IDEAL	Huerfano	Feb 24,1910	Nov 7,1929	
IDLEDALE	Jefferson	Sep 1,1930		Formerly named Starbuck.
IGNACIO	La Plata	Jan 31,1882		
ILIFF	Weld Logan	Mar 21,1882 Apr 23,1896	Nov 27,1895	
ILLIUM	San Miguel	Feb 10,1891 Aug 1,1910	Jul 20,1894 Nov 30,1917	
ILSE	Custer	Aug 14,1884 Jan 23,1895 Dec 10,1920	May 4,1891 Apr 30,1919 Sep 30,1929	
INCHE	Arapahoe	Sep 14,1891	Dec 10,1891	
INDEPENDENCE	Teller	May 12,1899	Jul 1954	P. O. moved from Macon.
INDIAN HILLS	Jefferson	Jun 2,1925		
INDIANAPOLIS	Las Animas	Aug 11,1887	May 16,1889	
INSMONT	Park	Jun 5,1902	Dec 15,1917	
INTERLAKEN	Lake	Apr 29,1887 Mar 20,1891	Jul 10,1890 Apr 21,1894	

OFFICE	COUNTY	ESTABLISHED	DISCONTINUED	REMARKS
IOLA	Gunnison	Jun 24,1896	Aug 16,1963	P. O. moved from Kezar
IONE	Weld	Jun 16,1927	1958	
IONIA	Mesa	Mar 2,1899	Oct 1,1899	Formerly Copper
IRIS	Saguache	Oct 30,1894 May 7,1895	Apr 8,1895 Mar 15,1902	Ghost Town
IRONDALE	Arapahoe	Dec 11,1889	Sep 19,1895	
IRONHILL	Lake	Jun 18,1883	Oct 30,1883	
IRONSIDES	Boulder	Apr 22,1898	Rescinded	
IRONTON	Ouray	May 2,1883 Jan 18,1894	Apr 11,1893 Aug 7,1920	
IRVING	Douglas	Jun 24,1913	Apr 15,1920	Formerly Case
IRWIN	Gunnison	Sep 12,1879 Jul 16,1895	Apr 29,1895 Jun 5,1900	
IRWIN CANYON	Las Animas	Mar 9,1920	Sep 30,1924	
ISLAND STATION	Arapahoe	Aug 29,1872	Mar 1,1894	Name changed to Henderson.
IVANHOE	Pitkin	Apr 26,1888 Jul 31,1899 Aug 22,1913	Jun 13,1894 Jun 15,1912 Aug 10,1918	
IVYWILD	El Paso	Feb 14,1871	Jul 31,1895	
JACK RABBIT	Moffat	Dec 20,1916	May 31,1923	
JACKS CABIN	Gunnison	Jan 25,1909	Mar 30,1918	Formerly named Howeville.
JACKSON	Gunnison	Mar 21,1873 (Not listed in 1888-1890 Postal Guides.)	Feb 20,1893	
JAMESTOWN	Boulder	Jan 8,1867 Aug 1934	Jul 15,1930	
JANEWAY	Pitkin	Aug 16,1887	Nov 30,1900	Ghost Town
JANSEN	Las Animas	Jun 23,1902 Sep 2,1911 Apr 1932	May 31,1911 Jun 15,1913	

OFFICE	COUNTY	ESTABLISHED	DISCONTINUED	REMARKS
JAROSO	Las Animas	Dec 16,1890	Nov 16,1894	
JAROSO	Costilla	Mar 10,1911		
JASPER	Rio Grande	Nov 20,1882 Jun 25,1913 May 11,1920	Jul 30,1910 Feb 18,1918 Feb 15,1927	P. O. moved from Cornwall.
JEFFERSON	Kansas Terr. Arapahoe	Jan 18,1860	Dec 6,1860	
JEFFERSON	Jefferson	Mar 25,1872	Dec 12,1873	Name changed to Morrison.
JEFFERSON	Park	Sep 3,1861 Oct 3,1879	Apr 4,1863	
JENNISON	Hinsdale	Jan 15,1875 Apr 11,1877	Dec 20,1875 Dec 10,1877	
JENNISON	San Juan Hinsdale	May 20,1878	Apr 25,1879	Changed to Timber Hill
JIMMY CAMP	El Paso	May 17,1878	Feb 14,1879	
JOES	Yuma	Oct 22,1912		
JOHNSTOWN	Weld	Apr 17,1903		
JOJUNIOR	Montrose	Dec 16,1914	?	Rescinded (?)
JONES	Mesa	Apr 3,1883	May 25,1883	Changed to Arlington
JOSIE	Summit	Jul 21,1882	Jan 4,1883	Changed to Naomi
JOYA	Conejos	May 27,1904	May 28,1904	Rescinded
JOYCOY	Baca	Aug 13,1915	Mar 15,1927	Changed to Pritchett
JOYLAN	Jefferson	Jan 28,1918	Jul 7,1920	Changed to Starbuck
JUAL	Dolores	Jan 28,1918	Sep 14,1918	
JUANITA	Archuleta	May 2,1904	Jun 15,1912	
JULESBURG (III)	Weld Logan Sedgwick	May 26,1886		

OFFICE	COUNTY	ESTABLISHED	DISCONTINUED	REMARKS
JULESBURGH (I)	Nebraska Terr. Weld	May 29,1860	Sep 10,1862	Located at Jules Ranch P. O. moved to Clearwater
JULESBURGH (II)	Weld	Jan 20,1864	May 3,1866	P. O. moved from Clearwater P. O. moved to Fort Sedgwick (present site of Weir siding)
		Aug 2,1866	Aug 31,1868	
		Apr 8,1869	Nov 27,1871	
		Dec 10,1873	Apr 10,1877	
		May 24,1877	Jul 7,1879	
		May 31,1880	Feb 1,1881	
		Mar 28,1881	Jan 23,1882	
		Apr 7,1882	Jan 7,1885	P. O. moved to Denver Junction Site later re-named Weir
JUNCTION	Jefferson	Aug 28,1861	Oct 22,1863	
JUNCTION CITY	Routt	May 13,1912	Dec 12,1916	P. O. moved to Coalview. Re-named Haybro
JUNCTION HOUSE	Gilpin (?) Weld	Dec 14,1864	Jul 16,1866	P. O. moved to Fort Morgan.
JUNIATA	Pueblo	Jun 15,1869	Aug 31,1893	
JUNIPER	Fremont	Jan 10,1881	Oct 17,1881	
JUNIPER	Routt Moffat	Feb 9,1906	Sep 4,1919	Name changed to Juniper Springs.
JUNIPER SPRINGS	Moffat	Sep 4,1919	Oct 1946	Formerly named Juniper.
KAUFFMAN	Kimball (Nebr) Weld	Sep 12,1914*	Apr 1934	* Date P. O. transferred to to Colorado.
KAISERHEIM	Park	Apr 2,1914	Feb 4,1918	Name changed to Grousemont.
KALBAUGH	Fremont	Nov 2,1898	Feb 15,1900	
KALOUS	Weld	Apr 12,1915	Apr 15,1931	
KANNAH	Gunnison	Jun 29,1882	Sep 11,1882	
KANT	Las Animas	Jul 20,1921	Aug 15,1925	
KANZA	Elbert	Jul 19,1907	Apr 14,1917	

OFFICE	COUNTY	ESTABLISHED	DISCONTINUED	REMARKS
KARVAL	Lincoln	Mar 2,1911		
KATRINA	Las Animas	Apr 10,1907	Sep 12,1907	P. O. moved to Morley.
KAZAN	Las Animas	Feb 10,1920	May 9,1931	
KEARNS	Archuleta	Aug 15,1913	May 15,1919	
		Sep 13,1919	Oct 31,1925	
KEATING	Custer	Dec 18,1914	Nov 6,1924	
KEBLE	Pueblo	Apr 25,1899	Jul 29,1899	Rescinded
KEENSBURG	Weld	Apr 10,1907		
KELIM	Larimer	Mar 2,1915	Mar 15,1923	
		Apr 16,1923	Oct 31,1925	
KELKER	El Paso	Apr 30,1912	Aug 31,1914	
KELLY	Logan	Aug 26,1909	Nov 30,1912	
		May 26,1913	Aug 15,1916	
KENDRICK	Lincoln	Jan 25,1906	1955	
KENOSHA	Park	May 16,1891	Oct 2,1893	
KENWOOD	Fremont	Apr 16,1926	Dec 31,1929	Formerly Pyrolite
KEOTA	Weld	Sep 11,1888	Jan 8,1890	
		Jan 22,1909		
KERSEY	Weld	Dec 20,1894		Formerly named Orr.
KESTER	Park	Aug 10,1874	Nov 11,1886	
		May 16,1887	Dec 21,1891	
KEYSOR	Elbert	May 24,1906	Apr 1938	
KEYSTONE	Douglas	Apr 8,1869	Oct 28,1872	
KEYSTONE RANCH	Douglas	Apr 7,1863	Jun 16,1865	
KEZAR	Gunnison	May 17,1882	Jun 24,1896	P. O. moved to Iola.
KILBURN	Kiowa	Jul 17,1890	Oct 2,1891	
KILLBURN	Larimer	Jun 4,1895	Nov 2,1898	

OFFICE	COUNTY	ESTABLISHED	DISCONTINUED	REMARKS
KILROY	Las Animas	Nov 15,1917	Rescinded	
KIM	Las Animas	Jan 30,1917		
KIMBRELL	Saguache	Mar 11,1881	Oct 14,1881	
KING	Park	Apr 14,1884	Oct 24,1896	
KINGS CANYON	Jackson	Jun 13,1928	Oct 1936	
KINKEL	Pueblo	Dec 19,1907	Oct 7,1911	Name changed to Burnt Mill.
KINSEY	Grand	Oct 24,1891 (The order of change was rescinded, and the name Kinsey does not appear in the Postal Guides.)	Jun 19,1895	Formerly named Kremmling. Re-named Kremmling.
KIOWA	Douglas Elbert	Feb 14,1868		
KIRK	Arapahoe Adams Yuma	Nov 18,1887		
KIRKWELL	Baca	Jun 1,1917	Dec 24,1921	
KIT CARSON	Greenwood Bent Cheyenne	Dec 29,1869 Feb 14,1882	May 17,1881	
KITTREDGE	Jefferson	Apr 2,1923		
KLINE	La Plata	Apr 22,1904	Mar 31,1953	Changed to Marvel
KOENIG	Weld	Jan 9,1913 May 19,1923	Aug 31,1922 Dec 31,1930	
KOKOMO	Summit	May 5,1879	1966	Townsite Buried.
KONNANTZ	Stanton (Kans) Baca	Jan 4,1895* Apr 21,1921 (Last listed in the 1918 Postal Guide.)	Aug 15,1918 Apr 30,1924	* Date transferred to Colorado.
KRAFT	Chaffee	Feb 14,1882	May 8,1888	Name changed to Browns Canon. Later, Brown Canon.

OFFICE	COUNTY	ESTABLISHED	DISCONTINUED	REMARKS
KRAIN	Chaffee	Mar 24,1917	Jun 14,1919	
KREMMLING	Grand	Feb 12,1885 Jun 19,1895	Oct 24,1891	Name changed to Kinsey. Re-named Kremmling
KUHNS CROSSING	Elbert	Apr 10,1879	Jan 31,1920	
KUKKUK	Kit Carson	Apr 24,1907	Apr 15,1908	
KUNER	Weld	Jul 22,1908	Sep 30,1920	
KUTCH	Lincoln Lincoln Elbert	Jul 17,1899 Jun 3,1905	Oct 9,1899 Jan 30,1971	Formerly Sanborn
LA BOCA	New Mexico La Plata	* (* Date not available)	Oct 1937	
LA GARITA	Saguache	Jun 24,1874 Nov 13,1886 Apr 7,1897	May 18,1875 Dec 7,1894	
LA JARA	Conejos	Jul 15,1884		Formerly known as LaJara Station as distinguished from "old" La Jara.
LA JUNTA	Bent Otero	Jan 26,1876 Sep 20,1878	Jul 27,1877	Formerly named Otero.
LA PLATA	La Plata	Jul 24,1882	Dec 23,1885	
LA PORTE	Larimer	Jul 15,1862 Oct 5,1866	Dec 12,1864 Dec 21,1894	Spelling changed to Laporte.
LA SALLE	Weld	May 6,1886		
LA SAUSES	Conejos	Jun 25,1890	Feb 28,1895	Spelling changed to Lasauses.
LA VETA	Huerfano	Aug 17,1876		Formerly named Spanish Peak.
LABOCA	La Plata	Mar 2,1895	Mar 16,1896	
LADO	Conejos	Feb 25,1884	Mar 9,1885	
LADORE	Routt Moffat	Jun 3,1889 (Not listed in 1916 Postal Guide.)	Mar 25,1924	Spelling changed to Lodore.

OFFICE	COUNTY	ESTABLISHED	DISCONTINUED	REMARKS
LAFAYETTE	Boulder	Feb 4,1889		
LAIRD	Washington	Jul 12,1887	Feb 17,1892	P. O. moved to Seebarsee
	Yuma	Jan 25,1899		Renamed Laird
LAJARA	Conejos	Mar 5,1875	May 15,1884	P. O. moved to Newcomb.
LAKE CITY	Hinsdale	Jun 18,1875		
LAKE GEORGE	Park	May 15,1891	Sep 30,1905	
		Sep 27,1910		
LAKE STATION	Greenwood	Jul 27,1870	Oct 12,1871	Stage Station
LAKESHORE	Hinsdale	Oct 19,1896	May 14,1904	
LAKESIDE	Summit	Sep 14,1882	Sep 20,1886	
LAKETON	Elbert	Oct 9,1884	Mar 27,1886	
LAKEVIEW	Jefferson	Dec 3,1892	Feb 3,1894	
		(Not listed in Postal Guides.)		
LAKEVISTA	Montezuma	Jul 27,1914	Feb 15,1918	
LAKEWOOD	Boulder	Oct 1,1912	Dec 31,1920	
LAKEWOOD	Jefferson	Apr 21,1892	Sep 15,1900	
		Jul 1937	Apr 1942	Converted to a branch of Denver.
LAMAR	Pueblo	Aug 12,1885	Jul 9,1886	
LAMAR	Bent	Jul 16,1886		Formerly named Blackwell.
	Prowers			
LAMARTINE	Clear Creek	Nov 27,1889	?	Ghost Town
		(Not listed in 1910 or later Postal Guides.)		
LAMB	Jefferson	Jun 11,1890	Feb 15,1908	
LAMPORT	Baca	Jun 8,1908	May 31,1927	
LANARK	Saguache	Mar 29,1898	Dec 27,1898	

OFFICE	COUNTY	ESTABLISHED	DISCONTINUED	REMARKS
LANDSMAN	Elbert Arapahoe Kit Carson Arapahoe Adams Yuma	Mar 27,1883	May 31,1918	
LANGDON	Teller	Dec 21,1907	Nov 24,1911	Name changed to Crystola.
LANGFORD	Boulder	Aug 5,1881 May 1,1895	May 19,1892 Aug 31,1899	P. O. moved to Marshall. Changed to Gorham
LANSING	Arapahoe Adams Yuma	Sep 17,1886	Feb 28,1910	
LAPLATA	La Plata	Apr 21,1894 Dec 9,1918	Aug 31,1918 Aug 1936	Ghost Town
LAPORTE	Larimer	Dec 21,1894		Formerly spelled La Porte.
LARAND	Jackson	Oct 8,1914	Aug 15,1916	
LARIAT	Rio Grande	Aug 5,1881	Apr 16,1884	Name changed to Henry, then later to Monte Vista.
LARIMER	Huerfano	Jul 1,1907	Jan 21,1914	P. O. moved to Mustang
LARKSPUR	Douglas	Dec 13,1871 Aug 26,1892 (Not listed in 1893 Postal Guide.)	Jul 27,1892	Formerly Huntsville
LAS ANIMAS	Bent	Apr 4,1871 May 1,1877	Apr 11,1877 Jun 8,1883	Different townsite from West Las Animas which became the present day town of Las Animas.
LAS ANIMAS	Bent	Sep 4,1886		Formerly named West Las Animas.
LASAUSES	Conejos	Feb 28,1895	Jul 31,1920	Formerly spelled La Sauses.
LASCAR	Huerfano	Jan 27,1916	Apr 1947	Formerly named Concord
LAUB	Las Animas	Dec 15,1916	Apr 30,1923	
LAURA	Logan	Apr 16,1908	Jun 30,1916	
LAURETTE	Park	Nov 14,1861	Dec 21,1865	Name Changed to Buckskin. Ghost Town
LAURIUM	Summit	May 6,1895	Apr 1,1899	

OFFICE	COUNTY	ESTABLISHED	DISCONTINUED	REMARKS
LATHAM	Weld	Nov 25,1863 Mar 14,1867	Oct 22,1864 May 16,1870	Formerly named Cherokee City. P. O. moved to Evans.
LAVALLAY	Costilla	Aug 14,1903	Aug 15,1918	Place was named San Francisco.
LAVENDER	Bent	Jun 20,1873	Apr 6,1874	
LAVENDER	Dolores	Aug 10,1888 Nov 5,1913	Dec 31,1909 Feb 27,1915	
LAVETA PASS	Costilla	Jan 5,1904	Apr 13,1911	P. O. moved to Veta Pass.
LAWRENCE	Gunnison Ouray	Feb 5,1883	Feb 11,1884	P. O. moved to Dallas.
LAWRENCE	El Paso	Feb 3,1892	Apr 22,1898	
LAWSON	Clear Creek	Jun 29,1877	1967	
LAY	Routt Moffat	Aug 1,1881 Sep 29,1892	Jan 7,1892	Converted Aug 4,1962 to a rural station of Craig.
LAZEAR	Delta	Jan 29,1912		
LE ROY	Logan	Jul 2,1888	Aug 2,1895	Spelling changed to Leroy
LEADER	Adams	Mar 26,1910	Dec 31,1940	
LEADVILLE	Lake	Jul 16,1877		
LEAL	Grand	Sep 17,1904	Sep 30,1930	
LEAVICK	Park	Dec 29,1896	Aug 31,1899	Ghost Town
LEBANON	Pueblo	Apr 16,1875	Jun 6,1876	
LEBANON	Montezuma	Sep 29,1908	May 1939	
LEES	Pueblo	Aug 3,1897	May 14,1904	
LEFT HAND	Boulder	Apr 25,1872	Dec 26,1879	P. O. moved to Gold Hill.
LEHMAN	Grand	Mar 31,1903	Oct 4,1911	P. O. moved to Stillwater.
LENA	Arapahoe	Oct 4,1895	Jun 17,1896	

OFFICE	COUNTY	ESTABLISHED	DISCONTINUED	REMARKS
LENADO	Pitkin	Feb 4,1891 Oct 2,1905	Sep 8,1893 Jan 2,1907	
LEON	Mesa	Apr 13,1883	Aug 3,1883	
LEONARD	San Miguel	May 23,1900	Jan 1941	
LEOPARD	San Miguel	Oct 6,1890	Apr 6,1892	Later named Sams.
LEROY	Logan	Aug 2,1895	Jun 31,1918	Formerly spelled Le Roy.
LESLIE	Washington	Jun 6,1888	Mar 2,1896	
LESTER	Huerfano	Mar 5,1910	May 31,1929	Also known as Bunker Hill.
LEVINSON	Weld	Apr 12,1906	Jun 29,1906	
LEWIS	Montezuma	Sep 7,1911		
LIBERTY	Rio Grande	Oct 11,1887	Apr 30,1898	Formerly named Parma. Later re-established as Parma.
LIBERTY	Saguache	Nov 1,1900 Oct 14,1920	Oct 31,1919 Mar 31,1921	Ghost Town
LILLIAN SPRINGS	Weld	Jul 23,1863	Apr 9,1864	
LILY	Routt Moffat	Sep 17,1889 Aug 3,1903	Aug 22,1898 Jun 1937	
LIME	Pueblo	Apr 13,1898	Aug 1943	
LIMON	Lincoln	Nov 14,1903		Formerly named Limon Station.
LIMON STATION	Lincoln	Aug 6,1889	Nov 14,1903	Name changed to Limon.
LINCOLN CITY	Summit	Aug 1,1861	Jul 10,1894	Formerly Paige City
LINDLAND	Jackson	Sep 18,1922	Jun 1937	
LINDON	Arapahoe Adams Washington	Sep 21,1888 (Spelled LindEn in the 1889-1892 Postal Guides.)		Formerly Harrisburg
LINK	Las Animas	Jan 11,1910	Feb 29,1912	

OFFICE	COUNTY	ESTABLISHED	DISCONTINUED	REMARKS
LINWOOD	Las Animas	Apr 17,1876	Nov 11,1886	Formerly Dodsonville
LITTELL	Fremont	Dec 7,1911	Jan 15,1915	
LITTLE BEAVER	Rio Blanco	Sep 13,1919	Jul 15,1925	
LITTLE ORPHAN	Huerfano	May 1,1865	Sep 12,1865	Changed to Badito
LITTLE THOMPSON	Larimer	Apr 5,1875	Apr 4,1878	Changed to Berthoud.
LITTLETON	Arapahoe	Apr 8,1869		
LIVERMORE	Larimer	Dec 1,1871		
LIVING SPRINGS	Arapahoe	Jul 5,1865	Nov 27,1867	
LIZARD HEAD	Dolores	Jul 23,1892	Oct 31,1895	
LIZARD HEAD	San Miguel	Mar 1,1898	Jun 27,1898	Rescinded
		Jul 25,1898	Nov 3,1898	Rescinded
LOBATOS	Conejos	Mar 14,1902	Oct 14,1911	Formerly Cenicero
		Oct 14,1912	Dec 13,1920	
LOCKETT	Saguache	May 22,1889	Jan 14,1905	
LOCO	Kit Carson	Mar 11,1903	May 31,1922	
LODGE	Gunnison	Apr 13,1911	Feb 14,1920	
LODORE	Moffat (transferred to Utah)	Mar 25,1924		Formerly Ladore
LOGAN	Arapahoe	May 14,1887	Jul 31,1901	
LOGCABIN	Larimer	Jun 24,1903	Jun 1942	
LOMA	Saguache Conejos	Apr 1,1867	Jan 28,1873	Changed to Del Norte
LOMA	Saguache	Jul 23,1873	Jul 22,1875	
LOMA	Mesa	Aug 2,1905		Formerly Mainard
LOMBARD	Clear Creek	Dec 30,1914	Jul 15,1919	

OFFICE	COUNTY	ESTABLISHED	DISCONTINUED	REMARKS
LONDON	Park	Jun 25,1883	Aug 27,1886	
LONE DOME	La Plata Montezuma	Oct 25,1883	Dec 6,1894	Spelling changed to Lonedome.
LONE OAK	Las Animas	Jan 23,1922	Jan 14,1928	Formerly Gotera
LONEDOME	Montezuma	Dec 6,1894	Jan 2,1907	Formerly spelled Lone Dome.
LONGS PEAK	Larimer	Jul 23,1909	Aug 1936	
LONGMONT	Boulder	Apr 14,1873		P. O. moved from Burlington
LONGVIEW	Jefferson	Apr 4,1911	Oct 1937	P. O. formerly named Dome Rock.
LORETTO	Arapahoe	Sep 28,1896	1966	Converted to a station of Denver.
LOS CERRITOS	Conejos	Jun 3,1889	Apr 15,1914	
LOS MOGOTES	Saguache	Jul 28,1888	Jan 8,1890	
LOS PINOS	Saguache	Nov 20,1872	Feb 23,1877	P. O. moved to Cochetopa.
LOS PINOS	Gunnison Montrose	Feb 23,1877	Jan 13,1881	P. O. moved from Uncompaghre
LOS PINOS	La Plata	Jan 18,1889	Feb 25,1899	P. O. moved to Bayfield
LOS SAUSES	Conejos	Jul 21,1882	Feb 15,1883	
LOST TRAIL	Hinsdale	Jan 28,1878 May 14,1883 Jun 27,1892 (Not listed in Postal Guides.)	Sep 30,1879 Aug 14,1884 May 10,1894	
LOUISVILLE	Boulder	May 21,1878		
LOUVIERS	Douglas	Jun 20,1907		
LOVE	El Paso Teller	Dec 29,1894	Jul 15,1902	
LOVELAND	Larimer	Apr 4,1872	Jan 24,1873	
LOVELAND	Larimer	Jan 10,1878		Formerly Big Thompson
LOWLAND	El Paso	Aug 13,1908	Jan 15,1909	Changed to Wayne

OFFICE	COUNTY	ESTABLISHED	DISCONTINUED	REMARKS
LOYD	Moffat	Feb 12,1929 (Last listed in the 1953 Postal Guide.)	?	
LOYTON	Rio Grande Conejos	Sep 10,1884	Oct 2,1884	Formerly Blainvale Name changed to Stunner.
LUCERNE	Weld	Jun 23,1892		
LUDLOW	Las Animas	Feb 8,1896	Jul 1954	
LUDLUM	Yuma	Sep 16,1889 (Continuous listing thru the 1893 Postal Guide.)	Dec 24,1890	
LUJANE	Montrose	Sep 1,1905	Jul 15,1910	
LULU	Grand	Jul 26,1880 (Spelled LulA in the Postal Guides.)	Nov 26,1883	Ghost Town
LUSLO	Lincoln	Aug 18,1904	Nov 30,1904	
LYCAN	Baca	Jun 27,1913		
LYMAN	Arapahoe	Mar 2,1885	Feb 15,1895	P. O. moved to Elyria. Location now within Denver.
LYONS	Boulder	May 18,1882		
LYTLE	El Paso	Aug 12,1885	Mar 5,1920	Formerly named Turkey Creek.
MACES HOLE	Pueblo	Apr 23,1873	Oct 25,1876	Name changed to Beulah.
MACK	Mesa	Apr 21,1904		
MACON	El Paso Teller	Feb 20,1895	May 12,1899	P. O. moved from Altman. P. O. moved to Independence.
MADRID	Las Animas	Oct 3,1882 Oct 23,1893* Jan 6,1896	Sep 29,1892 Oct 25,1893 Nov 30,1917	P. O. moved to Smith Canyon. *P. O. returned to Madrid.
MAGIC MOUNTAIN	Jefferson	Jul 16,1960	Jun 1,1962	Established as a rural station of Golden.
MAGNOLIA	Boulder	May 16,1876	Dec 31,1920	

OFFICE	COUNTY	ESTABLISHED	DISCONTINUED	REMARKS
MAHER	Delta Montrose	Apr 7,1884		
MAHONVILLE	Lake Chaffee	Feb 26,1876	Sep 18,1879	P. O. moved to Buena Vista
MAINARD	Mesa	May 24,1901 Jan 6,1905	Oct 15,1902 Aug 2,1905	Name changed to Loma.
MAINE RANCH	Bent	Mar 5,1872	Dec 22,1875	
MAITLAND	Huerfano	Jan 31,1898 (Not listed in the 1915 Postal Guide.)	May 1935	
MAJESTIC	Las Animas	Aug 21,1900	Dec 31,1914	
MAJORS	El Paso	May 27,1911	Nov 30,1912	
MALACHITE	Huerfano	Nov 27,1880	Apr 15,1915	
MALDONADO	Las Animas	May 27,1901	Jan 14,1905	
MALTA	Lake	Oct 26,1875 May 2,1890	Sep 13,1887 1955	
MAMRE	Weld	Jun 4,1886	Sep 13,1886	
MANASSA	Conejos	Feb 3,1879		
MANCOS	La Plata Montezuma	Feb 19,1877		
MANCOS CREEK	Montezuma	Jul 16,1961	Jun 16,1962	Established as a Rural Station of Cortez.
MANHATTAN	Larimer	Mar 19,1887	Dec 31,1900	
MANITOU	El Paso	Oct 3,1872	Feb 2,1885	Name changed to Manitou Springs.
MANITOU	El Paso	May 20,1892	Jan 1936	Name changed to Manitou Springs.
MANITOU PARK	El Paso	Mar 19,1888	Feb 20,1890	Formerly Summit Park. Changed to Woodland Park.
MANITOU PARK	El Paso	Jun 30,1890	Feb 17,1892	

OFFICE	COUNTY	ESTABLISHED	DISCONTINUED	REMARKS
MANITOU SPRINGS	El Paso	Feb 2,1885	May 20,1892	Name changed to Manitou
MANITOU SPRINGS	El Paso	Jan 1936		Formerly named Manitou
MANOA	Fremont	May 14,1900	Dec 31,1907	
MANZANARES	Costilla	Feb 19,1901	Mar 31,1902	
MANZANOLA	Otero	Nov 4,1895		Formerly named Catlin
MARBLE	Gunnison	Mar 19,1890	Feb 4,1892	Name changed to Clarence.
		Mar 2,1892*	Nov 1942	*Re-named Marble. Clarence and Marble were adjoining townsites.
MARGARET	Costilla	May 22,1899	Mar 31,1900	
MARIGOLD	Fremont Teller	Oct 31,1895	Jun 30,1902	
MARION	Delta	Feb 6,1885	Aug 27,1886	
MARION	Garfield	Aug 6,1889	Dec 19,1891	
		Feb 10,1909	Jun 30,1909	
		Dec 10,1909	Jan 31,1912	Ghost Town
MARNEL	Pueblo	Sep 24,1917	Nov 30,1923	
MARSHALL	Boulder	Aug 2,1878	Oct 5,1880	
		May 19,1892	Apr 10,1893	P. O. moved from Langford
MARSHALL PASS	Saguache	Mar 6,1919	Jan 1941	
		Mar 1942	Jan 1953	
MARSHALLPARK	Clear Creek	Jul 25,1902	Nov 14,1903	
MARSHALTOWN	Saguache	Jul 13,1880	Jan 26,1882	Name changed to Sargents.
MARTIN	Grand	Aug 24,1898	Jan 1935	
MARTINSEN	Las Animas	Jun 3,1889	May 20,1891	
MARTYNIA	Prowers	May 27,1892	Jul 25,1893	
MARVEL	La Plata	Apr 1,1953		Formerly Kline

OFFICE	COUNTY	ESTABLISHED	DISCONTINUED	REMARKS
MARVINE	Rio Blanco	May 14,1895	Jun 22,1899	
		Aug 19,1913	Feb 1934	
MASON	Larimer	Jul 8,1880	Oct 5,1880	
MASONVILLE	Larimer	Sep 1,1896		
MASSADONA	Moffat	Jul 10,1917	Nov 1932	
MASTERS	Weld	Feb 15,1900	1968	
MATHESON	Elbert	Feb 17,1915		Formerly named Mattison.
MATTISON	Elbert	Feb 13,1889	Sep 19,1895	
		May 12,1906	Feb 17,1915	Name changed to Matheson
MAXEY	Las Animas	Jan 19,1889	Oct 9,1894	
	Baca	Jun 6,1895	Jul 31,1920	
MAYBELL	Routt	Oct 14,1884		
	Moffat			
MAYDAY	La Plata	Sep 4,1913	Dec 31,1914	
MAYNE	Huerfano	Jul 27,1905	Dec 31,1907	
MAYSVILLE	Chaffee	Jul 28,1879	Dec 23,1893	
MCCLAVE	Bent	Oct 29,1908		
MCCOLLIN	Lincoln	Jun 10,1915	Nov 30,1917	
MCCOY	Eagle	May 23,1891		
MCELMO	Montezuma	Mar 11,1892	Mar 15,1911	
		Mar 16,1912	Apr 1932	
MCFERRAN	El Paso	Jan 19,1889	Jul 30,1896	Name changed to Newfield.
MCGREGOR	Routt	Jul 1,1915	Dec 1942	
MCGUIRE	Huerfano	Nov 4,1905	Apr 13,1911	P. O. moved to Camp Shumway.
MCMILLIN	Bent	May 1,1886	Apr 16,1887	Changed to Toledo.
MCMILLAN	Huerfano	Sep 7,1900	Sep 15,1904	
MCPHEE	Montezuma	Sep 17,1924	Jul 1948	

OFFICE	COUNTY	ESTABLISHED	DISCONTINUED	REMARKS
MCQUIETY	La Plata	Mar 16,1894	Aug 7,1895	Never operated
MEAD	Weld	Mar 1,1907		
MEARS	Chaffee	Sep 29,1879 Jan 31,1883	Jun 6,1882 Apr 25,1888	
MEARS	Chaffee	Sep 25,1907	Rescinded	
MEDANO SPRINGS	Costilla	Jan 29,1874 Jun 27,1877	May 11,1875 Jun 20,1879	
MEDILL	Cheyenne	Dec 1,1910	May 15,1920	
MEDFORD SPRINGS	Bent	Nov 8,1916	May 31,1922	
MEDLEN	Jefferson	Aug 15,1896	May 31,1901	
MEEKER	Summit Garfield Rio Blanco	Aug 23,1880		P. O. moved from White River (Agency)
MEILY	Chaffee	Jun 2,1882 Apr 9,1884	Oct 30,1883 Jun 16,1885	
MEEKTON	Washington	Jul 7,1910	Nov 30,1918	
MELVILLE	Elbert	Jan 24,1889	Jan 21,1890	
MELVIN	Arapahoe	May 4,1888	Dec 26,1895	
MENGER	Las Animas	Jul 15,1891	Nov 15,1901	Formerly Wenger
MENOKEN	Montrose	Oct 1,1891	Jun 2,1892	P. O. moved from Brown. P. O. returned to Brown.
MERCIER	Pueblo	Sep 22,1906	Nov 30,1913	
MEREDITH	Otero	Nov 29,1889	Jun 25,1890	Changed to Ordway.
MEREDITH	Pitkin	Jan 25,1893		
MERINO	Weld Logan	Feb 21,1883		Formerly Buffalo.
MESA	Mesa	Apr 12,1883	Mar 4,1884	Changed to Fruita.

OFFICE	COUNTY	ESTABLISHED	DISCONTINUED	REMARKS
MESA	Mesa	Apr 29,1887		
MESA VERDE NATIONAL PARK	Montezuma	May 19,1924		
MESAVIEW	Las Animas	Oct 11,1921	Sep 30,1922	
MESEROLE	La Plata	Sep 12,1882	Jul 28,1884	
MESITA	Costilla	May 27,1910		
MESSEX	Washington	Jun 18,1907	Dec 1942	
MEYER	Costilla	Aug 25,1885	Dec 10,1885	
MICANITE	Fremont	Sep 30,1904	Sep 30,1925	
MICHEOLS	Montrose	Dec 17,1919 (Not listed in Postal Guides.)	?	
MICHIGAN	Larimer	Jul 26,1880	Feb 23,1882	
MICHIGAN HOUSE	Jefferson	Feb 28,1863	May 5,1863	
MIDDLE BOULDER	Boulder	Sep 13,1871	Mar 2,1874	Name changed to Nederland.
MIDLAND	El Paso Teller	Jun 27,1892 Feb 21,1895	Jan 4,1895 Aug 31,1899	
MILDRED	Montezuma	Mar 18,1895	May 30,1903	
MILDRED	Yuma	May 21,1910	Jul 1954	
MILL CITY	Clear Creek	Jul 5,1861 Mar 12,1866	Feb 10,1863 May 26,1879	Re-named Dumont.
MILLARD	Montezuma	Sep 17,1907	Jun 30,1909	
MILLBROOK	Custer	Mar 2,1893 (Not listed in Postal Guides.)	Nov 7,1895	
MILLETT	Washington	Apr 8,1890	Dec 27,1890	Name of this place was changed to Platner.
MILLIKEN	Weld	Nov 10,1909		

OFFICE	COUNTY	ESTABLISHED	DISCONTINUED	REMARKS
MILNER	Routt	Jan 22,1920 Jan 27,1921	Nov 18,1920	Formerly named Pool. Converted Feb 25,1966 to a rural branch of Steamboat Springs
MINARET	Gunnison	Feb 25,1890	Nov 14,1896	
MINDEMAN	Otero	Jun 9,1917	Feb 1935	Formerly named Symons.
MINER	Larimer	Mar 10,1888	Sep 5,1894	
MINERAL HOT SPRINGS	Saguache	May 9,1911	Jan 1948	
MINERAL POINT	La Plata San Juan	Oct 29,1875 Apr 23,1879	Oct 14,1878 Jan 28,1897	Ghost Town
MINNEAPOLIS	Las Animas Baca	Aug 12,1887	Nov 15,1899	Formerly Corinth
MINTURN	Eagle	Sep 17,1889		
MIRAGE	Saguache	Feb 13,1895	Jan 31,1927	Formerly named Cotton Creek.
MISSOURI CITY	Kansas Terr. Gilpin	Mar 24,1860	Jan 3,1863	
MITCHELL	Eagle	Apr 2,1883	Mar 31,1909	P. O. moved from Rondebush.
MOBLEY	Routt	Mar 17,1906	Jan 2,1907	
MODEL	Las Animas	Oct 26,1912		Formerly named Roby.
MODOC	Boulder	Jun 18,1874	Oct 31,1879	P. O. moved to Ni Wot.
MOFFAT	Saguache	Aug 20,1890		
MOGOTE	Conejos	Aug 27,1897	Dec 31,1920	
MOLDING	Dolores	Sep 16,1919	Feb 29,1924	
MOLINA	Mesa	Apr 25,1895 May 3,1906	Sep 1,1896	Formerly named Snipes.
MONARCH	Chaffee	May 14,1883	Nov 30,1903	Formerly named Chaffee.
MONARCH	Grand	Feb 12,1907 Oct 12,1912	Jan 15,1909 Feb 15,1922	

OFFICE	COUNTY	ESTABLISHED	DISCONTINUED	REMARKS
MONON	Stanton (Kans) Baca	Nov 1,1901*	Apr 15,1918	P. O. moved from Kansas. *Date transferred to Colorado.
MONTANA	Kansas Terr. Arapahoe	Jan 18,1859	Oct 1,1859	
MONTCLAIR	Arapahoe Denver	Jul 3,1888	Mar 31,1912	Converted to station of Denver (1912-1916 and 1951---)
MONTE VISTA	Rio Grande	Feb 18,1886		Formerly named Henry. Originally named Lariat.
MONTEZUMA	Summit	Jun 15,1871		
MONTGOMERY	Park	Jun 7,1882	May 3,1888	Formerly named Montgomery City. Ghost Town.
MONTGOMERY CITY	Park	Jul 21,1862	Oct 31,1872	P. O. moved to Dudley.
MONTROSE	Gunnison Montrose	Feb 14,1882		
MONTVILLE	Costilla	Feb 28,1887	Jan 31,1900	Formerly named Orean.
MONUMENT	El Paso	Apr 8,1869		
MOONEY	Huerfano	Mar 26,1896	Apr 15,1896	
MOORE	Las Animas	Jul 11,1904	Nov 17,1904	
MOQUI	Montezuma	Jun 18,1900	Apr 15,1914	
MORAINE	Larimer	Mar 22,1880	Jan 27,1902	Name changed to Moraine Park.
MORAINE PARK	Larimer	Jan 27,1902	Feb 15,1921	Formerly named Moraine.
MORAPOS	Moffat	Oct 14,1912	Sep 30,1931	
MORGAN	Weld	Nov 26,1879	Feb 15,1883	P. O. moved to Deuel.
MORGAN	La Plata Montezuma	Oct 24,1887	May 4,1891	
MORGAN	Conejos	Aug 25,1900	May 14,1901	Changed to Freedom
MORLAND	El Paso	Dec 9,1891	Feb 4,1892	Formerly named Fremont. Re-named Fremont.

OFFICE	COUNTY	ESTABLISHED	DISCONTINUED	REMARKS
MORLEY	Las Animas	Jan 11,1882 Aug 27,1884 Sep 26,1888 Sep 12,1907 (Last listed in the 1953 Postal Guide.)	Aug 3,1882 Feb 16,1885 Aug 31,1907 ?	P. O. moved from Katrina.
MORRIS	Garfield	Jan 15,1902	Apr 15,1903	
MORRIS	Kit Carson	Mar 18,1907	Mar 15,1914	
MORRISON	Jefferson	Dec 12,1873 Oct 1950	Jun 6,1908	P. O. moved from Jefferson. Name changed to Mount Morrison. Re-named Mount Morrison.
MOSBY	El Paso	Mar 24,1910	Nov 30,1913	
MOSCA	Costilla Alamosa	Dec 30,1890		Formerly Streator
MOSCO	Costilla	May 24,1880	Feb 1,1882	
MOUND	El Paso	Mar 3,1893 (Not listed in Postal Guides.)	May 10,1894	
MOUNT CARBON	Gunnison	Aug 26,1884 Mar 16,1901	Jul 28,1891 Jun 26,1909	Name changed to Baldwin. Each period of operation was at a different location.
MOUNT HARRIS	Routt	Apr 1,1915	1958	Ghost Town
MOUNT MORRISON	Jefferson	Jun 6,1908	Oct 1950	Formerly named Morrison. Re-named Morrison.
MOUNT PEARL	Cheyenne	Jul 27,1911	Jan 31,1923	
MOUNT PRINCETON	Chaffee	Sep 17,1889 Sep 17,1889	Jun 19,1899 Jun 19,1899	
MOUNT SNEFFELS	Ouray	Oct 31,1879	Apr 3,1895	Name changed to Sneffels
MOUNT STREETER	Moffat	Dec 26,1919	Nov 15,1921	
MOUNT VERNON	Kansas Terr. Jefferson	May 9,1860 Jan 31,1867 Jun 29,1869 Mar 10,1880 Jan 13,1885	Sep 29,1866 Mar 19,1867 Oct 11,1875 Jul 27,1882 Jul 9,1885	

OFFICE	COUNTY	ESTABLISHED	DISCONTINUED	REMARKS
MOUNTAIN CITY	Kansas Terr. Gilpin	Jan 17,1860	Oct 8,1869	P. O. moved to Central City
MOUNTAIN PARK	Jefferson	Aug 16,1965		Established as a non-personnel rural branch of Golden.
MOUNTAINDALE	Park	Jan 5,1880	Oct 11,1899	
MOUNTAINVALE	Mesa	Sep 14,1884 (First listed in the 1886 Postal Guide.)	Aug 31,1903	
MOUNTEARL	Larimer	Oct 28,1896	Jul 27,1899	
MT PRINCETON HOT SPRINGS	Chaffee	Aug 21,1926	Jun 1936	
MUD CREEK	Bent	Sep 4,1911	Mar 30,1918	
MUDDY CREEK	Pueblo	Dec 8,1870	Nov 19,1886	
MULLENVILLE	Park	Jun 28,1880	Jan 31,1882	
MULVANE	Bent Prowers	Jun 8,1888 (Spelled MulRane in 1890-1892 Postal Guides.)	Feb 20,1893	
MURIEL	Huerfano	Aug 18,1903 Jul 12,1904	May 31,1904 Jan 31,1906	
MURNANE	La Plata	Nov 10,1882	Jul 8,1886	
MUSTANG	Huerfano	Jan 21,1914	Mar 1940	Formerly Larimer
MYERS	El Paso	Aug 11,1891 (Not listed in Postal Guides.)	May 10,1894	
MYRTLE	Pueblo	Feb 23,1906	Jul 15,1913	
MYSTIC	Routt	Jun 17,1910	Dec 1942	
NAMAQUA	Larimer	Jan 28,1868	Jan 3,1879	
NANTES	Weld	Aug 19,1887	Feb 9,1888	
NAOMI	Summit	Jan 4,1883	Apr 3,1888	Formerly Josie
NAST	Pitkin	May 4,1909	Aug 10,1918	

OFFICE	COUNTY	ESTABLISHED	DISCONTINUED	REMARKS
NATHROP	Chaffee	Sep 8,1880		Formerly Chalk Creek
NATURITA	Gunnison Montrose	Sep 15,1882		Formerly Chipeta
NAVAHO SPRINGS	Montezuma	Dec 24,1910	Apr 1,1915	Changed to Towaoc
NAVAJOE	Conejos	Sep 17,1878	Nov 6,1879	
NEDERLAND	Boulder	Mar 2,1874		Formerly named Middle Boulder.
NEEDLETON	San Juan La Plata	May 26,1882 May 5,1892 Oct 20,1896	Mar 18,1892 Jun 22,1896 Jan 31,1910	
NEELEY	Custer	Feb 16,1888	Dec 12,1888	
NEPESTA	Pueblo	Jun 7,1876	Dec 31,1929	
NEVA	Chaffee	May 17,1882	Oct 6,1882	
NEVADA	Kansas Terr. Gilpin	Jan 12,1861	Dec 16,1869	Name changed to Bald Mountain.
NEW CASTLE	Garfield	Apr 23,1888		Formerly named Chapman.
NEW FORT LYON	Bent	Jan 17,1908	May 31,1908	Old Fort abandoned.
NEW HAVEN	Logan	Dec 7,1910	Jun 30,1916	
NEW LIBERTY	Weld	Jul 17,1876	Jun 18,1884	Name changed to New Windsor.
NEW MEMPHIS	Douglas	Jan 8,1872	May 18,1874	Name changed to Castle Rock.
NEW RAYMER	Weld	Nov 13,1909		Formerly named Raymer.
NEW WATTENBURG	Weld	Mar 9,1911	Feb 29,1916	
NEW WINDSOR	Weld	Jan 18,1884	Aug 19,1911	Formerly named New Liberty. Name changed to Windsor.
NEWCOMB	Conejos	May 15,1884	May 13,1886	P. O. moved from "Old" La Jara.
NEWETT	Chaffee	Apr 22,1895 Apr 30,1903 (*Rescinded)	Apr 30,1903* Aug 10,1918	Formerly Higgins
NEWFIELD	El Paso	Jul 30,1896	May 28,1898	Formerly named McFerran.

OFFICE	COUNTY	ESTABLISHED	DISCONTINUED	REMARKS
NEWMIRE	San Miguel	Apr 4,1895	May 17,1913	Name changed to Vanadium.
NEWTON	Arapahoe Adams Yuma	Aug 6,1889	Apr 15,1918	
NI WOT	Boulder	Apr 2,1873 Oct 31,1879	Oct 2,1879 May 2,1895	P. O. moved to Altona. P. O. moved from Modoc. Spelling changed to Niwot.
NICCORA	San Juan	Jul 16,1877	Nov 26,1877	
NICHOLS	Rio Grande	Dec 22,1903	Apr 2,1904	Rescinded
NIEGOLDSTOWN	San Juan	Jan 10,1878	Aug 15,1881	Ghost Town
NIGGERHEAD	Huerfano	Sep 2,1913		Rescinded
NINIAVIEW	Bent Las Animas Bent	Sep 20,1915 (Last listed in the 1965 Postal Guide.)	?	
NIWOT	Boulder	May 2,1895		Formerly spelled Ni Wot.
NOEL	San Miguel	Jul 23,1909 Oct 30,1919	Apr 30,1919 Jun 30,1923	P. O. moved from Dallas Divide.
NOLAND	Boulder	Jul 16,1890 Feb 21,1899	Jun 11,1895 Aug 31,1901	
NORMA	Rio Grande	Dec 16,1896	Dec 15,1899	
NORMAN	Costilla	Jun 25,1890	Oct 16,1890	
NORRIE	Pitkin	Nov 16,1894 Jul 1,1907	Jul 17,1906 Aug 10,1918	
NORTH AVONDALE	Pueblo	Aug 17,1917		Converted Jul 31,1964 to a rural station of Pueblo.
NORTH CREEDE	Mineral	Nov 28,1908	Apr 15,1919	P. O. moved from Amethyst
NORTH POLE	El Paso	Aug 1,1956		Established as a rural branch of Colorado Springs.
NORTH STAR	Gunnison	Oct 11,1889	May 18,1894	
NORTH VETA	Huerfano	Jan 13,1920 Feb 18,1927	Feb 28,1923 Aug 1934	

OFFICE	COUNTY	ESTABLISHED	DISCONTINUED	REMARKS
NORTHDALE	Dolores	May 23,1918 Dec 17,1920	Aug 19,1920 Oct 1946	
NORTHGATE	Jackson	Jan 16,1912	Feb 15,1918	
NORTHSTAR	Gunnison	Oct 16,1900	Apr 30,1903	
NORTHWAY	Prowers	May 29,1916	Aug 30,1919	
NORTON	Elbert	Jun 29,1899	Jun 15,1915	
NORWOOD	San Miguel	Dec 22,1887		
NOWLINSVILLE	Baca	May 29,1916	Jun 14,1919	
NUCLA	Montrose	Dec 12,1904		
NUGGET	Gilpin	Nov 21,1895	Mar 15,1901	
NUNDA	Huerfano	May 7,1883	Oct 24,1888	
NUNN	Weld	Sep 28,1905		
NYBURG	Pueblo	Aug 6,1889	Jul 31,1918	
O. Z.	El Paso	Jan 29,1877	Aug 8,1889	Name changed to Ramah.
OAK CREEK	Routt	Feb 5,1907		
OAKES	Arapahoe	Jun 9,1890	May 31,1905	
OAKVIEW	Huerfano	Dec 3,1907	May 31,1930	Also known as Tropic.
OHIO	Gunnison	Jun 15,1880		
OFFICER	Las Animas	Feb 24,1917	Jul 1938	
OJO	Huerfano	Jun 14,1880	Aug 10,1881	
OJO	Huerfano	Apr 5,1913	Aug 15,1928	
OKLARADO	Baca	May 12,1916	Aug 1935	
OLATHE	Montrose	Jun 4,1896		Formerly named Colorow, then Brown.
OLAVA	Park	Oct 1936	Jan 1948	Changed to Grant.

OFFICE	COUNTY	ESTABLISHED	DISCONTINUED	REMARKS
OLESON	Adams	Jul 18,1916	Jul 7,1931	
OLIO	Jefferson	Feb 16,1872	Aug 26,1872	
OLNEY	Otero	Jun 28,1890	Mar 24,1909	Name changed to Olney Springs.
OLNEY SPRINGS	Otero Crowley	Mar 24,1909		Formerly named Olney.
OMAR	Weld	Apr 17,1915 Mar 21,1922	Apr 30,1917 May 15,1923	
OMER	Otero	Aug 30,1900	Jul 31,1909	
ONECO	Routt	Jul 12,1900	Dec 14,1901	
ONINE	Baca Las Animas	Jun 6,1918	Jun 30,1921	
OPAL	Bent	Oct 28,1913	Jul 31,1923	
OPHIR	Ouray San Miguel	May 17,1878 Jun 12,1920	Oct 31,1918 Jan 31,1921	
OPHIR	San Miguel	Jun 3,1922		P. O. moved from Ames. The site of "Old" Ophir was abandoned in order to relocate on the Rio Grande Southern railroad.
ORCHARD	Weld Morgan	Mar 6,1882		
ORANOLA	Elbert	Jul 7,1888	Feb 17,1889	
ORDWAY	Otero Crowley	Jun 25,1890		Formerly Meredith
OREAN	Costilla	Jun 22,1881	Feb 28,1887	Name changed to Montville.
ORIENT	Saguache	Oct 15,1894	May 15,1905	
ORIENTAL	Saguache	Mar 25,1881	Feb 25,1884	
ORISKA	Kit Carson	Dec 22,1910	Dec 31,1917	
ORO CITY	Kansas Terr. Lake	Feb 16,1861	Sep 19,1895	Ghost Town

OFFICE	COUNTY	ESTABLISHED	DISCONTINUED	REMARKS
ORODELFAN	Boulder	Jun 9,1876	Jan 3,1881	
ORR	Weld	Mar 16,1884	Dec 20,1894	Name changed to Kersey.
ORSBURN	Elbert	Mar 2,1885	Jan 28,1896	
ORSON	Gunnison	Oct 3,1882	Jan 8,1883	
ORSON	Mesa	Dec 15,1890	Jun 20,1894	
ORTIZ	Conejos	May 23,1890 Feb 1935	Aug 15,1931 Feb 1943	
OSAGE	Pueblo	Apr 4,1884	Oct 24,1888	Known earlier as Osage Avenue.
OSAGE AVENUE	Pueblo	Apr 16,1873	Jan 31,1882	Re-established as Osage.
OSBORN	Boulder	Sep 20,1880	Feb 4,1885	
OSGOOD	Weld	Sep 2,1910	Jun 30,1928	
OSIER	Conejos	May 15,1882 Dec 22,1887 Nov 2,1889	Mar 11,1887 Jul 29,1889 May 31,1928	
OTIS	Larimer	Feb 15,1881	May 16,1881	
OTIS	Weld Washington	Jan 11,1886		
OURAY	La Plata San Juan Ouray	Oct 28,1875 May 9,1876	Mar 20,1876	
OVERLAND	Arapahoe Denver	Apr 12,1892	Feb 14,1920	Located within Denver.
OVERSTEG	Gunnison	Aug 1,1882	Mar 15,1905	
OVERTON	Pueblo	Apr 9,1892	Dec 15,1900	
OVID	Sedgwick	Dec 12,1907		
OWEN	Lincoln	Sep 26,1908	Dec 31,1915	
OWL	Larimer Jackson	Dec 26,1899	Oct 31,1918	

OFFICE	COUNTY	ESTABLISHED	DISCONTINUED	REMARKS
OXFORD	Bent Otero	Apr 27,1882	Sep 6,1890	Name changed to Fowler.
OXFORD	La Plata	Jan 13,1908 (Last listed in the 1953 Postal Guide.	?	Formerly Grommet
PACIFIC	El Paso	Mar 10,1880 (Not listed in Postal Guides.)	?	
PACTOLUS	Gilpin	Mar 9,1911	Oct 15,1912	
PADRONI	Logan	Nov 10,1909		
PAGODA	Routt	Feb 15,1890	Apr 1947	
PAGOSA JUNCTION	Archuleta	Jul 25,1899 (Last listed in the 1953 Postal Guide.)	?	Date of P. O. discontinuance unknown. Also known as Gato.
PAGOSA SPRINGS	Conejos Archuleta	Jun 7,1878		
PAIGE CITY	Summit	Jun 28,1861	Aug 1,1861	Changed to Lincoln City.
PAISAJE	Conejos	Jun 25,1906	Dec 31,1920	
PALISADE	Mesa	Nov 1,1924		Formerly spelled Palisades.
PALISADES	Mesa	Jan 26,1891	Nov 1,1924	Spelling changed to Palisade.
PALLAS	Routt	Jul 15,1895 Apr 22,1904 Aug 21,1912 May 23,1922	Aug 31,1903 Mar 23,1906# Aug 15,1919 Mar 13,1926@	Formerly named Conger. # Changed to Huggins. Huggins was discontinued and later re-established as Pallas. @P. O. moved to Pinnacle.
PALMER	Fremont	Feb 10,1880	Jan 31,1887	Formerly Hayden Creek. Changed to Hendricks.
PALMER	El Paso	Mar 22,1887 Sep 11,1894*	Apr 26,1887 Jun 17,1912@	P. O. formerly named Weissport. Name changed to Palmer Lake. *Re-named Palmer. @Re-named Palmer Lake.

OFFICE	COUNTY	ESTABLISHED	DISCONTINUED	REMARKS
PALMER LAKE	El Paso	Apr 26,1887 Jun 17,1912	Sep 11,1894	Name changed to Palmer. Re-named Palmer Lake.
PANDO	Eagle	Dec 26,1891 Oct 4,1902 May 19,1905 1942*	Jan 12,1893 Dec 19,1902 Jun 1942 Apr 1946	* Branch of Denver during World War II.
PANDORA	Ouray San Miguel	Aug 5,1881 Mar 28,1902	Nov 12,1885 Oct 15,1902	
PAOLI	Logan Phillips	Jun 8,1888 Mar 9,1910	Feb 11,1890	
PAONIA	Gunnison Delta	Jun 7,1882		
PARACHUTE	Garfield	Jul 27,1885	Aug 19,1904	Name changed to Grand Valley.
PARADOX	Gunnison Montrose	Jan 9,1882		
PARGIN	La Plata	Jul 24,1901	Jan 15,1903	
PARK	Park	Nov 26,1879	Apr 14,1891	
PARK SIDING	Jefferson	Dec 27,1890	May 21,1896	
PARKDALE	Fremont	Aug 16,1880 Feb 1,1882 Sep 3,1883 Feb 5,1889	Nov 28,1881 Jul 3,1883 Jan 1,1889 Jul 31,1970	
PARKER	Douglas	Mar 17,1882		Formerly named Pine Grove.
PARKVILLE	Summit	Dec 13,1861	Oct 22,1866	
PARKVILLE	Saguache	Jan 12,1885	Mar 2,1886	Formerly Sedgwick
PARLIN	Gunnison	Aug 23,1880		P. O. moved from Tumichi.
PARMA	Rio Grande	Mar 20,1886 Mar 27,1906	Oct 11,1887 Jun 15,1910	Name changed to Liberty. Liberty was discontinued and later re- established as Parma.

OFFICE	COUNTY	ESTABLISHED	DISCONTINUED	REMARKS
PARROTT	La Plata	May 5,1876	Nov 12,1885	Named Parrott City.
		Jan 6,1887	Oct 31,1898	Ghost Town.
PARSHALL	Grand	Nov 17,1906		
PATCHES	Las Animas	Jun 26,1917	Jul 14,1928	
PATT	Las Animas	Mar 11,1919	Mar 1944	
PAULEY	Huerfano	Jan 6,1920	Jun 29,1929	
PAULUS	Jackson	Dec 16,1920	Dec 1933	
PAWNEE	Morgan	Oct 26,1903	Mar 1944	Town was named Union.
PAXTON	Montrose	Nov 3,1905	Apr 15,1907	
PAYMASTER	Montezuma	Mar 20,1900	Jun 20,1900	Rescinded
PEACEFUL VALLEY	Boulder	Jun 2,1917	Aug 1935	
PEACH BLOW	Eagle	Nov 24,1890	Aug 21,1909	P. O. moved to Sloss.
PEARL	Larimer Jackson	Jan 19,1889	Aug 30,1919	Ghost Town.
PEARMONT	Grand	Apr 8,1907	Jul 31,1918	
PECKHAM	Weld	Aug 11,1898	Jun 15,1911	
		Jun 19,1916	Feb 18,1921	Rescinded (?)
		?	Feb 1932	
		(Listed continually in Postal Guides thru 1932.)		
PEETZ	Logan	Nov 20,1908		Formerly named Mercer.
PELLA	Boulder	Apr 5,1871	Nov 12,1885	
PEMBERTON	Douglas	Jan 23,1896	Apr 14,1902	P. O. moved to Westcreek.
PENEOLD	Jackson	Mar 1937	May 1937	Changed to Gould
PENN	Boulder	Mar 6,1882	Jul 18,1882	
PENROSE	Fremont	May 8,1909		Formerly named Glendale.

OFFICE	COUNTY	ESTABLISHED	DISCONTINUED	REMARKS
PEORIA	Arapahoe	Mar 3,1906	Jan 15,1914	
PERIGO	Gilpin	Mar 2,1895	Jul 20,1896	
		Aug 27,1897	Mar 15,1905	
PERIN	La Plata	Apr 4,1902	Mar 24,1903	Same place as Perins.
PERINS	La Plata	Apr 1,1907	Aug 15,1922	Same place as Perin.
		Oct 6,1924	Aug 14,1926	
PERRY	Douglas	Jun 21,1890	Mar 23,1895	
		(Not listed in annual Postal Guides.)		
PERRY	Saguache Rio Grande	Dec 16,1896	Nov 16,1898	
PERRY PARK	Douglas	Mar 11,1892	Jan 3,1906	
PERSHING	Routt	Jun 17,1918	Jan 1943	Formerly named Crater.
PETERSBURGH	Arapahoe	May 4,1876	Jul 16,1887	
PETERSBURGH	Arapahoe	Jul 13,1880	Jul 17,1905	
PETRA	Larimer	May 17,1882	Sep 4,1882	Changed to Stout
PEYTON	El Paso	Feb 14,1889		
PHILLIPSBURG	Jefferson	Jul 2,1896	Oct 22,1896	
PHIPPSBURG	Routt	Mar 3,1909		
PICEANCE	Rio Blanco	Jun 25,1892	Aug 15,1923	
		Jan 10,1924	Apr 15,1926	
PICTOU	Huerfano	Sep 12,1889	Dec 1932	
PIEDRA	Conejos Archuleta	May 16,1879 Jan 27,1880	Jan 6,1880 Jun 30,1927	
PIEDRA	Rio Grande	Jan 27,1875	May 24,1878	
PIEPLANT	Gunnison	Aug 24,1904	May 14,1906	
PIERCE	Weld	Nov 4,1903		

OFFICE	COUNTY	ESTABLISHED	DISCONTINUED	REMARKS
PIKEVIEW	El Paso	Aug 28,1902	1957	P. O. moved from Edgerton.
PILOT	Cheyenne	Sep 11,1899 Jan 22,1900	Dec 12,1899 Sep 30,1903	
PINE	Jefferson	Mar 28,1882 Apr 11,1919 Oct 1,1960** Jul 22,1961@	Dec 14,1918 Oct 1,1960* Jul 22,1961	Railroad station named Pine Grove. *P. O. moved to Conifer. **Re-opened as a Rural Station of Conifer. @ Returned to active status.
PINE BLUFF	Mesa	Jun 6,1913	Dec 31,1914	
PINE GROVE	Douglas	Dec 8,1873 Dec 18,1877	Nov 7,1877 Mar 17,1882	Name changed to Parker.
PINE RIVER	La Plata	Jul 15,1878	Apr 14,1894	Spelling changed to Pineriver.
PINECLIFFE	Boulder	Mar 8,1909		
PINERIVER	La Plata	Apr 14,1894	Sep 12,1895	Spelling changed from Pine River.
PINEWOOD	Larimer	Feb 6,1879	Jun 30,1921	
PINKHAMTON	Larimer	Oct 24,1879	Sep 15,1904	
PINNACLE	Routt	Apr 22,1898 Mar 20,1915 Mar 13,1926 (Last listed in the 1947 Postal Guide.)	Feb 14,1911 Mar 13,1926 ?	P. O. moved to Trout Creek. P. O. moved from Pallas.
PINNEO	Weld Washington	Nov 15,1883 Feb 13,1892 Sep 25,1896 Jan 4,1920	Feb 12,1892 Jul 9,1895 Dec 31,1898 Dec 1931	
PINON	Montrose	Feb 21,1896	Jun 15,1905	
PINON	Pueblo	Feb 21,1907	Jun 30,1921	P. O. moved from Dawkins (¼ mile)
PITKIN	Gunnison	Sep 1,1879		P. O. moved from Quartzville.
PITTSBURGH	Gunnison	Jul 22,1881	Dec 30,1896	
PLACERVILLE	Ouray San Miguel	Apr 22,1878		

OFFICE	COUNTY	ESTABLISHED	DISCONTINUED	REMARKS
PLACITA	Pitkin	Oct 25,1899	Dec 15,1903	
		Oct 10,1928	Dec 1934	Ghost Town
PLAIN	Summit	Jan 21,1898	Aug 31,1899	
PLAINS	Prowers	Jan 11,1908	Sep 15,1908	
		Aug 23,1911	Aug 16,1920	
		Aug 30,1920	Mar 15,1921	
PLAINVIEW	Jefferson	Aug 25,1909	Aug 31,1918	
		Nov 21,1918	Jul 1952	
PLATEAU	Mesa	Nov 23,1883	Oct 27,1887	
PLATEAU CITY	Mesa	Aug 26,1901	Jan 1941	Formerly named Eagalite.
PLATNER	Washington	Jun 15,1892	Nov 19,1903	Known earlier as Millett.
		Apr 7,1909	1955	
PLATORO	Conejos	Mar 12,1888	May 15,1895	
		Apr 9,1898	Apr 30,1919	
PLATTE	Park	Nov 5,1894	Dec 12,1894	Formerly named Platte Station.
				Re-named Platte Station.
PLATTE CANON	Douglas	Oct 11,1877	Dec 19,1879	P. O. moved to Deane.
PLATTE CANON	Jefferson	Mar 11,1881	May 21,1893	P. O. moved from Enterprise.
				Name changed to Waterton.
PLATTE STATION	Park	Sep 27,1878	Nov 5,1894	Name changed to Platte.
		Dec 12,1894	Dec 18,1894	Re-named Platte Station.
				(Stage station)
PLATTE VALLEY	Weld	Jan 31,1876	Nov 2,1881	Name changed to Hardin.
PLATTEVILLE	Weld	Feb 11,1875		P. O. moved from St. Vrain.
PLEASANT VALLEY	Fremont	Mar 19,1877	Jul 26,1882	Name changed to Howard.
PLEASANT VIEW	Montezuma	? (First listed in the 1941 Postal Guide.)		See Ackmen.
PLUM BUSH	Washington	Aug 16,1910	Jun 15,1918	

OFFICE	COUNTY	ESTABLISHED	DISCONTINUED	REMARKS
PLUM VALLEY	Las Animas	Jan 9,1917	Sep 1935	
PLUMER	Ouray	May 28,1900	Dec 14,1901	
POINT LOOKOUT	Montezuma	?	?	
		(First listed in the 1941 Postal Guide. Last listed in the 1949 Postal Guide.)		
POINT OF ROCKS	Huerfano	May 12,1864	May 16,1865	
PONCHA SPRINGS	Chaffee	Nov 22,1924		Formerly named Poncho Springs.
PONCHA SPRINGS	Lake Chaffee	Mar 13,1877 Mar 16,1923	Sep 30,1922 Nov 22,1924	Formerly named South Arkansas. Name changed to Poncha Springs.
POOL	Routt	Mar 17,1900	Jan 22,1920	Name changed to Milner.
PORTER	La Plata	Oct 7,1891	Sep 15,1908	
PORTLAND	Ouray	Jan 11,1878 Mar 31,1896	Mar 25,1896 Apr 24,1896	
PORTLAND	Fremont	Mar 29,1900	Oct 1952	
POUGHKEEPSIE	San Juan	Jan 12,1880	Aug 15,1881	
POWDERHORN	Gunnison	Jan 12,1880 May 18,1881	Apr 22,1881	
POWELL	Las Animas	Jun 4,1883	Jun 8,1896	
PRAIRIE	Washington	Jul 7,1910 Jan 20,1913	Aug 15,1912 Mar 31,1917	
PRESTON	Summit	Jul 13,1875 Feb 11,1884	Jan 18,1884* Dec 26,1889	Formerly Delaware City. *P. O. moved to Braddock.
PRICE	Conejos	Sep 27,1880	Aug 31,1882	
PRICE CREEK	Moffat	May 28,1912	Jul 1942	
PRIDE	Baca	Dec 18,1914	Jun 15,1920	
PRIMERO	Las Animas	Dec 11,1901	Jun 1933	
PRIMOS	Boulder	May 17,1907	Feb 15,1913	

OFFICE	COUNTY	ESTABLISHED	DISCONTINUED	REMARKS
PRITCHETT	Baca	Mar 15,1927		Formerly Joycoy
PROCTOR	Logan	Nov 21,1908	1964	
PROGRESS	Las Animas Baca	Sep 26,1888	Nov 19,1895	
PROSPECT	Gunnison	Nov 9,1886	Dec 24,1890	
PROVIDENCE	Gunnison	May 17,1898	Mar 31,1900	Ghost Town.
PROWERS	Bent	Mar 11,1881 Feb 24,1891 May 20,1898	Aug 4,1886 Jul 11,1893 Jun 1933	
PRUDEN	Saguache	Mar 5,1895	Dec 31,1900	
PRYOR	Huerfano	Feb 26,1898		
PUEBLO	Kansas Terr. Pueblo	Dec 13,1860		
PUEBLO WEST	Pueblo	Oct 20,1969		Established as a rural branch of Pueblo.
PULASKI	Las Animas	Jan 27,1874	Nov 2,1886	P. O. moved to Hoehne.
PULLEN	Larimer	May 15,1888	Jul 12,1894	
PUMA	Routt	Apr 17,1896	Aug 10,1897	Formerly named Trull. Re-named Trull.
PURCELL	Weld	Dec 23,1911 (Last listed in the 1949 Postal Guide.)	?	
PULTNEY	Otero	May 19,1890	Jun 11,1890	
PUZZLER	Boulder	May 10,1898	Nov 14,1903	
PYKE	Saguache	Nov 8,1900	Sep 15,1902	
PYRAMID	Routt Rio Blanco	Apr 24,1896 Nov 21,1896	Oct 10,1896 Jan 1933	Settlement on county line, change in P. O. location caused county change.

OFFICE	COUNTY	ESTABLISHED	DISCONTINUED	REMARKS
PYROLITE	Fremont	Apr 20,1915	Apr 16,1926	Formerly named Radiant. Changed to Kenwood.
QUARRY	Montezuma	Jun 30,1892	Apr 30,1912	
QUARTZ	Gunnison	Aug 7,1882	Mar 29,1886	
QUARTZVILLE	Gunnison	Jun 9,1879	Sep 1,1879	P. O. moved to Pitkin.
QUEBEC	Huerfano	Jul 13,1880	Feb 18,1884	Name changed to Scissors.
QUEEN BEACH	Kiowa	Nov 9,1908	Sep 30,1911	
QUERIDA	Custer	Jan 12,1880 Apr 29,1891 Aug 27,1897	Nov 29,1887 May 21,1895 May 14,1906	Ghost Town
QUIMBY	Arapahoe	Oct 8,1895	Oct 20,1900	
RADIANT	Fremont	Dec 20,1904	Apr 20,1915	Name changed to Pyrolite
RADIUM	Grand	Feb 9,1906		Converted Dec 6,1963 to a rural station of Kremmling.
RAGGED MOUNTAIN	Gunnison	Apr 11,1919	Mar 30,1956	
RAGO	Washington	Mar 7,1912	Apr 1951	
RALSTON	Jefferson	Apr 4,1887	Oct 27,1887	Same place as Ralstons.
RALSTONS	Jefferson	Mar 16,1863 Apr 11,1867	Aug 31,1866 Jan 21,1870	Same place as Ralston.
RAMAH	El Paso	Aug 8,1889		Formerly named O. Z.
RAND	Grand Larimer Jackson	Sep 3,1883 Jun 2,1887	Nov 13,1886	
RANGELY	Garfield Rio Blanco	Sep 10,1885		Formerly spelled Rangley.
RANGLEY	Garfield	Aug 26,1884	Sep 10,1885	Spelling changed to Rangely.
RAPSON	Las Animas	Apr 4,1911 Sep 12,1913 Aug 10,1920	May 15,1912 Jul 31,1917 Nov 1934	

OFFICE	COUNTY	ESTABLISHED	DISCONTINUED	REMARKS
RATHBONE	Summit	Sep 19,1891	Jul 11,1895	Ghost Town.
RATON	Las Animas	Jan 31,1878	Apr 19,1881	Name changed to Alfalfa.
RATTLESNAKE BUTTES	Huerfano	Apr 15,1918	Nov 1938	
RAVEN	Garfield	Aug 11,1898	May 1939	
RAVENS	Mesa	Feb 5,1885	May 21,1886	P. O. moved to Ravensbeque.
RAVENSBEQUE	Mesa	May 21,1886	Mar 23,1888	P. O. moved from Ravens. Name changed to De Beque.
RAVENWOOD	Huerfano	Mar 4,1910	May 1939	
RAWLINGS	Bent	Apr 24,1886	Jul 7,1887	
RAYMER	Weld	Jun 27,1888	May 14,1895	
READ	Delta	Apr 22,1898	Mar 1934	
RED CLIFF	Summit Eagle	Feb 4,1880	Feb 7,1895	Changed to Redcliff
RED ELEPHANT	Clear Creek	Dec 19,1878	Apr 22,1881	
RED LION	Weld	Nov 19,1886	May 13,1887	
RED LION	Logan	May 7,1888 Jun 20,1910	Sep 19,1890 Jan 1936	
RED MOUNTAIN	Grand	Apr 8,1878	Sep 5,1878	
RED MOUNTAIN	Gunnison	Dec 13,1880	Nov 7,1881	
RED MOUNTAIN	San Miguel Ouray	Jan 29,1883 Apr 27,1896	Mar 16,1895 Feb 28,1913	Ghost Town.
REDCLIFF	Eagle	Feb 7,1895		Formerly Red Cliff.
RED FEATHER LAKES	Larimer	Jul 2,1924 Aug 4,1926	Jan 31,1925	
RED MESA	La Plata	Apr 24,1907	?	Formerly Garland (?) There is no record for a Garland in La Plata county.

OFFICE	COUNTY	ESTABLISHED	DISCONTINUED	REMARKS
REDSTONE	Pitkin	May 19,1898 May 16,1925 Jun 1,1959	Sep 1918 Mar 1943	Converted Aug 1,1962 to a rural station of Carbondale.
REDVALE	Montrose	Dec 1,1909		
REDWING	Huerfano	May 22,1914		Converted Sep 2,1966 to a rural station of Walsenburg.
REGNIER	Baca	Sep 25,1900 A new postmaster was appointed on February 27,1920, but the office is not listed under Colorado in the 1920 or later Postal Guides. However, a Regnier is listed under Oklahoma.	?	
RENARAYE	Montezuma	Jul 10,1915	Jan 15,1929	
RENE	Otero	Feb 16,1912	Sep 30,1921	
RESOLIS	Elbert	Jul 26,1890	Jan 15,1914	
RESORT	Jefferson	Jan 15,1880 Aug 5,1881	Jan 3,1881 May 11,1886	P. O. moved to Vermilion Later named Dawson then Foxton.
REXFORD	Summit	Jan 9,1882	Nov 10,1883	
RHONE	Mesa	Sep 11,1894	Dec 15,1904	Formerly spelled Roan.
RICHARDS	Baca	Jan 27,1912	Apr 1938	
RICO	Ouray Dolores	Aug 25,1879		
RIDGE	Jefferson	Jul 3,1912	Jul 1954	
RIDGEWAY	Ouray	Oct 1,1890		
RIFLE	Garfield	Apr 23,1884		
RILAND	Eagle Garfield	Apr 24,1913	Jan 1947	

OFFICE	COUNTY	ESTABLISHED	DISCONTINUED	REMARKS
RINN	Weld	Jan 12,1901	Jan 2,1907	
RIO BLANCO	Rio Blanco	Jul 1950		Formerly spelled Rioblanco. Converted Oct 9,1964, to a rural station of Rifle
RIO GRANDE	Costilla	Mar 13,1874	Apr 18,1877	
RIOBLANCO	Rio Blanco	May 6,1899	Jul 1950	Spelling changed to Rio Blanco.
RITO ALTO	Saguache	Feb 7,1872	Feb 18,1884	
RIVAS	Moffat	Jul 26,1924	Sep 30,1925	
RIVER BEND	Elbert	Jan 4,1875 (Last listed in 1937 Postal Guide.)	?	Date discontinued unknown.
RIVER PORTAL	Montrose	Jan 9,1906	May 14,1910	
RIVERSIDE	Lake Chaffee	May 22,1872	Jun 19,1905	
ROACH	Larimer	Dec 28,1929	Jan 1942	
ROAN	Mesa	Aug 9,1893	Sep 11,1894	Spelling changed to Rhone.
ROARING FORK	Gunnison	Apr 13,1880	Jul 29,1880	
ROBB	Yuma	Dec 21,1889 Apr 13,1920	Oct 27,1893 Nov 15,1920	
ROBINSON	Summit Eagle Summit	Feb 17,1881 Jan 8,1883	Jan 8,1888 Feb 28,1911	Formerly named Ten Mile.
ROBY	Las Animas	Nov 6,1911	Oct 26,1912	Previously named Poso. Name changed to Model.
ROCK BUTTE	Douglas	Sep 20,1869 Jan 17,1872	Oct 3,1871 Oct 22,1874	
ROCK CLIFF	Saguache	Aug 10,1874	Jul 29,1880	
ROCK CREEK	Pueblo	May 11,1909	Apr 30,1915	
ROCK RIDGE	Douglas	Feb 12,1872	Mar 22,1892	Formerly Frosts Ranch.

OFFICE	COUNTY	ESTABLISHED	DISCONTINUED	REMARKS
ROCKDALE	Fremont	Mar 17,1882	Apr 12,1882	Name changed to Rockvale.
ROCKLAND	Logan	Apr 23,1888	Feb 4,1891	
ROCKLAND	Huerfano	Dec 19,1914	May 20,1915	Name changed to Solar.
ROCKVALE	Fremont	Apr 12,1882		Formerly named Rockdale.
ROCKVILLE	Boulder	Jul 16,1877	May 7,1878	Known later as Rowena.
ROCKWOOD	La Plata	Jul 8,1878 Nov 8,1895 Apr 20,1923	Jul 15,1895 Apr 14,1917 Mar 1940	This discontinuance may not have been effected.
ROCKY	Park	Dec 23,1874	Oct 31,1898	P. O. moved from Sulphur Springs.
ROCKY	Mesa	Aug 12,1905	Nov 25,1905	
ROCKY FORD	Bent Otero	Dec 1,1871		
RODLEY	Baca	May 21,1910	Nov 1937	
ROGERS	Arapahoe	May 24,1886	Sep 21,1888	
ROGERSVILLE	Ouray	Mar 19,1883	Jun 15,1883	
ROGGEN	Weld	Nov 15,1883		
ROLLINSVILLE	Gilpin	Jan 31,1871		
ROMEO	Conejos	Jul 24,1901 Sep 14,1908	Sep 10,1908	
ROMLEY	Chaffee	Jan 15,1886 Jun 19,1914 Feb 9,1920	Oct 18,1893 Aug 30,1919 Oct 30,1924	
RONDEBUSH	Summit Eagle	Dec 15,1880	Apr 2,1883	P. O. moved to Mitchell.
ROSA	El Paso	Jan 11,1895	May 7,1895	
ROSEMONT	Teller	Mar 31,1903	Nov 15,1926	
ROSES CABIN	Hinsdale	Jun 27,1878	Sep 19,1887	Ghost Town.

OFFICE	COUNTY	ESTABLISHED	DISCONTINUED	REMARKS
ROSITA	Fremont Custer	Jul 8,1874	1967	Almost a Ghost Town.
ROSWELL	El Paso	Feb 1,1889	Apr 30,1908	Now within Colorado Springs city limits.
ROUBIDEAU	Delta	Feb 27,1909	Jul 15,1918	
ROUND OAK	Huerfano	Mar 16,1908	Jul 20,1910	
ROUSE	Huerfano	Jan 2,1889	Nov 30,1929	
ROUTT	Routt	Oct 3,1884 Apr 23,1888 Nov 25,1890 Feb 14,1930	Jan 11,1887 Sep 11,1889 Mar 22,1892 Apr 1953	
ROWE	Prowers	Nov 30,1898	Sep 29,1900	
ROWENA	Boulder	Mar 16,1894 Aug 5,1911	May 31,1911 Jul 31,1918	Known earlier as Rockville.
ROYAL GORGE	Fremont	Oct 1949		Converted Apr 30,1966 to a rural branch of Canon City.
RUBY	Gunnison	Oct 31,1879 Nov 1,1893	Jan 8,1880 Apr 27,1895	Ghost Town.
RUBY CITY	Ouray	May 17,1878	Jul 31,1879	Ghost Town.
RUCTION	Larimer	Aug 1,1889	Sep 16,1889	
RUDOLPH	Montrose	Jan 27,1886	Jun 23,1886	
RUEDI	Eagle	Aug 6,1889	Nov 1941	
RUFF	Baca	Sep 16,1889	May 18,1896	
RUGBY	Las Animas	Mar 16,1900	Apr 1947	
RUIN CANYON	Montezuma	Sep 3,1920	Jul 31,1928	
RULE	Bent	Mar 12,1909	Jun 30,1921	
RUNNING CREEK	Douglas Elbert	Apr 14,1868 Oct 4,1876	Jun 26,1876 Mar 12,1883	
RUSH	El Paso	Feb 15,1908		

OFFICE	COUNTY	ESTABLISHED	DISCONTINUED	REMARKS
RUSSELL	Costilla	May 12,1876 Oct 11,1904 Jun 1936 (Not listed in the 1915 Postal Guide.)	Apr 30,1904 Jul 31,1931 1955	Also known as Placer.
RUSSELL GULCH	Gilpin	Sep 29,1879	Jun 1943	
RUSSELLVILLE	Douglas	May 22,1862	Sep 8,1862	Changed to Franktown
RUSTIC	Larimer	Oct 18,1880	Oct 31,1887	
RYE	Pueblo	Mar 7,1881		
SAGE	Gunnison	Nov 22,1880	Sep 18,1882	
SAGO	Montezuma	Jul 20,1922	Dec 15,1925	
SAGUACHE	Saguache	Apr 1,1867		
SAINT CHARLES	Pueblo	May 28,1866 Sep 26,1876	Jul 11,1876 Jan 3,1881	
SAINT CLOUD	Larimer	May 9,1884	Feb 14,1913	Changed to Cherokee Park.
SAINT ELMO	Chaffee	Jun 23,1880	Oct 1952	
SAINTS JOHN	Summit	Aug 8,1876	Feb 1,1881	Ghost Town
SAINT KEVIN	Lake	Jan 15,1886	Dec 24,1890	
SAINT MARYS	Huerfano	Aug 7,1867 May 5,1876 Jul 6,1891	Nov 18,1872 Jul 21,1889 Dec 31,1907	
SAINT PETERS	El Paso	Nov 14,1905 (Listed under Elbert county in the 1906 and 1907 postal guides.)	Dec 31,1907	
SAINT VRAINS	Weld	Sep 30,1915	Mar 15,1918	Do not confuse with St. Vrain.
SALEM	Arapahoe	Aug 28,1894	Jan 15,1919	
SALIDA	Chaffee	Mar 28,1881		Formerly named Arkansas.
SALINA	Boulder	Nov 19,1874	Jan 1,1925	

OFFICE	COUNTY	ESTABLISHED	DISCONTINUED	REMARKS
SALT CREEK	Pueblo	Oct 5,1880 May 25,1904	Oct 26,1893 May 31,1908	
SAMS	Montrose	Apr 18,1903	May 5,1903	Rescinded. Error by P. O. D. wrong county.
SAMS	San Miguel	May 7,1903 Jul 27,1927	Dec 31,1919 Oct 1950	
SAN ACACIO	Costilla	Nov 11,1909		
SAN ANTONIA	Las Animas	Jul 21,1875	Aug 7,1876	Name changed to Apishapa.
SAN ANTONIO	Conejos	Nov 26,1880	Jan 24,1881	Name changed to Antonito.
SAN BERNARDO	San Miguel	Jun 29,1892 Jan 29,1907	Nov 20,1905 Apr 7,1907	P. O. moved from Trout Lake.
SAN ISABEL	Saguache	Feb 7,1872	May 15,1912	
SAN ISABEL	Custer	Aug 1936	Jan 1939	
SAN JOSE	Las Animas	Oct 6,1873	Dec 18,1878	Changed to Grinnell
SAN JUAN	Hinsdale Mineral Hinsdale Mineral	Jun 24,1874 Feb 28,1900 Jul 5,1922	Mar 18,1895 May 14,1904 Mar 8,1923	Settlement actually in Mineral County. Rescinded.
SAN LUIS	Costilla	Feb 25,1862		
SAN MIGUEL	Ouray San Miguel	Jul 16,1877	Sep 19,1895	
SAN PABLO	Costilla	Jan 7,1893		
SAN PEDRO	Las Animas	Jan 31,1879	May 23,1879	P. O. moved to Starkville.
SAN RAFAEL	Conejos	May 17,1890	Jan 24,1895	
SANATORIUM	Jefferson	Mar 9,1923	Sep 1,1928	Name changed to Spivak.
SANBORN	Bent Lincoln	May 17,1878	Jun 3,1905	Changed to Kutch
SAND ARROYO	Baca	Oct 20,1915	Dec 31,1917	

OFFICE	COUNTY	ESTABLISHED	DISCONTINUED	REMARKS
SANFORD	Conejos	Jun 2,1888 Apr 9,1889	Feb 6,1889	P. O. moved from Ephraim ½ mi.
SANGRE DE CHRISTO	Saguache	Apr 19,1876	Feb 28,1884	
SANTA CLARA	Huerfano	Dec 17,1873 Oct 21,1875 Sep 16,1889	Jun 4,1875 May 21,1883 Jul 18,1894	
SAPINERO	Gunnison Montrose Gunnison	Nov 23,1882		Converted Aug 11,1967 to a rural branch of Gunnison.
SARGENTS	Saguache	Jan 26,1882		Formerly named Marshalltown.
SARINDA	Weld	Jul 28,1875	Feb 7,1882	
SATANK	Pitkin Garfield	Jun 27,1882	Jul 14,1904	
SAUGUS	Lincoln	Jan 4,1908	Jan 31,1914	
SAWPIT	San Miguel	Feb 21,1896 (Not listed in 1915 Postal Guide.)	Mar 31,1926	Formerly Seymour
SHISTOS	Saguache	Oct 30,1894	May 7,1895	
SCHLEY	Elbert	Jun 27,1899	Oct 15,1913	Formerly named Clemmons.
SCHLUETER	Washington	Sep 10,1912	Jul 31,1913	
SCHOLL	Grand	Nov 27,1901	Jan 31,1930	
SCHRAMM	Yuma	Apr 11,1913 Jul 13,1922	May 16,1914 Dec 31,1925	
SCISSORS	Huerfano	Feb 18,1884	Sep 26,1894	Formerly named Quebec Name changed to Capps.
SCOFIELD	Gunnison	Sep 20,1880	Nov 19,1886	Ghost Town
SCRANTON	Arapahoe	Aug 12,1887	Jul 25,1888	
SEDALIA	Douglas	Apr 8,1872		
SEDGWICK	Saguache	Aug 23,1880	Jan 12,1885	Changed to Parkville

OFFICE	COUNTY	ESTABLISHED	DISCONTINUED	REMARKS
SEDGWICK	Weld Logan Sedgwick	Sep 10,1885 Apr 30,1896	May 11,1894	Formerly named Henderson.
SEEBARSEE	Yuma	Feb 17,1892	Jan 25,1899	Formerly Laird. Re-named Laird.
SEGREGANSET	Kiowa	Jul 7,1914	Jul 31,1917	
SEGUNDO	Las Animas	Jul 17,1901		
SEGURO	Huerfano	Jan 4,1895	Sep 14,1901	
SEIBERT	Elbert Kit Carson	Oct 17,1888		
SELAK	Grand	Jun 11,1883	Sep 29,1893	
SELLAR	Pitkin	Apr 12,1888 Dec 30,1896 Jan 25,1901 May 22,1902 May 11,1910	Dec 17,1896 Jul 5,1898 Apr 15,1901 Aug 14,1909 Aug 10,1918	
SEMPER	Jefferson	Dec 28,1882	Aug 31,1900	
SERENE	Weld	Jan 25,1923	Sep 1942	
SETON	Baca	Jun 3,1915	Jan 22,1916	Name changed to Setonsburg.
SETONSBURG	Baca	Jan 22,1916	May 31,1920	Formerly named Seton.
SEVEN CASTLES	Eagle	Dec 11,1913	Aug 10,1918	
SEVERANCE	Weld	Mar 8,1894 Jan 20,1897 Sep 18,1907	Nov 10,1896 Jun 30,1902	
SEWARD	El Paso Teller	Aug 6,1896	Oct 12,1899	Name changed to Clyde.
SEYMOUR	San Miguel	Jul 13,1892	Feb 21,1896	Changed to Sawpit.
SHARPSDALE	Huerfano	Nov 23,1883 Feb 12,1895 Aug 1,1914	Oct 19,1894 Jun 30,1913 Aug 1934	
SHAVANO	Chaffee	Aug 4,1880	Nov 30,1880	

OFFICE	COUNTY	ESTABLISHED	DISCONTINUED	REMARKS
SHAVANO	Chaffee	Jan 4,1930	Sep 20,1930	Ghost Town
SHAW	Lincoln	Feb 24,1908	1955	
SHAWNEE	Park	Apr 19,1900		Formerly named Slaghts.
SHEEPHORN	Eagle	Jan 17,1895	Jan 1951	
SHEFFIELD	Arapahoe	Feb 25,1891	Jan 20,1892	P. O. changed to Denver Mills.
SHELTON	Boulder	May 13,1904	Sep 23,1904	
SHENANDOAH	Montrose	Apr 23,1892 Aug 26,1893	Jul 25,1893 Jul 17,1896	
SHERIDAN LAKE	Bent Kiowa	Sep 20,1887 Oct 27,1887 (Listed as "Sheridan" in the 1888 Postal Guide.)	Oct 15,1887	Formerly named Bee. Re-named Bee. Again named Sheridan Lake.
SHERMAN	Montrose (?) Eagle	Jun 30,1890	Jul 5,1892	
SHERMAN	Hinsdale	Jun 19,1877 May 16,1895	Nov 13,1886 Apr 5,1898	
SHERROD	Gunnison	Jul 18,1904	Apr 30,1906	
SHIELDS	Arapahoe	Aug 6,1887 Jul 28,1890	Aug 24,1889 Sep 22,1894	
SHIRLEY	Saguache	May 31,1881	May 11,1882	
SHOSHONE	Garfield	Sep 3,1907	Jun 30,1910	
SIDNEY	Gunnison Pitkin	Jan 4,1881	Mar 20,1882	
SIDNEY	Routt	Aug 10,1888	Dec 1941	
SIGMAN	Adams	Jun 25,1926	Mar 1935	
SIGNAL	El Paso	May 1,1896	May 23,1898	
SILLSVILLE	Gunnison	Nov 7,1903 Feb 17,1908	Oct 15,1907 Jun 15,1910	
SILOAM	Pueblo	Mar 31,1891	Jun 1943	

OFFICE	COUNTY	ESTABLISHED	DISCONTINUED	REMARKS
SILT	Garfield	Oct 27,1898		
SILVER CLIFF	Custer	Oct 30,1878		
SILVER LAKE	Summit	Nov 22,1862	Jan 15,1864	
SILVER LEDGE	San Juan	Sep 6,1904	Mar 30,1905	
SILVER PARK	Custer	Jul 28,1879	Feb 2,1881	
SILVER PLUME	Clear Creek	Dec 1,1875	Jan 1896	Formerly named Brownsville. Name changed to Silverplume
SILVERDALE	Chaffee	Jan 23,1882	May 25,1882	
SILVERPLUME	Clear Creek	Jan 1896		Formerly spelled Silver Plume.
SILVERTHORNE	Summit	Jan 1,1962		Established as a rural station of Dillon.
SILVERTON	La Plata San Juan	Feb 1,1875		
SIMLA	Elbert	Aug 12,1907 (First listed in the 1911 Postal Guide.)		
SIMPSON	Adams Washington Adams	Jun 24,1910	Sep 1943	
SINBAD	Montrose Mesa Montrose	Dec 19,1914	Feb 1933	
SITTON	Pueblo	Dec 22,1906	Aug 31,1917	
SKINNER	Chaffee	Feb 20,1897	Feb 1,1899	
SKULL CREEK	Moffat	Feb 8,1929	Jan 16,1950	P. O. moved to Blue Mountain.
SKYWAY	Mesa	Jun 4,1927 (Last listed in the 1943 Postal Guide.)	?	
SLAGHTS	Park	Feb 23,1882	Apr 19,1900	Formerly named Fairville. Name changed to Shawnee.

OFFICE	COUNTY	ESTABLISHED	DISCONTINUED	REMARKS
SLATER	Carbon (Wyo.) Routt Moffat	Dec 24,1888*		* Date transferred to Colorado.
SLICK ROCK	San Miguel	Aug 1941 ?	Oct 1946	Re-established after Jul 1,1955
SLIGO	Weld	Oct 27,1908	Sep 1941	
SLOSS	Eagle	Aug 21,1909	Jul 31,1931	P. O. moved from Peachblow.
SMITH CANYON	Las Animas	Jun 30,1892 Sep 29,1892	Sep 28,1892 Oct 23,1893	P. O. moved from Madrid. P. O. moved back to Madrid.
SMUGGLER	San Miguel	Apr 6,1895	Dec 5,1928	
SNEFFELS	Ouray	Apr 3,1895	Oct 6,1930	Formerly named Mount Sneffels.
SNIPES	Mesa	Jan 9,1897	May 3,1906	Name changed to Molina.
SNOWDEN	Lake	Nov 24,1890	Aug 31,1893	Formerly Hope.
SNOWMASS	Gunnison	Jul 21,1882	Aug 13,1883	
SNOWMASS	Pitkin	Feb 19,1901 Oct 7,1904 Apr 8,1914	Apr 14,1904 Jan 31,1914	
SNYDER	Weld Morgan	Jun 16,1882		
SODA SPRINGS	Lake	Aug 25,1879	Oct 31,1902	
SOLAR	Huerfano	May 20,1915	Nov 10,1926	Formerly Rockland
SOMERSET	Gunnison	Mar 19,1903		
SOPRIS	Las Animas	Jul 25,1888	Jan 3,1969	
SORRENTO	Cheyenne	Jul 29,1907	Feb 14,1918	
SOUTH ARKANSAS	Lake	Apr 22,1868	Mar 13,1877	P. O. moved to Poncho Springs.
SOUTH BOULDER	Gilpin	Dec 14,1865	Nov 22,1869	
SOUTH CANON	Garfield	Aug 21,1905	Sep 30,1916	
SOUTH DENVER	Arapahoe	Nov 20,1889	May 13,1896	Re-established in 1900 as a station of Denver.

OFFICE	COUNTY	ESTABLISHED	DISCONTINUED	REMARKS
SOUTH FORK	Rio Grande	Feb 10,1876 May 5,1892 Nov 9,1910	May 23,1883 Sep 9,1909	
SOUTH PARK	Park	Jun 18,1874	Jun 24,1879	
SOUTH PLATTE	Weld	Jun 20,1873	Jan 9,1883	
SOUTH PLATTE	Jefferson	Jan 31,1899	Oct 1937	Formerly named Symes.
SOUTH PUEBLO	Pueblo	Aug 26,1874	Jun 4,1887	
SOUTH SIDE	Pueblo Bent	Feb 22,1869	Sep 12,1877	
SOUTHWATER	El Paso	Jan 4,1872	Oct 1,1878	Also known as Borst's. P. O. moved from Bassetts Mills. P. O. moved to Husted.
SPANISH	Saguache	May 25,1898	Nov 21,1898	
SPANISH BAR	Kansas Terr. Clear Creek	Dec 13,1860	Jul 9,1885	Name changed to Fall River.
SPANISH PEAK	Huerfano	Jun 15,1871	Aug 17,1876	Name changed to La Veta.
SPANISH PEAKS	Huerfano	Apr 21,1920	Oct 30,1920	
SPAR	Hinsdale Mineral	Aug 16,1892	Aug 23,1895	
SPARGO	Montezuma	Nov 17,1920	Feb 29,1924	
SPARKILL	Pitkin	Feb 1,1882	Oct 18,1887	
SPARKS	Moffat	Nov 26,1913	Aug 15,1914	
SPARROW	Pueblo	Oct 18,1883	Dec 23,1885	
SPENCE	Washington	Aug 20,1910	Jan 31,1920	
SPENCER	Gunnison	Sep 10,1894 Dec 14,1905	Jul 31,1905 Sep 14,1907	
SPERRYVALE	Pueblo	Jan 5,1901	Apr 15,1901	
SPICER	Grand Larimer Jackson	Apr 29,1884	Jul 1954	

OFFICE	COUNTY	ESTABLISHED	DISCONTINUED	REMARKS
SPIVAK	Jefferson	Sep 1,1928		Formerly named Sanatorium. Converted 1966 to a branch of Denver.
SPINNEY	Park	Feb 14,1889 Feb 4,1908	Aug 31,1904 Sep 1,1908	
SPRING	Gunnison	Apr 19,1881	Oct 31,1881	
SPRING GULCH	Pitkin	Sep 10,1891	Apr 19,1895	P. O. name changed to Gulch.
SPRING VALLEY	Douglas	Mar 27,1865	Jul 3,1885	
SPRINGDALE	Boulder	May 3,1881	Jul 5,1911	
SPRINGER	Park	Aug 23,1901 Jun 2,1902	Jan 10,1902 Oct 15,1902	Rescinded
SPRINGFIELD	Las Animas Baca	Jun 2,1887		
SPRINGVALE	Las Animas	Jul 21,1874	Nov 9,1875	
SPRINGVILLE	?	?	?	Listed in "Chase-Cabeen." No other record.
SPURGIN	Weld	Dec 7,1916	Dec 16,1927	Changed to Vim.
SQUARETOP	Archuleta	Jun 11,1917	Aug 15,1918	
SQUAW CREEK	Eagle	Jul 14,1884	Jan 14,1888	Renamed Allenton.
SQUAW POINT	Dolores	Nov 3,1920	May 15,1926	
SQUIRREL CREEK	El Paso	Jan 24,1911	Jul 31,1916	
ST VRAIN	Nebraska Terr. Weld	Jan 18,1859	Feb 11,1875	P. O. moved to Platteville. Do not confuse with Saint Vrains.
STAGE CANYON	Las Animas	Feb 11,1919	Nov 30,1920	
STAMFORD	Las Animas	May 2,1883 Jul 27,1905	Jun 14,1902 Apr 15,1920	
STANDISH	Gunnison	Sep 10,1885	Oct 25,1886	
STANLEY	Costilla	Jan 8,1890	Sep 2,1891	Formerly Coryell
STARBUCK	Jefferson	Jul 7,1920 (Not listed in the 1926 & 1927 Postal Guides.)	Sep 1,1930	Formerly Joylan. Name changed to Idledale.

OFFICE	COUNTY	ESTABLISHED	DISCONTINUED	REMARKS
STARKVILLE	Las Animas	May 23,1879		Formerly San Pedro.
STARR	Phillips	Feb 2,1907	Jun 11,1907	Rescinded.
STATE BRIDGE	Eagle	Nov 8,1909	Apr 15,1915	
STEAMBOAT SPRINGS	Routt	May 20,1878		
STEFFENS	Yuma	Aug 25,1915	Nov 15,1919	
STERLING	Park	Dec 23,1862	Nov 17,1865	
STERLING	Weld Logan	Feb 24,1874		
STEVENS	Gunnison	Jun 9,1881	Mar 21,1882	
STEVENSON	Las Animas	Feb 15,1888	Oct 30,1888	
STEWART	Bent Kiowa	Apr 23,1888	Apr 25,1899	
STILLWATER	Grand	Oct 4,1911	Oct 30,1930	Formerly Lehman
STOCKADE	Bent	Mar 21,1873	Jan 30,1874	
STOCKVILLE	Las Animas	May 19,1873	Jun 1,1875	
STOCKYARDS	Arapahoe Denver	Apr 16,1898	Jan 15,1904	Converted to a station of Denver.
STONE CITY	Pueblo	Oct 14,1912	1957	Formerly named Cabin Springs.
STONEHAM	Weld	Aug 2,1888	Jan 12,1892	
STONEHAM	Weld	May 27,1907 Jun 8,1910	Oct 15,1908	
STONER	Montezuma	Apr 4,1917 (Last listed in the 1953 Postal Guide.)	Nov 30,1954	
STONEWALL	Las Animas	Aug 6,1878	Jan 31,1918	
STONINGTON	Las Animas Baca	Jan 20,1888		
STOUT	Larimer	Sep 4,1882	Jul 31,1908	Formerly Petra

OFFICE	COUNTY	ESTABLISHED	DISCONTINUED	REMARKS
STRANGE	Las Animas	Mar 21,1881	Oct 5,1883	
STRASBURG	Arapaphe Adams	May 25,1908		
STRATTON	Kit Carson	Mar 24,1906		Formerly named Claremont.
STREATOR	Costilla	Apr 23,1888	Dec 30,1890	Changed to Mosca
STRONG	Huerfano	Mar 31,1905	May 31,1929	
STRONTIA	Douglas	Oct 3,1903	Dec 1,1903	Rescinded.
STRONTIA SPRINGS	Douglas	Sep 27,1911	Feb 1932	Formerly named Deane and Deansbury. Ghost Town.
STUART	Kiowa	Mar 18,1911	Nov 20,1912	
STUNNER	Conejos	Oct 2,1886	Nov 17,1894	Formerly named Loyton
STUNNER	Conejos	Jun 25,1913	Jan 31,1914	
SUBLIME	El Paso	May 28,1903	Aug 31,1907	
SUFFOLK	El Paso	Feb 5,1879	Sep 11,1886	
SUGAR CITY	Otero Crowley	May 27,1900		Formerly Wait
SUGAR LOAF	Boulder	Sep 30,1867 Feb 12,1869	Jun 26,1868 Apr 1944	
SULPHUR	Rio Blanco	Jul 2,1902	Jan 15,1926	
SULPHUR SPRINGS	Park	Feb 7,1873	Dec 23,1874	P. O. moved to Rocky.
SULPHUR SPRINGS	Grand	Jun 26,1894	Feb 12,1912	Formerly named Hot Sulphur Springs. Re-named Hot Sulphur Springs.
SULTANA	San Miguel	Jan 25,1899 Oct 22,1900	Aug 31,1899 Oct 14,1903	
SUMMIT	Rio Grande	Feb 10,1876 Oct 16,1879	Sep 24,1879 Nov 17,1880	Name changed to Summitville.
SUMMIT PARK	El Paso	Sep 1,1873 Mar 17,1890	Mar 19,1888 Jul 15,1892	Name changed to Manitou Park. Later to Woodland Park.

OFFICE	COUNTY	ESTABLISHED	DISCONTINUED	REMARKS
SUMMITVILLE	Rio Grande	Nov 17,1880 Oct 1935	Apr 30,1912 Apr 1948	Formerly named Summit
SUNBEAM	Moffat	Oct 1,1912	Jul 1942	
SUN VIEW	El Paso	Oct 15,1877 Mar 19,1889	Jan 23,1885 May 27,1896	
SUNFLOWER	Conejos	Jun 3,1889	Jan 14,1892	
SUNLIGHT	Garfield	Oct 19,1897 Mar 11,1899	Dec 13,1898 Sep 2,1912	Ghost Town
SUNNYSIDE	Hinsdale	Apr 7,1886	Jan 3,1891	
SUNOL	Fremont	Sep 8,1892	Oct 18,1894	
SUNSET	Boulder	Sep 25,1883 Mar 11,1918	Apr 30,1917 Nov 15,1921	
SUNSHINE	Boulder	Feb 26,1875	Aug 31,1913	
SUPERIOR	Boulder	Dec 14,1896 Apr 14,1900	Mar 15,1900	
SURBER	El Paso	Jun 11,1895	Jul 31,1916	
SUTTLE	Gunnison	Aug 25,1882	Apr 12,1883	
SWALLOWS	Pueblo	Nov 12,1892 Sep 1,1926	Apr 24,1896 Oct 1947	P. O. moved from Taylorville.
SWAN	Summit	Aug 4,1880	Feb 23,1898	
SWANDYKE	Summit	Nov 30,1898	Sep 30,1910	
SWEETWATER	Kiowa	May 28,1908	Aug 15,1918	
SWIFT	Lincoln	Dec 17,1910	Dec 31,1919	
SWINFORD	Adams	May 28,1912	Oct 15,1913	
SWINK	Otero	Feb 7,1906		Formerly named Fairmount.
SYLVANITE	San Juan	Sep 20,1893	Oct 26,1894	
SYLVANITE	Chaffee	May 16,1898	Jul 28,1898	
SYMES	Jefferson	Feb 9,1887	Jan 31,1899	Name changed to South Platte.

OFFICE	COUNTY	ESTABLISHED	DISCONTINUED	REMARKS
TABASCO	Las Animas	Sep 26,1901	Mar 14,1925	Town spelling "Tobasca."
TABEGAUCHE	Huerfano	Feb 22,1869	Sep 20,1869	
TABERNASH	Grand	Sep 30,1905		
TABLE MOUNTAIN	Pueblo	Sep 12,1879	Oct 4,1880	
TABLE ROCK	El Paso	Dec 15,1873	Nov 11,1893	
TABOR	Lake	Apr 14,1879	Jan 27,1881	
TABOR	Arapahoe	Aug 20,1888 (Not listed in any Postal Guide.)	Apr 11,1890	
TACLAMUR	Fremont	Oct 18,1901	Sep 14,1905	
TACOMA	Lake	Sep 20,1883 Nov 3,1885	Oct 30,1883 Mar 12,1886	
TACOMA	La Plata	Sep 25,1906 (Last listed in the 1953 Postal Guide.)	?	
TACONY	Pueblo El Paso Pueblo	Mar 25,1915	Aug 1942	
TALPA	Huerfano	Oct 16,1890 Nov 9,1904	Oct 31,1904 Dec 31,1912	Formerly Huerfano Canon
TARRYALL	Kansas Terr. Park	Jan 4,1860	Sep 29,1863	Ghost Town
TARRYALL	Park	Sep 19,1896 Dec 19,1914	Sep 30,1909 May 1933	New location. Site known as Puma City.
TAYLOR	Summit Eagle	Sep 28,1882	Jul 31,1886	Formerly Cooper Re-named Cooper
TAYLORVILLE	Pueblo	Jun 17,1878	Nov 12,1892	P. O. moved to Swallows.
TELLER	Larimer Grand	Jul 19,1880	Dec 16,1885	Ghost Town
TELLER	Hinsdale Mineral	Apr 29,1892	Mar 15,1912	Town was named Bachelor. That name was not acceptable to P. O. D.

OFFICE	COUNTY	ESTABLISHED	DISCONTINUED	REMARKS
TELLURIDE	Ouray	Jul 26,1880	Aug 17,1880	P. O. moved to Folsom.
	San Miguel	Dec 13,1880		P. O. returned to Telluride. Previously named Columbia.
TELLURIUM	Hinsdale	Aug 24,1875	Oct 4,1880	
TEN MILE	Summit	May 16,1879	Feb 17,1881	Changed to Robinson
TENNESSEE PASS	Eagle	Feb 6,1890	Jul 27,1893	Formerly Cooper
TENNESSEE PASS	Lake	Jul 14,1912	1960	
TERCIO	Las Animas	Jul 5,1902	Oct 1949	
TERRACE	Conejos	Dec 18,1894	Apr 14,1900	
TETONS	Saguache	Aug 30,1880	Jun 7,1881	
TEXAS	Fremont	May 12,1882	Jan 21,1884	P. O. moved to Hillside. Same site as Texas Creek.
TEXAS CREEK	Fremont	Aug 27,1872	Mar 31,1882	
TEXAS CREEK	Fremont	Sep 10,1885		P. O. formerly named Ford which was on the South Bank of Arkansas River.
TEXAS RANCH	Bent	Dec 19,1871	Jun 16,1873	
THATCHER	Las Animas	Nov 9,1883	Dec 3,1884	
		Jan 29,1885	Oct 13,1888	
		Dec 30,1890	May 20,1911	
		Aug 29,1911		
THE MEADOWS	Bent	Apr 10,1873	Oct 2,1876	
THEDALUND	Adams	Jul 17,1917	Jul 31,1926	
THEISEN	Routt	Jun 3,1909	Dec 31,1911	
THOMASVILLE	Pitkin	Mar 31,1890	Aug 10,1918	Formerly Calcium
THORNBURG	Rio Blanco	Oct 10,1900	Dec 1937	
THORNTON	Mineral	Jun 24,1895	May 26,1901	Name changed to Wagon Wheel Gap.
THURMAN	Arapahoe	Jul 6,1888	?	Converted to a branch of Denver.
	Adams	(Last listed in the 1953		
	Washington	Postal Guide.)		

OFFICE	COUNTY	ESTABLISHED	DISCONTINUED	REMARKS
TIFFANY	La Plata	Dec 3,1907 (Last listed in the 1953 Postal Guide.)	?	
TIGER	Summit	Dec 26,1919	Nov 1940	
TIGIWON	Eagle	Jun 5,1929	Nov 1942	
TIMBER HILL	Hinsdale	Apr 25,1879	Jan 3,1881	Formerly Jennison
TIMBERTON	Park	May 26,1898	Oct 27,1898	Rescinded
TIMNATH	Larimer	Jul 10,1884		
TIMPAS	Otero	May 27,1891	Oct 23,1970	
TIN CUP	Gunnison	Feb 28,1880	May 7,1895	Formerly named Virginia City. Spelling changed to Tincup.
TINCUP	Gunnison	May 7,1895	Jan 31,1918	Formerly spelled Tin Cup.
TINDALE	Jefferson	Nov 2,1891	Feb 6,1893	
TIOGA	Huerfano	Nov 21,1907	Apr 1954	
TIPPERARY	Weld	Jul 14,1915	Jan 15,1917	
TIPTOP	Gilpin	Apr 18,1890	Dec 24,1890	
TIPTOP	Grand	Jul 26,1909	Aug 31,1910	
TITUSVILLE	Fremont	Oct 12,1881	Aug 13,1883	
TOBE	Las Animas	Dec 17,1910 Not listed in the 1915 and 1916 Postal Guides. A double listing on the micro-film may indicate a break in service during that time.	1960	
TOLEDO	Bent Prowers	Apr 16,1887	Sep 16,1889	Formerly McMillin
TOLIFARO	Gunnison	Feb 20,1896	Apr 16,1898	
TOLLAND	Gilpin	Oct 26,1904	Jul 1944	P. O. moved from Baltimore.
TOLLERBURG	Las Animas	Mar 18,1909	May 30,1931	
TOLTEC	La Plata	Jan 26,1887	Nov 21,1887	

OFFICE	COUNTY	ESTABLISHED	DISCONTINUED	REMARKS
TOLTEC	Huerfano	Apr 13,1911	Jan 1954	
TOMICHI	Gunnison	Aug 23,1880 Oct 27,1898 (Last listed in the 1893 Postal Guide.)	Aug 31,1893 Nov 30,1899	Formerly named Argenta.
TOOF	Fremont	Apr 21,1881	Jan 8,1883	Name changed to Beaver Creek.
TOPONAS	Routt	Jul 25,1888		
TORRES	Las Animas	Sep 25,1894	Jun 31,1918	
TORRINGTON	El Paso Teller	Sep 14,1896	Nov 14,1903	
TOSH	Routt	Oct 8,1915	Jan 15,1917	
TOURAINE	Teller	Nov 9,1899	Apr 10,1901	Changed to Cameron
TOURIST	Huerfano	Oct 20,1887	Nov 29,1887	P. O. formerly named Walsenburgh.' Re-named Walsenburgh.
TOURTELOTTE	Pitkin	Mar 19,1899	Nov 5,1894	
TOWAOC	Montezuma	Apr 1,1915		Formerly named Navaho Springs.
TOWNER	Bent Kiowa	Feb 20,1888		
TOWNSEND	Arapahoe	Jan 14,1890	Sep 29,1893	
TOWNSITE	Baca	Mar 18,1900	Dec 31,1902	Same location as Carrizo P. O.
TRAIL RIDGE	Larimer	Jul 1937	Apr 1954	
TRAPPERS LAKE	Garfield	May 26,1927	Dec 1934	
TRIMBLE	La Plata	Jan 29,1883 May 6,1886 Dec 28,1896	Jan 14,1886 Oct 19,1896 Sep 15,1900	
TRINCHERA	Las Animas	Feb 14,1889		
TRINIDAD	Huerfano Las Animas	Jun 17,1862 Feb 6,1866	Sep 19,1864	P. O. moved from Grays Ranch.
TROUBLESOME	Grand	Mar 15,1878 Mar 26,1914	Apr 19,1904 Jun 1935	
TROUT	Ouray	Jun 9,1881	Mar 21,1882	

OFFICE	COUNTY	ESTABLISHED	DISCONTINUED	REMARKS
TROUT CREEK	Routt	Mar 13,1926	Mar 1935	P. O. moved from Pinnacle.
TROUT LAKE	Ouray	Jun 14,1882	Nov 12,1885	
	San Miguel	Apr 8,1890	Jun 29,1892	P. O. moved to San Bernardo.
TROUTVILLE	Eagle	Dec 6,1909 (Last listed in the 1953 Postal Guide.)	?	
TROY	Las Animas	Oct 27,1887	Jul 1942	Formerly Humbar
TRUJILLO	Archuleta	Feb 20,1900	Sep 30,1905	
TRULL	Routt	Jun 16,1888	Apr 17,1896	Changed to Puma.
		Aug 10,1897	Nov 15,1922	Re-named Trull.
TRUMP	Park	May 1,1928	Dec 1931	
TRURO	Park	Aug 11,1887	Sep 11,1895	
TUCK	Baca	Feb 16,1916	Jun 9,1917	Changed to Utleyville
TUCKER	Gunnison	Dec 28,1896 (Not listed in Postal Guides.)	Nov 10,1897	
TOMICHI	Gunnison	Oct 24,1879	Aug 23,1880	P. O. moved to Parlin. Also spelled Tomichi. Re-established as Tomichi.
TUNGSTEN	Boulder	Jul 10,1916	Jan 1950	
TUNNEL	Mesa	Oct 10,1902	Dec 31,1903	
TURKEY CREEK	Jefferson	Dec 16,1874	Aug 24,1875	
TURKEY CREEK	El Paso	Jul 16,1877	Oct 25,1881	Place name changed to Lytle.
TURNER	Gunnison	Apr 19,1881	Oct 14,1881	
TURRET	Chaffee	Feb 28,1898	Jul 31,1920*	* Rescinded (?)
		Jul 20,1920	Nov 1939	Ghost Town
TUTTLE	Elbert Kit Carson	Mar 27,1883	Jul 31,1918	
TWELVE MILE	Grand	Jun 19,1879	Aug 5,1880	

OFFICE	COUNTY	ESTABLISHED	DISCONTINUED	REMARKS
TWIN LAKES	Lake	Dec 19,1879		Formerly named Dayton
TWO BUTTES	Baca	Mar 1,1910		
TYLER	Douglas	Nov 27,1895	Jul 30,1897	
TYNER	Larimer	Oct 24,1879	Jul 20,1881	
TYRONE	Las Animas	Aug 1,1929	Dec 6,1968	Formerly named Yetta.
ULA	Fremont Custer	Dec 1,1871	May 4,1891	Ghost Town
UNAWEEP	Mesa	Aug 21,1883 Apr 25,1895	Sep 18,1890 Sep 22,1898	
UNCAPAGHRE	La Plata	Dec 20,1875	Mar 20,1876	Changed to Uncompaghre
UNCOMPAGHRE	La Plata San Juan	Mar 20,1876	Feb 23,1877	Formerly Uncapaghre Changed to Los Pinos
UNCOMPAGHRE	Gunnison Montrose	Oct 14,1880	Nov 30,1906	
UNDERCLIFFE	Pueblo	Jan 20,1879	Sep 30,1925	Formerly Huerfano
UNDERHILL	Costilla	Mar 28,1872	May 20,1873	
UNITED STATES AIR FORCE ACADEMY	El Paso	Jun 28,1958		
UNIVERSITY PARK	Arapahoe	Jun 19,1890 May 18,1904	Jan 15,1904 Dec 31,1915	Converted to Station 39 of Denver. Changed in 1957 to University Park Station.
URANIUM	Montrose	Aug 29,1900	Feb 15,1922	
URAVAN	Montrose	Oct 1,1936		
URMSTON	Jefferson	Mar 25,1891	Aug 15,1900	
UTE	Gunnison	Feb 3,1882	May 26,1882	Changed to Grand Junction
UTE	Huerfano	Aug 12,1888	Apr 27,1900	Name changed to Huerfano

OFFICE	COUNTY	ESTABLISHED	DISCONTINUED	REMARKS
UTE	Montrose	May 24,1912	Apr 1951	
UTLEYVILLE	Baca	Jun 9,1917		Formerly Tuck
VADNER	Conejos	Sep 18,1884	Jul 31,1885	
VAIL	Eagle	Oct 1,1962* Jan 28,1966**		* Established as a Rurual Station of Minturn. ** Became independent post office.
VALDAI	Larimer	Jun 14,1889	May 11,1892	
VALDEZ	Las Animas	Apr 20,1910	1962	
VALLECITO	La Plata	Nov 15,1901 Jun 6,1917 Oct 1939	Dec 30,1916 Rescinded (?) Mar 1942	P. O. known earlier as Viceto. Same location (?)
VALLEY	Kit Carson	Jun 2,1898	Aug 15,1901	
VALLERY	Morgan	Dec 21,1907 Feb 12,1910	Feb 15,1909 Aug 15,1919	
VALLORSO	Las Animas	Sep 14,1918	Jul 1954	
VALMONT	Boulder	Sep 14,1865	Jun 29,1901	
VALVERDE	Arapahoe Denver	Oct 14,1889	Feb 29,1908	Location within Denver.
VANADIUM	San Miguel	May 17,1913	Aug 1942	Formerly named Newmire.
VANCE	San Miguel	Oct 26,1894	Sep 30,1909	
VANSVILLE	Kit Carson	Sep 14,1907	Nov 20,1907	Rescinded
VARROS	Las Animas	Sep 21,1902	Feb 14,1903	
VEGA	Mesa	May 23,1891	Apr 15,1914	
VEGA RANCH	Las Animas	Sep 21,1916	Jun 14,1924	
VERDE	Pueblo	Apr 9,1903	Oct 31,1912	
VERDUN	Prowers	Feb 2,1920	Jun 15,1920	
VERMILION	Jefferson	Jan 3,1881	Jun 7,1881	P. O. moved from Resort.

OFFICE	COUNTY	ESTABLISHED	DISCONTINUED	REMARKS
VERNE	Delta	Oct 12,1903	Dec 30,1903	
VERNON	Arapahoe Adams Yuma	May 23,1892		P. O. moved from Condon.
VESUVIUS	Boulder	Apr 15,1908	Jun 30,1908	
VETA PASS	Huerfano	Jun 15,1889 (Not listed in the Postal Guides.)	Oct 16,1890	
VETA PASS	Costilla	Apr 13,1911	Jun 1935	Formerly Laveta Pass
VETERAN	Saguache	May 17,1888	Apr 16,1894	
VICETO	La Plata	Mar 19,1890	Oct 15,1891	Same location as Vallecito.
VICKSBURGH	Chaffee	May 3,1881	Jul 30,1885	
VICTOR	El Paso Teller	Jun 7,1894		
VIGIL	Las Animas	Nov 5,1894	Dec 31,1912	
VILAS	Las Animas Baca	Jun 20,1887		
VILLA GROVE	Saguache	Jan 19,1872 Jul 1950	Oct 12,1894	Formerly Garibaldi Changed to Villagrove Re-named Villa Grove
VILLA PARK	Arapahoe	Feb 15,1890	May 6,1895	Changed to Villapark
VILLAGE	Otero	Nov 1,1943	Mar 31,1956	**Established as a Rural Station of La Junta.**
VILLAGROVE	Saguache	Oct 12,1894	Jul 1950	Formerly Villa Grove Re-named Villa Grove
VILLAPARK	Arapahoe	May 6,1895	Apr 20,1901	Formerly Villa Park
VILLEGREEN	Las Animas	Apr 21,1917		
VIM	Weld	Dec 16,1927	Oct 1944	Formerly Spurgin
VIRGINIA	Douglas	Sep 29,1869	Feb 8,1871	Changed to Frosts Ranch
VIRGINIA	Gunnison	Jul 22,1879	Feb 28,1880	Name changed to Tin Cup.

OFFICE	COUNTY	ESTABLISHED	DISCONTINUED	REMARKS
VIRGINIA DALE	Larimer	Jan 9,1868 Sep 14,1874	Sep 28,1868	Converted Feb 10,1967 to a rural branch of Laporte.
VIRGINIUS	Ouray	Aug 16,1887	Apr 24,1894	
VOLLMAR	Weld	Nov 2,1910	Oct 31,1912	
VONA	Elbert Kit Carson	Jan 19,1889 Jun 25,1901 Jan 21,1907	Jul 9,1885 Oct 14,1905	
VROMAN	Otero	Jul 22,1918 (Last listed in the 1953 Postal Guide.)	?	Formerly named Weitzer.
VULCAN	Garfield	Oct 6,1892	Oct 23,1893	Formerly named Coalridge. Re-named Coalridge.
VULCAN	Gunnison	Aug 2,1895	Aug 15,1912	Ghost Town.
WABASH	Saguache	May 9,1911	Dec 1,1911	Changed to Gibson
WACHTEL	Weld	Mar 20,1913	Mar 15,1916	
WADLEIGH	Park	Jun 24,1895	Nov 11,1895	Rescinded
WAGES	Yuma	Mar 31,1917	Jul 1950	Formerly Ford
WAGON WHEEL GAP	Saguache Rio Grande Mineral	Aug 27,1875	Feb 2,1895	
WAGON WHEEL GAP	Mineral	Mar 26,1901	Sep 30,1957	Formerly Thornton. Converted Jun 1,1955 to a rural station of Creede. Summer P. O. 6/1 to 9/30.
WAIT	Otero	Feb 26,1900	Mar 27,1900	Changed to Sugar City
WAITLEY	Washington	Jun 15,1915	Feb 1937	
WAKEMAN	Logan Phillips	Sep 19,1887	May 15,1897	
WALDEN	Larimer Grand Larimer Jackson	Feb 28,1881		

OFFICE	COUNTY	ESTABLISHED	DISCONTINUED	REMARKS
WALDORF	Clear Creek	Jul 6,1908	Feb 29,1912	Ghost Town
WALES	Arapahoe	Aug 6,1887	Sep 21,1888	
WALLET	Kit Carson	Apr 8,1890	May 15,1907	
WALLROCK	Sweetwater (Wyoming) Routt	Jul 29,1902*	Jun 30,1903	* Date transferred to Colorado.
WALLS	La Plata	Apr 25,1896	Aug 13,1896	Rescinded
WALLSTREET	Boulder	Apr 18,1898	Sep 15,1921	Formerly Delphi
WALSEN	Huerfano	Mar 29,1902	Dec 1932	
WALSENBURG	Huerfano	Dec 22,1892		Formerly spelled Walsenburgh.
WALSENBURGH	Huerfano	Dec 14,1870 Nov 29,1887	Oct 20,1887 Dec 22,1892	Changed to Tourist Re-named Walsenburgh Spelling changed to Walsenburg.
WALSH	Baca	Dec 23,1926		
WAPITI	Summit	Mar 16,1894	Apr 15,1903	
WARD	Boulder	Sep 11,1894		Formerly named Ward District.
WARD DISTRICT	Boulder	Jan 13,1863	Sep 11,1894	Name changed to Ward.
WAREMONT	Pueblo	Jun 13,1916	Apr 15,1922	
WAREVILLE	Ouray	May 16,1877	Jul 17,1877	
WARRANTSVILLE	Huerfano	Jul 10,1876	Sep 13,1877	
WASHBURN	Arapahoe	Sep 12,1889 Dec 22,1892	Jul 13,1892 Jan 7,1893	Changed to Derblay Re-named Washburn Name changed to Hazeltine.
WASON	Rio Grande Mineral	Dec 26,1891	Apr 30,1904	
WATER VALLEY	Bent Kiowa	Sep 9,1887	Sep 12,1894	
WATERMAN	Garfield	May 21,1888 (Not listed in the Postal Guides.)	Rescinded ?	

OFFICE	COUNTY	ESTABLISHED	DISCONTINUED	REMARKS
WATERVALE	Las Animas	Jul 6,1888 Jun 13,1896 Aug 18,1903 Nov 19,1919	Jun 9,1893 Aug 31,1900 Dec 31,1917 Mar 31,1921	
WATKINS	Arapahoe Adams	Jan 3,1878 Nov 6,1894	Oct 14,1893	
WATONGA	Saguache	Jun 6,1910	Oct 31,1911	
WATSON	Pitkin	May 31,1889	Jun 14,1918	Name changed to Gerbazdale.
WAUNITA	Gunnison	Sep 10,1885 Jul 7,1886 Aug 11,1887 Aug 8,1896	Mar 12,1886 Nov 11,1886 Oct 23,1895 Apr 15,1908	P. O. moved from Elgin.
WAUNITA HOT SPRINGS	Gunnison	May 27,1910	Dec 1942	P. O. moved from Bowerman
WAVERLY	El Paso	May 1,1897 (Not listed in the Postal Guides.)	Rescinded (?)	
WAVERLY	Larimer	Feb 23,1906	May 15,1912	
WAYNE	El Paso	Jan 15,1909	Nov 30,1912	Formerly Lowland
WAYSIDE	Costilla	Feb 15,1875	Sep 10,1878	
WEBB	Prowers	May 31,1910	Nov 29,1919	
WEBSTER	Park	May 7,1877 Jun 1,1904	May 31,1904 Sep 30,1909	
WEIR	Sedgwick	Jun 21,1889	Dec 22,1890	Formerly site of Julesburgh II
WEISSPORT	El Paso	Jul 21,1875 Oct 21,1880	Aug 3,1880 Mar 22,1887	P. O. moved to Palmer (¼ mile)
WEITZER	Otero	Jun 27,1908	Jul 22,1918	Name changed to Vroman.
WELBY	Adams	Dec 19,1910	Mar 31,1911	
WELCOME	Delta	Jun 22,1910	Aug 31,1912	

OFFICE	COUNTY	ESTABLISHED	DISCONTINUED	REMARKS
WELD	Weld	Jan 18,1869	Dec 7,1870	Formerly named Fort Lupton (Located 1 mi. north of present Ft. Lupton.)
WELD	Weld	Jun 9,1900	Oct 27,1900	Rescinded
WELDON VALLEY	Weld	Mar 8,1880	Nov 19,1880	
WELDONA	Morgan	Jul 18,1907		Formerly named Deuel.
WELLINGTON	Larimer	Aug 25,1903		
WELLONS	Lincoln	Jun 10,1908	Jun 30,1916	
WELLSVILLE	Fremont	Dec 13,1880	Aug 13,1896	
WENGER	Las Animas	Jun 15,1891	Jul 15,1891	Name changed to Menger
WENTWORTH	Baca	Jun 15,1911	Jun 30,1921	
WENTZ	Weld	Nov 24,1891	Mar 14,1903	
WEST LAS ANIMAS	Bent	Nov 3,1873	Sep 4,1886	Name changed to Las Animas
WEST PORTAL	Grand	Oct 12,1923	Dec 1939	P. O. moved to Winter Park
WESTCLIFFE	Custer	Jul 14,1881 Jan 22,1886	Nov 21,1882	
WESTCREEK	Douglas	Apr 14,1902 Oct 26,1918 Feb 1935	Aug 31,1918 Jun 14,1919 Dec 6,1968	P. O. moved from Pemberton
WESTFORK	Montezuma	Apr 18,1903 Mar 7,1907	Mar 31,1905 Apr 20,1907	Rescinded.
WESTLAKE	Larimer	Apr 25,1895	Jul 22,1898	
WESTMINSTER	Adams	Jun 5,1908		Formerly Harris
WESTOLA	Morton (Kans) Baca	Aug 20,1914 (Another date of Feb 28,1918 is also given for the closing of this office.)	May 31,1917	
WESTON	Park	Nov 4,1879	Feb 24,1880	

OFFICE	COUNTY	ESTABLISHED	DISCONTINUED	REMARKS
WESTON	Las Animas	Sep 9,1889		Place formerly known as Quinto, and as La Junta. P. O. moved from Cordova.
WESTPLAINS	Logan	May 23,1910	Apr 1949	
WETMORE	Custer	Apr 19,1881		
WEZEL	Lincoln	Feb 8,1911	Jul 15,1919	
WHEAT RIDGE	Jefferson	Jul 7,1913		
WHEATLAND	El Paso	Aug 19,1869	Oct 26,1873	
WHEATLAND	Weld Larimer	Sep 24,1875 Oct 25,1878	Oct 1,1878 Feb 10,1881	P. O. moved from Hiltonville.
WHEELER	Summit	Apr 1,1880	May 14,1894	
WHEELMAN	Boulder	Jun 2,1900	Jul 31,1902	
WHITE	Lincoln	Mar 6,1901	Nov 30,1901	
WHITE CROSS	Hinsdale	Sep 28,1882	May 15,1912	Formerly Burrows Park
WHITE EARTH	Saguache	Jan 24,1876	Jun 24,1880	
WHITE PINE	Gunnison	Aug 12,1880	Apr 14,1894	Spelling changed to Whitepine.
WHITE RIVER	Summit	Sep 29,1871	Aug 23,1880	P. O. moved to Meeker from the White River Ute Indian Agency.
WHITE RIVER	Garfield Rio Blanco	Aug 15,1888	Mar 15,1908	
WHITE ROCK	Pueblo	May 17,1909	Aug 31,1927	
WHITEHORN	Chaffee Fremont	Jul 22,1897	Nov 15,1916	
WHITEPINE	Gunnison	Apr 14,1894 Apr 1949	Apr 30,1928 Jul 1954	Formerly spelled White Pine.
WHITEWATER	Mesa	Oct 9,1884		
WHITMAN	Weld	Apr 4,1882	Jul 18,1882	
WHITNEY	Boulder	Apr 27,1868	Jul 3,1871	

OFFICE	COUNTY	ESTABLISHED	DISCONTINUED	REMARKS
WIGGINS	Morgan	Dec 2,1896		Formerly named Corona
WIGWAM	El Paso	Jun 26,1882 Oct 1,1890	Sep 18,1890 May 31,1922	
WILBUR	Fremont	Sep 11,1894	Jul 15,1913	
WILD HORSE	Bent	Jan 5,1877	May 25,1877	
WILD HORSE	Cheyenne	Apr 13,1904		
WILDE	Bent Prowers	Aug 6,1887	Jun 10,1893	
WILDS	Larimer	Feb 11,1926	Mar 1934	
WILEY	Prowers	Apr 22,1907		
WILLARD	Logan	Sep 26,1888 Mar 30,1900 Apr 5,1910	Apr 19,1894 Feb 28,1901 1968	P. O. moved from Arnold.
WILLIAMSBURGH	Fremont	Jan 10,1882 (Last listed in the 1916 Postal Guide.)	?	
WILLOW	Saguache	May 12,1891	Jul 1,1891	P.O. moved to Creede.
WILLOW CREEK	Routt	Feb 12,1923 Nov 1934	Oct 31,1925 Nov 1943	
WILLOW GULCH	Dolores	Mar 21,1928 (These are the dates as given on the microfilm. The office is listed in the 1925-1927 Postal Guides.)	Dec 31,1927	
WILLOWVILLE	Jefferson	Jan 8,1879	Jul 10,1879	
WILSON	San Miguel	Feb 7,1895	Nov 15,1901	
WILSON	Pueblo	Jun 24,1911	Sep 15,1913	
WINDHAM	Ouray	Dec 9,1878	Jun 20,1881	
WINDSOR	Routt	Apr 26,1877	Jul 19,1880	
WINDSOR	Weld	Aug 19,1911		Formerly named New Windsor.

OFFICE	COUNTY	ESTABLISHED	DISCONTINUED	REMARKS
WINFIELD	Chaffee	Jul 5,1881	Sep 15,1912	
WINNVIEW	Arapahoe	Sep 1933	Nov 1942	
WINONA	Larimer	Feb 2,1889	May 18,1893	
WINSTON	Logan	May 18,1902 Jul 23,1908	Oct 15,1902 Dec 31,1918	
WINTER PARK	Grand	Dec 1939		P. O. moved from West Portal.
WITHERBEE	Yuma	May 28,1912	Aug 31,1918	
WOLCOTT	Eagle	Sep 12,1889		
WOLFCREEK	Elbert	Mar 15,1910	Mar 15,1919	
WOOD VALLEY	Pueblo	Jun 12,1862 Oct 12,1865 Jun 3,1868	Feb 24,1865 Sep 25,1867 Dec 15,1869	
WOODLAND PARK	El Paso Teller	Feb 20,1890		Formerly named Manitou Park, Summit Park.
WOODMEN	El Paso	Jan 20,1912	Apr 1949	
WOODROW	Morgan	Jun 18,1913	?	P. O. located close to county line. Probably the same as the Woodrow in Washington county.
WOODROW	Washington	Sep 10,1913		
WOODSTOCK	Gunnison	Aug 5,1881 Dec 6,1883	May 9,1882 Aug 12,1884	
WOODY CREEK	Pitkin	Sep 4,1920		
WOOTTON	Las Animas	Dec 4,1908	Jan 14,1922	
WORMINGTON	Las Animas	Apr 19,1919	Nov 1934	
WORTMAN	Lake	Sep 25,1900 May 25,1916	Aug 31,1908 Jan 15,1919	
WRAY	Weld Washington Yuma	Jun 26,1882 May 2,1883	Apr 9,1883	

OFFICE	COUNTY	ESTABLISHED	DISCONTINUED	REMARKS
WULSTENVILLE	Fremont	Jul 21,1871	Dec 4,1871	
YACHITA	Las Animas	Oct 6,1916	Jul 31,1918	
YALE	Kit Carson	Sep 10,1891	Nov 30,1905	
YAMPA	Routt	Jan 12,1883	Aug 28,1889	Name changed to Craig.
YAMPA	Routt	Oct 30,1894		
YANKEE	Clear Creek	Nov 2,1893	Feb 28,1910	
YARMONY	Eagle	Feb 3,1908	May 11,1908	Rescinded
YARMONY	Routt	Jan 6,1908	Jan 27,1908	Rescinded. This may be the same as the office in Eagle county.
YATES	Clear Creek	Sep 4,1882	Feb 8,1883	
YEISER	Las Animas	Apr 16,1904	Jul 31,1929	
YELLOW JACKET	Montezuma	May 5,1914		
YELLOWSTONE CREEK	Huerfano	Aug 5,1915 (Not listed in the Postal Guides.)	Apr 15,1916	
YETTA	Las Animas	Aug 5,1916	Aug 1,1929	Name changed to Tyrone.
YODER	El Paso	Apr 21,1904		
YOMAN	Elbert	Feb 11,1904	May 12,1904	
YORKVILLE	Fremont	Nov 4,1875 (Last listed in the 1883 Postal Guide.)	?	
YOUGHAL	Moffat	Jul 16,1919	Feb 1934	
YOUNG	La Plata	Nov 7,1882	Mar 19,1883	
YUMA	Weld Washington Yuma	Nov 24,1885		
ZAPATO	Costilla	Apr 30,1879 Jun 22,1880 Sep 14,1898	Jun 12,1880 Sep 7,1898 Sep 15,1900	

OFFICE	COUNTY	ESTABLISHED	DISCONTINUED	REMARKS
ZILAR	Weld	May 5,1892	Oct 30,1894	
ZIRKEL	Larimer Jackson	May 5,1899	Dec 30,1911	
ZITA	Weld	Feb 21,1910	Sep 16,1910	Changed to Galeton
ZUCK	Prowers	Dec 26,1891	Mar 29,1895	P. O. moved to Barton.

Mrs. J. A. Piper
173 1⁄2 St.
Lincoln
Nebraska.

D.P.O.

"The West End,"

ROUSE, LeBOSQUET & HANSEN, Proprietors,

DURANGO, COLO.

Dr E. Stiner
Rawlins
Wyoming Ter

After 5 days, return to

J. T. ROBERTS,

CLAREMONT, COLO.

C. S. Morey Mer Co
Denver
Colo

S E C T I O N   B

BRANCHES, STATIONS, AND RURAL ESTABLISHMENTS

In the last 100 years of Colorado's postal history 152 named branches, stations, and rural establishments have existed or are still in existence.   In addition, 103 numbered stations, 5 lettered stations (all letter "A"), 16 C.O.D. (Collect On Delivery) stations, and 24 M.O.S. or M.O.U. (Money Order Unit) have existed.   Recent years have seen only a few post offices established, probably due in part to the low rate of remuneration for postmasters operating one of the small post offices.   However, there has been a large increase in the number of named and contract stations and in the conversion of existing post offices to Rural Stations or Branches.

This section of "Postal History of Colorado" deals with the branches and stations.   The section is in two parts.   The first portion is an alphabetical listing of the named branches, stations, and rural establishments with the status under which they exist or existed, and their parent post office.   The second portion is a listing by parent office,   giving the name or number, the status under which it existed, the dates of establishment and discontinuance, and any other known information about the office.

Information on the stations and branches is difficult to obtain. Some are not listed in the Postal Guides, and the reports of establishment and discontinuance are not in the "Records of Postmaster Appointments" which proved to be so useful in compiling the section on regular post offices. The desired information is often found in the Postal Bulletin, and from that source the basic information was abstracted.   A fortunate event was the discovery in the Denver Post Office of the "official" records for the stations and branches in Colorado.   These records, like the Records of Appointment contain dates of establishment, discontinuance, and the names of the clerks in charge of the office.   These records, although more comprehensive than any other source, still leave some openings that can only be partially filled from other sources.   Thus, some offices may have opened earlier, or closed later than recorded.   As with the "regular" post offices, the authors would appreciate any further knowledge the reader may possess about this segment of Colorado postal history.

Where specific dates remain undetermined, a single year date, under "Established", indicates the earliest Postal Guide in which the station or branch is listed. Likewise, a single year date under "Discontinued" indicates the latest Postal Guide in which the station or branch is listed. All stations and branches are assumed to be in the same county as the parent office unless otherwise stated in the remarks column.

Research has shown that the numbered stations of a parent office were so designated merely as a method of keeping the various stations separated. They were discontinued and re-established at will with a re-establishment often having no relation to the previously discontinued office with the same number. In many cases, the re-establishment was not even in the same part of town. As is indicated in the list, many numbered stations were established to handle the business of a discontinued named post office or station, but not necessarily at the same location. The post office records are sketchy in regards to these exact relationships.

The physical locations of the various branches and stations are listed where known. An attempt has been made to tie the locations to the various dates of operation, but the official records do not always include this information thus it is probable that many of the branches and stations have existed at locations additional to those reported.

In earlier years most of the branches and stations were classified; that is, they were operated by employees of the post office department. In recent years most are operated as contract offices, manned by non-post office personnel on a part time basis and paid accordingly. In most cases, numbered classified offices are not the same as the contract offices of later years with the same number, and they are listed separately. However, some offices were redesignated from classified to contract and operated with the same personnel and at the same location. Where this is known to have happened, no separate listing has been made.

The C.O.D., M.O.S., and M.O.U. stations may very well have operated at specific windows in the parent post office. The military establishment M.O.S.'s and M.O.U.'s are believed to have operated at the post exchanges, their function being that of only processing postal money orders and not of cancelling mail. These offices are listed in the postal guides, but without explanation. Cancellations from these offices are known, but are believed to be philatelic favors and not to have been regularly used on mail except as an identifying mark associated with the money order transactions.

Cancellations from offices such as "Dead Letter Office", "General Accounting Office", "Bear Valley Delivery Annex", etc., are known on cover. However, it is our opinion that these were intended as a dating or recording device for interdepartmental correspondence and transactions and were not a part of the regular system for handling mail.

Around the turn of the century some R.F.D. (Rural Free Delivery) route carriers cancelled mail. The purpose, mechanics, and the location where such cancellations were applied (on the route or in the office) is a subject of much controversy, and is under research by other students. With regards to Colorado, several such covers are known and more are suspected to exist. To date we have seen cancellations that include Broomfield R.F.D., La Junta R.F.D., La Salle R.F.D., Platteville R.F.D., and Durango R.F.D. Reports of others would be appreciated.

Another unusual series of cancellations exist from Colorado Springs. These read "Colorado Springs, Colo., Clerk No. 2" (also Clerks Nos. 3, 4, 5, and 6). The significance of these markings is unknown at present.

As matters of information, Rural Station status was changed to Rural Branch status in change No. 35, U. S. Postal Bulletin #20516 dated February 10,1966. ZIP Codes first appeared in change No. 3 of the U.S. Postal Bulletin #20367 dated June 20,1963.

Abbreviations and definitions of the terms used in this section are as follows:

BR	BRANCH - A sub-facility located outside the city limits of the parent office
STA	STATION - A sub-facility located within the city limits of the parent office
CLBR or CLSTA	CLASSIFIED BRANCH or CLASSIFIED STATION - A branch or station operated by the Post Office Department and manned by Post Office Department employees
CNBR or CNSTA	CONTRACT BRANCH or CONTRACT STATION - A branch or station under contract to private individuals and staffed by non-Post Office Department personnel, and having no general or box delivery and no postmarking equipment
RB	RURAL BRANCH - Located at some point other than the parent office city and operated on a contract basis by non-Post Office Department personnel, but providing the same services as a 4th class post office
RS	RURAL STATION - A previous designation for Rural Branch
C.O.D.	COLLECT ON DELIVERY
M.O.S.	MONEY ORDER STATION
M.O.U.	MONEY ORDER UNIT
IRS or IRB	INDEPENDENT RURAL STATION or INDEPENDENT RURAL BRANCH

148

THE NAMED STATIONS AND BRANCHES OF COLORADO

OFFICE	TYPE	PARENT OFFICE	REMARKS
ADAMS CITY	BR STA	Commerce City	
AIR BASE	BR	Colorado Springs	
AIR BASE	BR	La Junta	
AIR BASE	BR	Pueblo	
AIRPORT	RS	Pueblo	Changed to Station No. 6
ALAMEDA	BR	Denver	
ALCOTT	STA	Denver	
ALTURA	BR BR	Denver Aurora	Transferred to branch of Aurora
AMACHE	BR	Lamar	
AMERICAN PHILATELIC SOCIETY CONVENTION	STA	Denver	Not listed in Postal Guides
AMERICAN TOPICAL ASSOCIATION CONVENTION	STA	Colorado Springs	Not listed in Postal Guides
ANNEX	STA	Colorado Springs	
ANNEX	STA	Englewood	Not listed in Postal Guides
APPLEWOOD	BR	Denver	
ASPEN-GERBAZ	RB	Aspen	
ASSOCIATION CAMP	RB	Estes Park	
AURORA	BR	Denver	Became an independent post office
BELMAR	BR	Denver	
BELMONT	STA	Pueblo	
BESSEMER	STA	Pueblo	Became Station A
BLACK FOREST	RB	Colorado Springs	

OFFICE	TYPE	PARENT OFFICE	REMARKS
BRANDON	RS RB	Eads	
BROADMOOR	BR	Colorado Springs	Cancellation error "Broadmoore"
BROOKRIDGE	BR STA	Littleton Englewood	Transferred to station of Englewood
BUCKLEY FIELD	BR	Denver	
BUCKSKIN JOE	RS	Canon City	
BUFFALO CREEK	RS RB	Pine	
CADET	STA	United States Air Force Academy	Previously M.O.U. No. 1
CAMP CARSON	BR	Colorado Springs	
CAPITOL HILL	STA	Denver	Became Cherry Creek Station
CAPITOL HILL	STA	Denver	Re-established at new location
CENTENNIAL	BR STA	Littleton Englewood	Transferred to station of Englewood
CHAFFEE	STA	Denver	Changed to North Pecos branch
CHERRY CREEK	STA	Denver	Previously Capital Hill station
CHIMNEY ROCK	RB	Pagosa Springs	
CHIPITA PARK	RB	Cascade	Summer post office only
COLLEGE	STA	Greeley	
COLLEGE HEIGHTS	STA	Durango	
COLLEGE VIEW	RS	Denver	
COLORADO CITY	BR	Colorado Springs	Establishment indefinitely postponed
COLORADO CITY	RS RB	Pueblo	Do not confuse with Colorado City post office in El Paso County

OFFICE	TYPE	PARENT OFFICE	REMARKS
COLORADO SIERRA	RB	Golden	Non-personnel
COMO	RS RB	Fairplay	
CRESCENT	RS RB	Golden	
CUCHARA	RS RB	La Veta	Summer post office only
DANIELS	RS BR	Golden	Became Edgemont branch
DAYTON	STA STA	Denver Aurora	Transferred to station of Aurora
DOWNTOWN	STA	Englewood	
DRENNAN	RS	Colorado Springs	
EAST COLFAX	STA	Denver	
EASTLAND	BR	Denver	
EAST TINCUP	RS	Golden	
EDGEMONT	BR	Golden	Previously Daniels branch
EDGEWATER	BR	Denver	
EIGHTH AVENUE	STA	Denver	
ELDORA	RB	Nederland	Summer post office only
ELK SPRINGS	RB	Craig	
EL RANCHO	RS RB	Golden	
ENGLEWOOD	BR	Denver	Became an independent post office
FAIR	STA	Sterling	
FAN FAIR	STA	Aurora	

OFFICE	TYPE	PARENT OFFICE	REMARKS
FEDERAL HEIGHTS	STA	Denver	
FITZSIMONS	BR	Denver	
FIVE POINTS	STA	Denver	
FORT CARSON	BR	Colorado Springs	Previously Camp Carson branch
FORT LYON	BR	Las Animas	Also see U. S. Fort Lyon
FORTIETH STREET	STA	Denver	
FOUNTAIN VALLEY SCHOOL	RS RB	Colorado Springs	
FRUITVALE	RS	Grand Junction	
GARCIA	RS RB	San Luis	
GARFIELD	RS RB	Salida	
GILSONITE	RS RB	Fruita	
GLENDALE	BR	Denver	
GLENDEVEY	RS RS RB	Jelm, Wyoming Walden	Became rural station of Walden
GRANITE	RB	Buena Vista	
GREEN MOUNTAIN	BR	Denver	
HEENEY	RS RB	Kremmling	
HERITAGE SQUARE	STA	Golden	
HIGHLANDS	STA	Denver	
HIGH MAR	STA	Boulder	
HILLSIDE	RS RB RB	Canon City Canon City Salida	Transferred to rural branch of Salida

OFFICE	TYPE	PARENT OFFICE	REMARKS
HOFFMAN HEIGHTS	BR STA	Denver Aurora	Transferred to station of Aurora
HOMELAKE	RB	Monte Vista	
INTERNMENT CAMP	BR	Trinidad	
IVYWILD	BR	Colorado Springs	
KNOB HILL	STA	Colorado Springs	
LAKESIDE	BR	Denver	
LAKEWOOD	BR	Denver	
LAY	RS RB	Craig	
LORETTO	STA	Denver	
LOWRY	STA	Denver	Became Lowry A. F. B. station
LOWRY AIR FORCE BASE	STA	Denver	Previously Lowry station
MAIN OFFICE	STA	Denver	Not in postal guides
MAGIC MOUNTAIN	RS	Golden	
MANCOS CREEK	RS	Cortez	
MEADOWLARK	BR	Denver	
MESA	STA	Pueblo	
MILNER	RB	Steamboat Springs	
MONTCLAIR	STA	Denver	
MOUNTAIN PARK	RB	Golden	Non-personnel
NAVAL CONVALESCENT HOSPITAL	BR	Glenwood Springs	N. P. O. 10206
NIWOT	BR	Boulder	Rescinded. Remained an independent post office.
NORTH AVONDALE	RS RB	Pueblo	

OFFICE	TYPE	PARENT OFFICE	REMARKS
NORTH END	STA	Colorado Springs	
NORTHGLENN	BR	Denver	
NORTH PECOS	BR	Denver	Previously Chaffee station
NORTH POLE	RS RB	Colorado Springs	
ORCHARD PLAZA	BR	Littleton	
OVERLAND PARK	STA	Denver	Summer post office only
PANDO	BR	Denver	World War II post office for Camp Hale
PARK HILL	STA	Denver	
PEOPLES	BR STA	Denver Aurora	Transferred to station of Aurora
PERL-MACK	BR	Denver	
PETERSON FIELD	BR	Colorado Springs	M.O.U. Branch
PINE	RS	Conifer	
PUEBLO ARMY DEPOT	BR	Pueblo	
PUEBLO WEST	RB	Pueblo	
RADIUM	RS RB	Kremmling	
REDSTONE	RS	Carbondale	
RED WING	RB	Walsenburg	
RIO BLANCO	RS RB	Rifle	
ROMPEX	STA	Denver	Not listed in Postal Guides (Rocky Mountain Philatelic Exhibition)
ROYAL GORGE	RB	Canon City	Summer post office only
SANTA FE DRIVE	STA	Denver	

OFFICE	TYPE	PARENT OFFICE	REMARKS
SAPINERO	RB	Gunnison	Summer post office only
SECURITY	BR	Colorado Springs	
SHAW HEIGHTS	STA	Westminster	
SILVERTHORNE	RS RB	Dillon	
SOCOPEX	STA	Colorado Springs	Not listed in Postal Guides (Southern Colorado Philatelic Exhibition)
SOUTH DENVER	STA	Denver	Previously Station A
SOUTHGATE	BR	Colorado Springs	
SOUTH PARK CITY	STA	Fairplay	
SPIVAK	BR	Denver	
STOCKYARDS	STA	Denver	
TERMINAL	STA	Denver	Became Terminal Annex
TERMINAL ANNEX	STA	Denver	Previously Terminal Station
THORNTON	BR	Denver	
TRANS-MISSISSIPPI PHILATELIC SOCIETY	STA	Denver	Not listed in Postal Guides
U. S. FORT LYON	BR	Las Animas	Also see Fort Lyon
UNIVERSITY PARK	STA	Denver	
VAIL	RS	Minturn	Became an independent post office
VETERANS ADMINISTRATION HOSPITAL	STA	Denver	
VILLAGE	RS	La Junta	
VILLA PARK	STA	Denver	
VIRGINIA DALE	RB	La Porte	

OFFICE	TYPE	PARENT OFFICE	REMARKS
WAGON WHEEL GAP	RS	Creede	
WELLSHIRE	BR STA	Denver	
WEST COLFAX	BR	Denver	
WEST END	STA	Colorado Springs	
WEST VILLAGE	BR	Aspen	
WESTWOOD	BR STA	Denver	
WINDSOR GARDENS	STA	Denver	

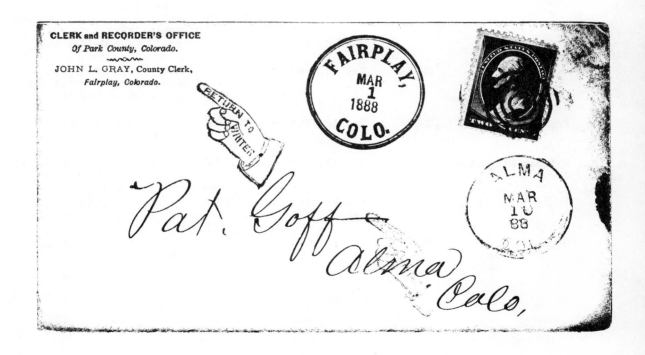

156

STATIONS AND BRANCHES OF COLORADO
BY PARENT OFFICE

OFFICE	TYPE	ESTABLISHED	DISCONTINUED	REMARKS
ALAMOSA C.O.D.	STA	Jan 2,1951	1951	
ARVADA No. 1	CNSTA	Sep 1,1960 May 1,1965	Feb 9,1965 Sep 30,1969	9800 West 59th Place Closed 6/30/69
No. 2	STA	Jan 24,1968	Jan 24,1968	5042 West 64th Ave. The contractor withdrew his bid on 2/16/68, be- fore the office opened.
ASPEN Aspen-Gerbaz	RB	Dec 4,1967		Aspen-Gerbaz trailer court
West Village	CLBR	Dec 4,1967		Snowmass-at-Aspen
Sta. A	CLSTA	Jan 20,1969		625 East Cooper Street
AURORA Altura	CNBR	Feb 16,1963 Jul 1,1966 Jun 2,1969	Sep 30,1964 Apr 30,1969	Previously a branch of Denver. 15751 East Colfax Ave. (Miles Plaza Superette) 15701 East Colfax Avenue (Plaza Motel) 15437 East Colfax Ave.
Dayton	CNSTA	Feb 16,1963		816 Dayton St. (Dayton Drug Store). Previously a branch of Denver
Fan Fair	CNSTA	Nov 16,1963	Sep 30,1966	333 Havana St., Closed 6/30/66
Hoffman Heights	BR CNSTA CLBR	Nov 15,1954 Apr 6,1957 Feb 16,1963 Jun 6,1964	Apr 5,1957 Feb 15,1963 Jun 6,1964	732 Peoria St., previously a branch of Denver 700 Peoria St. Changed to CLBR 722 Peoria St.
Peoples	STA	Feb 16,1963		2025 Clinton, previously CNBR of Denver

OFFICE	TYPE	ESTABLISHED	DISCONTINUED	REMARKS
BOULDER				
High Mar	CLSTA	Apr 17,1967		Moorhead Ave. and Table Mesa Drive
Niwot	CLBR	May 5,1967	May 5,1967	Rescinded, remained independent post office
C.O.D.	STA	Feb 16,1948	1951	
No. 1	STA	Mar. 1,1911	Jun 30,1911	Broadway, Pennsylvania and 13th Street
		Jul 1,1911	Dec 31,1926	1305 Pennsylvania Ave.
		Mar 1,1927		1124 13th St.
	CNSTA			1111 Broadway
No. 2	CNSTA	Oct 6,1956	Jun 30,1957	2677 Arapahoe (Kiddies Clothes Line)
		Jul 1,1957	Aug 31,1967	2580 Arapahoe, closed 5/31/67
No. 3	CNSTA	Oct 6,1956	Jan 9,1961	2570-90 Baseline Rd. (Hodels Drug) closed 9/15/60
		Aug 16,1961	Jun 30,1967	2490 Baseline Rd. (Red Owl Market) closed 2/25/67
No. 4	CNSTA	Jul 1,1958	Dec 30,1960	2603 North Broadway
		Feb 1,1961	Feb 25,1965	2670 North Broadway
		Feb 26,1965		2700 North Broadway
No. 5	CNSTA	Dec 1,1961	Nov 19,1962	Table Mesa Shopping Center
		Dec 1,1962	Jun 26,1964	Closed 3/26/64
BUENA VISTA				
Granite	RB	Mar 26,1966		Previously an independent post office
CAMP CARSON				
M.O.U. No. 1	STA	Jul 13,1942	1965	(Convalescent Hospital 6/5/56)
M.O.U. No. 2	STA	Jul 13,1945	Mar 31,1959	Closed 4/1/48
		1962	1965	
M.O.U. No. 3	STA	Dec 1,1942	Aug 31,1957	
		1962	1965	

158

OFFICE	TYPE	ESTABLISHED	DISCONTINUED	REMARKS
CAMP CARSON				
M.O.U. No. 4	STA	Nov 1,1943	1953	
		1962	1965	
M.O.U. No. 5	STA	Nov 1,1943	1953	
M.O.U. No. 6	STA	Jan 24,1944	1953	
M.O.U. No. 7	STA	Jan 24,1944	Nov 1,1954	
M.O.U. No. 8	STA	Jan 24,1944	Nov 1,1954	

(Note: All M.O.U.'s of Camp Carson continued under the name of Fort Carson, an office of Colorado Springs when the designation was changed from "Camp" to "Fort" Nov 1, 1954)

OFFICE	TYPE	ESTABLISHED	DISCONTINUED	REMARKS
CANON CITY				
Buckskin Joe	RS	Jun 1,1961	Feb 9,1966	Summer post office only
	RB	Feb 10,1966	Mar 31,1966	
Hillside	RS	Dec 5,1964	Feb 9,1966	Previously independent post office. Changed to a rural branch of Salida.
	RB	Feb 10,1966	Jul 25,1970	
Royal Gorge	IRB	Apr 30,1966		Previously independent post office. Summer post office only.
C.O.D.	STA	Jan 10,1944	1951	
CARBONDALE				
Redstone	RS	Jun 1,1959	Aug 1,1962	Closed 9/30/61
CASCADE				
Chipita Park	RB	Jun 1,1967		Summer post office only 6/1 to 9/30
COLORADO SPRINGS				
Air Base	BR	Oct 15,1942	Mar 31,1943	Changed to CLSTA
	CLSTA	Apr 1,1943	Dec 31,1946	Became Ent A.F.B. M.O.U.
American Topical Association Conv.	STA	Jun 15,1962	Jun 17,1962	Philatelic Exhibition station at the Antlers Hotel
Annex	CLSTA	Jun 18,1965	May 25,1968	Sierra Madre Ave. and Colorado Ave.

OFFICE	TYPE	ESTABLISHED	DISCONTINUED	REMARKS
COLORADO SPRINGS				
Black Forest	RS	Apr 16,1960	Feb 9,1966	
	RB	Feb 10,1966		
Broadmoor	CNBR	Aug 1,1959		Previously Sta. No. 6
Camp Carson	BR	Jun 25,1942	Nov 1,1954	Became Fort Carson Branch
Colorado City	BR	Jul 1,1916	Jul 1,1916	Establishment was indefinitely postponed.
Drennan	RS	?	1953	Discontinued about Oct 1, 1951
Fort Carson	CLBR	Nov 1,1954		Previously Camp Carson branch
Fountain Valley School	RS	May 18,1957	Feb 9,1966	Zip 80907 changed to Zip 80911 during 8/68
	RB	Feb 10,1966		
Ivywild	CNBR	Apr 1,1964	Jan 31,1967	1404 Tejon St., closed 12/31/65
Knob Hill	CLSTA	Aug 2,1958		
North End	STA	1955		
North Pole	RS	Aug 1,1956	Feb 9,1966	Seasonal post office 1/31/59. Santa's Workshop on Ute Pass Road.
	RB	Feb 10,1966		
Peterson Field	CNBR	Apr 16,1961		
Security	CLBR	Sep 1,1958		
SOCOPEX	STA	Oct 10,1970	Oct 11,1970	Philatelic Exhibition Station at Rustic Hills Shopping Center (Southern Colorado Philatelic Exhibition)
Southgate	CNBR	Sep 1,1960	Dec 31,1961	Closed 9/30/61
West End	CLSTA	Jul 1,1917		Previously Colorado City independent post office
C.O.D.	STA	May 1,1923	1953	

OFFICE	TYPE	ESTABLISHED	DISCONTINUED	REMARKS
COLORADO SPRINGS				
M.O.S. No. 1	STA	Jun 20,1943	1946	At Main Post Office
		Dec 20,1950		At Ent Air Force Base
M.O.S. No. 2	STA	Sep 15,1943	1946	At Peterson Field
Sta. A	STA	Dec 1,1911	Jun 30,1917*	Previously Sta. No. 1, 119 E. Fontanero St. 1528 N. Tejon St. (1916) * Became Sta. No. 6
Sta. A	CLSTA	Nov 1,1968		Yuma and Unita Sts.
No. 1	STA	Dec 1,1905	Nov 30,1911	Became Sta. A
		Oct 1,1912	Feb 29,1920	402 S. El Paso St.
		Mar 1,1920		729 W. Colorado Ave.
No. 2	STA	Dec 1,1905	Dec 31,1943	832 N. Tejon St.
No. 2	CNSTA	Mar 10,1949	Jun 30,1951	115 E. Fontanero St.
		Sep 4,1951	Sep 15,1952	
		Dec 13,1952	May 31,1965	
		Jun 1,1965	Aug 31,1968	1436 N. Hancock, closed 12/30/67
No. 3	STA	Dec 1,1905	Oct 31,1906	729 W. Huerfano St., later at 731 W. Huerfano St.
		Nov 1,1906	Dec 31,1942	1504 Colorado Ave., closed 3/31/41
No. 3	CNSTA	Apr 16,1966	Feb 21,1970	2419 N. Union Blvd.
		Mar 16,1970		
No. 4	STA	Jun 16,1910	Jul 19,1942	330 N. Institute St.
		Nov 1,1948	Feb 28,1951	2307 E. Platte Ave.
		Apr 16,1951	Apr 24,1952	2306 E. Platte Ave.
		Apr 25,1952	Jul 31,1958	2314 E. Platte Ave.
No. 4	CNSTA	Jul 1,1966	Aug 31,1968	1828 Alpine 1835 N. Circle Drive
No. 5	STA	May 1,1911	May 18,1942	432 W. Bijou St.
		Nov 1,1949	Nov 1,1950	210 Fillmore St.
No. 5	CNSTA	Apr 16,1961	Sep 27,1961	

OFFICE	TYPE	ESTABLISHED	DISCONTINUED	REMARKS
COLORADO SPRINGS				
No. 6	STA	Jul 1,1917	Dec 15,1938	Previously Station A, 119 E. Fontanero St., closed 9/30/37
		Jan 1,1939	May 24,1955	Lake Circle at Lake Ave.
		May 25,1955	Jul 31,1959	Changed to Broadmoor branch
COMMERCE CITY				
Adams City	CLBR	Oct 12,1963	May 3,1970	Previously independent post office
	CLSTA	May 4,1970		
CONIFER				
Pine	RS	Oct 1,1960	Jul 21,1961*	Previously independent post office * Changed to a second class post office
CORTEZ				
Mancos Creek	RS	Jul 16,1961	Jun 16,1962	
CRAIG				
Elk Springs	IRB	May 7,1966		Previously independent post office
Lay	RS	Aug 4,1962	Feb 9,1966	Previously independent post office
	RB	Feb 10,1966		
CREEDE				
Wagon Wheel Gap	RS	Jun 1,1955	Sep 30,1957	Previously independent post office
DENVER				
Alameda	CNBR	Sep 1,1964	Aug 30, 1967	263 South Sheridan
		Dec 13,1967	Dec 31,1968	5660 W. Alameda, closed 7/23/68
		Jul 1,1969	Jun 15,1971	285 S. Sheridan (Friendly Drug and Pharmacy) closed 11/30/70
Alcott	CLSTA	Jul 1,1904		Tennyson near 41st St. 3977 Tennyson 4515 W. 41st St. 3900 Tennyson
Altura	BR	Jun 1,1961	Feb 15,1963	15701 E. Colfax Ave., changed to branch of Aurora

OFFICE	TYPE	ESTABLISHED	DISCONTINUED	REMARKS
DENVER				
Amer. Philatelic Society Conv. Sta.	STA	Sep 8,1948	Sep 8,1948	Philatelic Exhibition station, operated for one day at the Shirley Savoy Hotel
Applewood	CNBR	Jun 16,1961 Jul 1,1962 Jul 1,1966	Jun 30,1962 Jun 30,1966 Jul 31,1967	2050 Youngfield 2090 Youngfield 2098 Youngfield, closed 4/29/67 (located in Jefferson County)
Aurora	CNBR	Jan 1,1940	Apr 27,1962	East side of Dallas St. between Colfax and 14th St. Became a first class post office.
Belmar	CLBR	Nov 14,1964		7801 W. Mississippi Ave. (located in Jefferson County)
Buckley Field	BR	Jul 6,1942	Oct 1,1946	Air Base in Arapahoe County
Capitol Hill	STA	Oct 1,1905 Aug 1,1925	Jul 31,1925 Nov 1,1963	1217-1219 E. Colfax Ave. 2227 E. Colfax Ave. changed to Cherry Creek station.
Capitol Hill	STA	1967		Previously East Colfax station, 1541 Marion St.
Chaffee	STA	Sep 1,1953	Sep 30,1964	East side of Tejon between 47th and Elk Place, became North Pecos Branch.
Cherry Creek	CLSTA	Nov 2,1963		245 Columbine, previously Capitol Hill station.
College View	RS	Aug 7,1946	Mar 31,1948	
Dayton	BR	Oct 16,1959	Feb 15,1963	816 Dayton St. (Dayton Drug) changed to branch of Aurora, Arapahoe County
East Colfax	STA	May 1,1944	1966	900-1300 blocks of East Colfax Ave. Moved and name changed to Capitol Hill Station.

OFFICE	TYPE	ESTABLISHED	DISCONTINUED	REMARKS
Eastland	CNBR	Nov 16,1961	Nov 1,1962	Located in Arapahoe County
Edgewater	BR CLBR	Jul 16,1937		Previously independent post office, 25th Ave. and Ames St. 2480 Gray St. (1971)
Eighth Avenue	STA	Mar 1,1909	Jul 31,1915	1022 West 8th Ave.
Englewood	BR	Dec 1,1913	Sep 14,1930	Became independent post office in Arapahoe County
Federal Heights	CNSTA	Aug 15,1970		2951 West 91st Place
Fitzsimons	BR CLBR	May 1,1923		In Fitzsimons Army Hospital, located in Adams County
Five Points	STA	Feb 1,1908	Dec 31,1915	Replaced by Sta. No. 8
Fortieth Street	STA	Feb 7,1904	Mar 31,1915	3901-3903 Downing Ave.
Glendale	CNBR	Mar 1,1959	Apr 15,1960	506 S. Colorado Blvd., closed 1/19/60
		Feb 16,1964	Aug 30,1968	690 S. Colorado Blvd., previously Sta. No. 13
		Sep 3,1968		4750 E. Cherry Creek Drive South
Green Mountain	CNBR	Apr 16,1966	Apr 10,1969	12292 W. Alameda Parkway
		May 1,1969		180 S. Union (located in Jefferson County)
Highlands	STA	Dec 1,1897		2935-2939 Gallup Ave. 2538 W. 32nd Ave. 3125 Federal Blvd.
Hoffman Heights	BR	Jul 1,1941	May 31,1954	708 Peoria St., closed 5/20/44
		Nov 15,1954	Feb 15,1963	
		Nov 15,1954	Feb 15,1963	Became station of Aurora, Arapahoe County

OFFICE	TYPE	ESTABLISHED	DISCONTINUED	REMARKS
Lakeside	CNBR	Oct 1,1959 Nov 16,1965	Jun 30,1965	5801 W. 44th Ave., Jefferson County
Lakewood	BR CLBR	Apr 1,1942		8755 W. 14th, previously an independent post office
Loretto	CLSTA	Mar 12,1966		3001 S. Federal, previously an independent post office
Lowry	STA	Jan 3,1939		Became Lowry A.F.B. sta- tion
Lowry Air Force Base	CLSTA	1957		Administration building, Lowry Air Force Base
Main Office	STA			1823 Stout St., not list- ed in Postal Guides, but cancels exist.
Meadowlark	CNBR	Jul 1,1963 Jan 16,1966	Dec 22,1965	9110 W. 6th Ave. (Hesteds) 9130 W. 6th Ave. (Hanson Shoe Store)
Montclair	STA	Apr 1,1912 Jul 1,1951	Sep 30,1916	1431 Krameria St. 1355 Kearney St.
Northglenn	CNBR	Nov 1,1962 Nov 1,1963 Jun 7,1968	Oct 31,1963 Jan 4,1968	106th Ave. at N. Washing- ton 603 Garland Dr. (Garland Shopping Center) 10465 Melody Dr. (Adams County)
North Pecos	CLBR	Oct 1,1964		Previously Chaffee sta- tion 1480 W. 71st Place 7156 Pecos St. (Adams County)
Overland Park	STA	1927	1932	Summer post office only
Pando	BR	Jun 1,1942	Oct 25,1945	Post Office for Camp Hale, Eagle County, pre- viously an independent post office.

OFFICE	TYPE	ESTABLISHED	DISCONTINUED	REMARKS
Park Hill	CLSTA	1951		3555 Hudson St.
Peoples	CNBR	May 16,1960	Feb 15,1963	2025 Clinton St., changed to CNSTA of Aurora, Adams County
Perl-Mack	CNBR	Sep 16,1960	Feb 9,1965	7150 Pecos St., closed 11/9/64
ROMPEX (Rocky Mountain Philatelic Exhibition Station)	STA	May 1,1959 May 4,1962 May 10,1963 May 1,1964 Aug 26,1965 Jun 10,1966 May 5,1967 May 10,1968 May 9,1969 May 1,1970 Apr 30,1971	May 3,1959 May 6,1962 May 12,1963 May 3,1964 Aug 29,1965 Jun 10,1966 May 7,1967 May 12,1968 May 11,1969 May 3,1970 May 2,1971	Shirley Savoy Hotel Albany Hotel Albany Hotel Albany Hotel Brown Palace Hotel Albany Hotel Albany Hotel Albany Hotel Albany Hotel Albany Hotel Albany Hotel
Santa Fe Drive	STA CLSTA	Sep 29,1923		1350 Santa Fe Drive
South Denver	STA	Aug 1,1889		Previously Station A 264-266 South Broadway 225 South Broadway
Spivak	CNBR	Jul 1,1967		Previously independent post office 6699 W. Colfax Ave. 6677 W. Colfax Ave., Space D (JCRS Center)
Stockyards	STA	Jan 16,1904		Livestock Exchange Building, 5910 Brighton Blvd.
Terminal	STA	Mar 22,1916	Aug 31,1931	Became Terminal Annex Station
Terminal Annex	CNBR	Apr 6,1957	Oct 5,1967	8810 N. Washington, Adams County
	CLSTA	Oct 6,1967		8804 N. Washington
Trans-Mississippi Philatelic Society Convention	STA	Oct 6,1961	Oct 8,1961	Shirley Savoy Hotel, philatelic exhibition station

OFFICE	TYPE	ESTABLISHED	DISCONTINUED	REMARKS
University Park	STA	Jul 1,1951		South University Blvd. between Wesley and Harvard. Later at 2095 S. Ogden St.
Veterans Administration Hospital	STA	1951	1961	
Villa Park	STA	Jul 1,1906	Dec 15,1915	2731 West Colfax Ave. Replaced by Sta. No. 38
Wellshire	CNBR	May 18,1957	Sep 1,1958	2238 S. Colorado Blvd. closed 7/10/58, became CNSTA No. 7
	CLBR	Oct 1,1960	Jul 20,1964	Grape St. between Evans and Warren
	CLSTA	Jul 21,1964		2171 S. Grape St.
West Colfax	CNBR	May 20,1967	Aug 30,1969	7024 West Colfax Ave. (Kincaid's Pharmacy) closed 6/30/69
Westwood	BR	May 1,1947	Jun 30,1947	3540 Morrison Road between Lowell and Nevada
	CLSTA	Jul 1,1947		275 S. Hazel Court
Windsor Gardens	CNSTA	Feb 1,1967		9660 E. Alameda Ave. (Windsor Gardens Drug)
C.O.D.	STA	Dec 1,1920	1953	
M.O.U. No. 1	STA	Dec 7,1942	Nov 20,1946	At Fitzsimons Branch
M.O.U. No. 2	STA	Aug 15,1960	Mar 7,1963	At Buckley Field
Sta. A	STA	Before 1896	Jul 31,1899	266 South Broadway, became South Denver station
No. 1	STA	Jul 1,1906	Mar 31,1907	625-627 15th Street
		Apr 1,1907	Aug 14,1907	640 15th Street
		Mar 1,1908	Apr 29,1921	May - Daniels and Fisher, 16th and Lawrence
	CLSTA	Apr 30,1921		Moved to new May-D&F store
		1956		May D&F 16th and Tremont

OFFICE	TYPE	ESTABLISHED	DISCONTINUED	REMARKS
No. 2	STA	Jul 1,1902	Jun 30,1934	1601 17th Street
		Apr 1,1936	Jun 30,1940	1059 Tejon Street
		Oct 1,1941	Feb 25,1942	
		Jul 1,1946	Jun 28,1948	
		Jul 1,1949	Dec 31,1950	
		Sep 4,1951	Jan 31,1952	5800 East Colfax Ave.
No. 2	CNSTA	Aug 27,1952		4100 East Colfax Ave.
No. 3	STA	Jul 1,1902	Jun 30,1911	701 E. 22nd Ave.
		Jul 1,1911	Mar 31,1927	1501 E. 22nd Ave.
No. 3	CNSTA	Jan 2,1962	Jul 31,1964	730 Colorado Blvd. (Boulevard National Bank)
		Sep 16,1954		4102 E. 8th Ave.
				3921 E. 8th Ave.
No. 4	STA	Jul 1,1906	Apr 16,1917	2400 East Colfax Ave.
		Jun 6,1917	Nov 30,1918	
		May 1,1920	Nov 22,1920	501 Corona Ave.
		Oct 10,1921	May 15,1923	1853 West 52nd Ave.
		Jul 12,1923	Jun 16,1927	
		Dec 6,1927	Jun 30,1930	
		Nov 1,1930	Mar 31,1935	
		Jun 5,1935	Jan 12,1942	
		1948	May 31,1954	Closed 12/9/52
No. 4	CNSTA	Jul 1,1955		1911 W. Mississippi Ave.
				1913 W. Mississippi Ave.
No. 5	STA	Jul 1,1906	Jul 3,1907	2644 Welton St.
		Oct 1,1907	Jan 27,1910	601 14th St.
		Feb 15,1910	Feb 4,1913	501 14th St.
		Nov 14,1913	Oct 31,1914	
		Nov 2,1914	Jun 30,1927	Denver Dry Goods Co.,
	CLSTA	Jul 1,1927		became CLSTA, 16th and Broadway
No. 6	STA	Jul 1,1906	Jun 30,1911	16th and Broadway
		Jul 1,1911	Nov 9,1917	235 16th St.
		Nov 10,1917	Mar 26,1918	1800 East Colfax Ave.
		Jul 20,1920	Aug 25,1925	800 16th St. (A.T. Lewis
		Feb 17,1926	Jan 5,1929	Department Store)
		Jul 8,1929	Jul 1,1939	
No. 6	CNSTA	Jan 16,1961	Aug 11,1967	1525 Sherman (State
		Aug 16,1967		Services Building)

OFFICE	TYPE	ESTABLISHED	DISCONTINUED	REMARKS
No. 7	STA	Jul 1,1906	Dec 4,1906	812 Santa Fe Ave.
		Dec 5,1906	Feb 28,1909	929 W. 8th Ave.
		Jul 16,1909	Feb 28,1923	4059 Tejon St.
		Jun 24,1924	Jan 17,1925	
		Feb 25,1925	Aug 31,1932	
		Nov 5,1932	Jan 26,1942	
		Jun 10,1943	Mar 26,1945	
		May 5,1948	Oct 15,1952	
		Nov 28,1952	May 17,1957	Became Wellshire CNBR
No. 7	CNSTA	Sep 1,1958		Previously Wellshire CNBR 2700 S. Colorado Blvd.
No. 8	STA	Jul 1,1902	May 21,1910	Boulevard F and West 26th St.
		Jul 1,1910	Sep 30,1915	2901 W. 25th Ave.
		Jan 1,1916	Apr 30,1935	Near Five Points Station
		Jul 1,1935	Oct 31,1942	
		Jan 2,1943	Jun 30,1961	2527 Welton St.
	CNSTA	Jul 1,1961		
No. 9	STA	Jul 1,1902	Mar 31,1920	3494 W. 32nd Ave.
		Apr 1,1920	Jun 30,1923	3940 W. 32nd Ave.
		Jun 20,1923?	Apr 29,1925	
		Jul 9,1925	Oct 31,1925	
		Feb 17,1926	Dec 31,1927	1800 Poplar St.
		Oct 23,1929	Jun 30,1931	(Colorado Womens College)
		Jul 6,1931	Apr 28,1941	
		May 20,1941	Nov 30,1942	
No. 9	CNSTA	1947?		1800 Pontiac St.
No. 10	STA	Jul 1,1902	Jan 26,1920	3100 Gilpin St.
		Aug 10,1920	Oct 30,1920	701 Santa Fe Drive
		Oct 10,1921	Jun 30,1943	
		Oct 1,1948	Feb 12,1951	
		May 22,1951	May 31,1954	2220 E. 34th Ave. Closed 6/30/53
		Nov 3,1954	Mar 31,1955	
		Jul 1,1955	Jan 19,1959	705 S. Colorado Blvd. Closed 10/22/58
No. 10	CNSTA	Oct 16,1959	Sep 1,1961	2521 E. 34th Ave. (Sarge Pharmacy)
		Nov 1,1961	?	3401 Columbine St.
		Mar 1,1963		JJJ Florist and Gift Shop 2501 E. 34th Ave. (1968)

OFFICE	TYPE	ESTABLISHED	DISCONTINUED	REMARKS
No. 11	STA	Jul 1,1906	Sep 30,1906	2805 E. 3rd Ave.
		May 15,1907	Jun 30,1911	335 W. 6th Ave.
		Jul 1,1911	Jun 30,1917	315 W. 6th Ave.
No. 11	CNSTA	Dec 1,1955	Apr 5,1957	8810 N. Washington, became Thornton CNBR
		Mar 22,1958	Nov 29,1958	1st Ave. and University Blvd. (Cherry Creek Shopping Center) Closed 8/31/58
		Jan 1,1963		3100 S. Sheridan
No. 12	STA	Jul 1,1906	Jun 30,1913	1400 Larimer St.
		Feb 16,1914	Oct 14,1914	1100 Santa Fe Dr.
		Dec 1,1914	Jun 30,1921	
		Aug 1,1921	Apr 8,1930	
		May 6,1930	Jun 7,1943	
		Jul 24,1943	Jul 1953	2700 Larimer St. became CNSTA
	CNSTA	Jul 1953	Apr 23,1966	
		Jul 1,1966		3300 Larimer St.
No. 13	STA	Oct 1,1906	Dec 5,1909	3655 Navaho St.
		Dec 6,1909	Feb 14,1957	3658 Navaho St., Closed 11/13/56
No. 13	CNSTA	Feb 1,1963	Nov 23,1963	765 S. Colorado Blvd., became Glendale CNBR
		Nov 16,1964		4830 Pecos St.
No. 14	STA	Sep 1,1904	Apr 30,1910	100 Broadway
		Jul 1,1910	May 6,1911	744 Knox Court
		Jul 1,1911	Dec 15,1913	4040 W. 50th Ave.
		Apr 16,1914	Sep 19,1917	
		Jan 1,1918	May 11,1922	
		Aug 3,1922	Mar 31,1923	
		May 24,1924	Oct 31,1937	
		Jan 10,1939	May 31,1954	1404 S. Broadway, closed 6/30/50
No. 14	CNSTA	Feb 1,1956		2005 S. Federal Blvd. (Hesteds) 1951 S. Federal Blvd. 1401 S. Federal Blvd. (1968)

OFFICE	TYPE	ESTABLISHED	DISCONTINUED	REMARKS
No. 15	STA	Jul 1,1906	Mar 12,1907	2002 Champa St.
		Apr 1,1907	Sep 10,1907	1801 Welton St.
		Dec 1,1907	Nov 7,1908	16th and Welton St.
		Oct 1,1909	Oct 4,1920	700 S. Pearl St.
		Nov 1,1922	Sep 30,1928	301 E. 7th Ave.
		Jul 8,1929	Jan 31,1944	
		Mar 6,1944	1957	1059 S. Gaylord
	CNSTA	1957		
No. 16	STA	Dec 15,1904	Jan 9,1935	2001 Larimer St.
		Jul 1,1935	Apr 9,1936	
		Dec 1,1937	Mar 27,1943	
		Aug 23,1949	May 31,1954	Closed 1/14/50
No. 16	CNSTA	Jan 16,1959	Dec 28,1970	4259 W. Florida Ave.
No. 17	STA	Jul 1,1906	Jun 30,1911	1024 E. 9th Ave.
		Jul 1,1911	Oct 19,1918	1032 E. 8th Ave.
		Jun 25,1923	Jun 30,1929	605 Knox Court
		Aug 26,1930	Oct 31,1931	
		Jan 21,1935	Mar 14,1938	
		Apr 1,1938	Dec 31,1942	
		Jul 1,1949	Jun 30,1951	
No. 17	CNSTA	Sep 22,1952	Mar 16,1965	1532 Broadway
		Aug 18,1969		12075 E. 40th Ave.
No. 18	STA	Oct 16,1905	May 12,1919	1701 Pearl St.
		Jun 26,1923	Mar 31,1930	
		Apr 21,1930	Oct 25,1939	
		Jan 17,1940	May 31,1954	Closed 9/9/42
No. 18	CNSTA	Jan 1,1964	Jan 1,1964?	3523 E. Colfax Ave.
		Jan 16,1964		2606-16 E. Colfax Ave.
No. 19	STA	Mar 16,1908	Oct 18,1913	
		Mar 1,1914	Mar 1,1914	Appointment of clerk cancelled
		Mar 3,1914	Sep 20,1918	
		Sep 21,1918	Nov 15,1918	2349 W. 44th Ave.
		Nov 14,1922	Nov 30,1943	
		Oct 1,1944	May 31,1954	Closed 6/13/51
No. 19	CNSTA	Apr 1,1965	Mar 31,1967	2200 W. Alameda Ave. (Alameda Shopping Center) closed 6/30/66
		Apr 15,1968	Aug 27,1968	2870 Colorado Blvd.

OFFICE	TYPE	ESTABLISHED	DISCONTINUED	REMARKS
No. 20	STA	Sep 1,1908	Jan 21,1919	1489 S. Pearl St.
		May 15,1922	Mar 9,1937	
		Jul 26,1937	Mar 31,1942	
		Jul 1,1942	Nov 15,1943	
		Nov 21,1949	Jun 30,1951	8100 E. 32nd Ave.
		Aug 14,1951		(Stapleton Air Field)
No. 21	STA	Oct 16,1911	Jan 23,1913	4489 Washington
		Dec 16,1913	Feb 4,1915	Became Sta. No. 36
		Apr 1,1915	Jul 23,1918	
		Sep 23,1918	Jun 30,1923	3799 Franklin St.
		Nov 13,1924	Apr 30,1926	
		Apr 11,1928	May 18,1931	
		Jul 1,1931	Jun 30,1935	
		Jan 16,1939	May 31,1954	Closed 3/13/40
No. 22	STA	Oct 16,1911	Dec 3,1915	
		Dec 6,1915	Apr 30,1918	
		Jun 1,1925	Feb 29,1932	
No. 23	STA	Jun 1,1912	May 12,1922	3434 E. 12th Ave.
		May 13,1922	Mar 31,1923	3001 E. Colfax Ave.
		Dec 10,1923	Mar 6,1924	
		Nov 13,1924	Sep 30,1926	
		Feb 6,1928	Sep 30,1937	
		Jul 10,1941	May 31,1954	Closed 5/9/42
No. 24	STA	Oct 1,1912	Apr 30,1920	1090 Broadway
		Mar 19,1925	Jul 21,1933	West 32nd and Clay (Drug Store)
		Aug 1,1933	May 31,1954	Closed 11/10/48
No. 25	STA	Oct 1,1912	Jun 15,1920	1962 Broadway
		Apr 16,1925	Oct 11,1926	
		Feb 4,1928	Sep 30,1932	
No. 26	STA	Feb 1,1913	Mar 31,1913	1400 S. Broadway
		Apr 1,1913	May 7,1934	4695 Josephine St.
		Aug 13,1934	May 31,1954	Closed 7/9/42
No. 27	STA	Feb 16,1913	Aug 31,1918	939 Cedar St.
		Jul 9,1925	May 31,1954	Closed 6/30/37

OFFICE	TYPE	ESTABLISHED	DISCONTINUED	REMARKS
No. 28	STA	Jun 1,1913	Apr 30,1920	1400 S. Broadway
		Aug 13,1925	Aug 6,1926	
		Sep 16,1929	Oct 26,1931	
		Oct 31,1931	Jul 7,1932	
No. 29	STA	Apr 16,1914	Oct 29,1914	3051 Columbine
		Nov 2,1914	Nov 9,1918	
		Aug 25,1925	May 31,1954	Closed 8/31/43
No. 30	STA	Jun 1,1914	Jan 23,1920	1700 E. 6th Ave.
		Feb 26,1920	Oct 1,1920	2341 E. Evans Ave.
		Sep 5,1929	?	290 S. Downing
	CNSTA		?	284 S. Downing
No. 31	STA	Jul 1,1914	May 31,1954	3243 W. Colfax Ave., closed 5/15/42
No. 32	STA	Jul 1,1914	Mar 31,1929	3774 Lowell Blvd., closed 3/28/22
		May 1,1931	Oct 2,1931	301 E. 7th Ave.
		Oct 28,1931	Feb 28,1934	
No. 33	STA	Jul 1,1914	Mar 31,1929	700 Knox Court, closed 4/4/22
		May 1,1931	May 31,1954	1775 Humboldt St., closed 12/1/41
No. 34	STA	Aug 1,1915	Aug 1,1915	801-803 Santa Fe Drive (cancelled)
		Aug 1,1915	Mar 31,1929	800-806 Santa Fe Dr.,closed 5/17/19
		May 1,1920	May 1,1920	Cancelled - no service performed
		Jul 16,1931	Jan 31,1932	8101 E. Colfax Ave.
No. 35	STA	Aug 1,1915	Mar 31,1929	999 S. Broadway (Gates Rubber Co.), closed 3/23/22
No. 36	STA	Aug 16,1915	Jan 10,1938	4489 Washington, previously Sta. No. 21
		Jan 25,1938	May 31,1954	Closed 10/20/42
No. 37	STA	Oct 16,1915	Nov 17,1915	1502 Colorado Blvd. (Jocelyn Department Store)
		Dec 1,1915	Mar 31,1929	Closed 9/1/20

OFFICE	TYPE	ESTABLISHED	DISCONTINUED	REMARKS
No. 38	STA	Jan 1,1916	Mar 31,1929	2626 W. Colfax Ave., established in place of Villa Park Sta., closed 7/28/20
No. 39	STA	Jan 1,1916		2343 E. Evans Ave. (postponed)
		Jan 17,1916	Mar 31,1929	Closed 6/30/18
No. 40	STA	Feb 1,1916	Jul 31,1917	1080 S. Gaylord St.
		Sep 21,1917	Mar 31,1929	Closed 7/31/18
No. 41	STA	Mar 1,1916	Jul 19,1916	4297 S. Broadway, established in place of Cherrelyn post office
		Feb 5,1917	Mar 31,1932	
DILLON				
Silverthorne	RS	Jan 1,1962	Feb 9,1966	
	RB	Feb 10,1966		
DURANGO				
College Heights	CNSTA	Dec 1,1961		Fort Lewis A & M College
EADS				
Brandon	RS	Mar 1,1963	Feb 9,1966	Previously an independent post office
	RB	Feb 10,1966		
ENGLEWOOD				
Annex	STA	?	?	Not listed in Postal Guides. Covers exist from 1964.
Brookridge	CNSTA	Jan 22,1966		5110 S. Broadway, previously CNBR of Littleton
Centennial	CNSTA	Jul 1,1962	Jun 7,1965	5050 S. Federal Blvd., previously BR of Littleton. Temporarily closed in 1965 because of flood damage.
		Sep 17,1965		
Downtown	CLSTA	Aug 22,1966		3330 S. Broadway
C.O.D	STA	May 1,1941	1951	

OFFICE	TYPE	ESTABLISHED	DISCONTINUED	REMARKS
No 1	CNSTA	Dec 16,1949 Mar 18,1955	Mar 12,1955	4295-97 S. Broadway 4360 S. Broadway
ENT AIR FORCE BASE M.O.S.	STA	Jan 2,1951	1953	Became M.O.U.
M.O.U.	STA	1953		Previously M.O.S.
ESTES PARK Association Camp	RB	May 1,1966		Previously independent post office. Summer post office only, 5/1 to 10/31. Became year around post office (RB) 11/1/70
FAIRPLAY Como	RS RB	Aug 31,1963 Feb 10,1966	Feb 9,1966	
South Park City	CNSTA	May 15,1959		Summer post office only, 5/15 to 10/1
FITZSIMONS M.O.U. No. 1	STA	1943	1945	
FORT CARSON (Refer to Camp Carson)				
FORT COLLINS C.O.D.	STA	Nov 16,1948	1951	
No. 1	CNSTA	Jan 1,1962 May 18,1968	Oct 7,1967	1671 S. College Ave. 111 W. Prospect Ave.
No. 2	CNSTA	Feb 16,1964		1117 W. Elizabeth Ave.
No. 3	CNSTA	Sep 1,1964		1025 Lemay Ave.
No. 4	CNSTA	Jun 16,1965 Mar 16,1967	Mar 15,1967	2320 S. College Ave. 2301 S. College Ave.
FORT LOGAN M.O.U. No. 1	STA	Jul 1,1942	Oct 31,1949	At main post office M.O.U. assigned to the Army Post from 9/10/42 until 6/13/46 when it became part of the Veterans Administration Hospital.

OFFICE	TYPE	ESTABLISHED	DISCONTINUED	REMARKS
FRUITA				
Gilsonite	RS	May 18,1957	Feb 9,1966	At refinery west of
	RB	Feb 10,1966		Fruita
GLENWOOD SPRINGS				
Naval Convalescent Hospital	BR	1945	1945	Naval P.O. No. 10206, located in Hotel Colorado
C.O.D.	STA	Jul 16,1949	1951	
M.O.U. No. 1	STA	Sep 16,1945	Mar 31,1946	
GOLDEN				
Colorado Sierra	RB	Aug 16,1966	Feb 28,1971	Non-personnel office, closed 11/19/70 (office was destroyed by a fire)
Crescent	RS	Oct 16,1959	Feb 9,1966	In Coal Creek Canyon
	RB	Feb 10,1966		east of Pinecliffe
Daniels	RS	Apr 8,1948	Dec 15,1949	11716 W. Colfax Ave.
	BR	Dec 16,1949	Jul 7,1951	11528 W. Colfax Ave.
		Jul 9,1951	Jun 30,1954	11507 W. Colfax Ave.
				11730 W. Colfax Ave.
				11526 W. Colfax Ave.
				Changed to Edgemont CNBR
East Tincup	RS	Jun 1,1960	Sep 1,1963	Believed to have closed earlier, summer post office only.
Edgemont	CNBR	Jul 1,1954	Jun 30,1959	Previously Daniels BR
		Jul 1,1969		1490 Sims St.
El Rancho	RS	Jul 1,1956	Feb 9,1966	
	RB	Feb 10,1966		
Heritage Square	STA	Jul 1,1971		Located at the former site of the Magic Mountain RS
Magic Mountain	RS	Jul 16,1960	Jun 1,1962	Summer post office only
Mountain Park	RB	Aug 16,1966		Non-personnel rural branch

OFFICE	TYPE	ESTABLISHED	DISCONTINUED	REMARKS
No. 1	STA	Jul 1,1962	Dec 31,1967	15940 S. Golden Road
	CNBR	Jan 8,1968		16350 S. Golden Road
GRAND JUNCTION				
Fruitvale	RS	Jul 1,1948	Aug 24,1950	
C.O.D.	STA	Jan 16,1924	1951	
No. 1	STA	Jul 1,1913	Dec 9,1915	901 Ouray Ave.
		Jan 1,1927	Feb 10,1946	723 N. 12th St.
		Oct 1,1947	Feb 14,1957	Drug Store, closed 7/6/56
		Apr 19,1958	Apr 1,1960	2140 N. 12th St.
	CNSTA	Feb 16,1961	Aug 31,1967	2232 N. 7th St. closed 5/27/67
No. 2	STA	Jan 2,1948	Jun 7,1948	956 Unaweep Ave.
		Jul 1,1948	Sep 30,1952	2121 Unaweep Ave.
		Nov 1,1952	Mar 15,1956	1624 Highway 50
	CNSTA	Apr 7,1956	Aug 31,1967	1620 Highway 50
No. 3	STA	May 16,1951	Sep 30,1952	902 North Ave.
		Sep 9,1953	Jun 30,1957	950 North Ave.
No. 3	CNSTA	Jul 1,1962	Aug 31,1967	2514 Broadway, closed 3/24/67
No. 4	CNSTA	Aug 20,1956	Jan 13,1967	2815 North Ave. 2847 North Ave., closed 4/30/66
GREELEY				
College	STA	Mar 16,1937	May 19,1943	915 16th St.
		Jul 1,1943	Jun 30,1969	1023 17th St.
	CNSTA	Jul 1,1969		2505 11th Ave. (See Sta. No. 1 ??)
C.O.D.	STA	May 16,1943	1951	
No. 1	STA	Jul 19,1948	Aug 24,1956	2626 8th Ave., closed 6/15/52
No. 1	CNSTA	Nov 16,1958		2505 11th Ave. (College Station ??)
No. 2	CNSTA	Sep 16,1964	Dec 31,1964	2904 10th St.
		Jan 1,1965		2434 10th St.

OFFICE	TYPE	ESTABLISHED	DISCONTINUED	REMARKS
GUNNISON				
Sapinero	RB	Aug 12,1967		Previously independent post office. Summer post office only, 3/1 to 11/30, effective 3/1/70 : 5/1 to 10/31
JELM, Wyoming (Refer to Walden)				
KREMMLING				
Heeney	RS	May 15,1960	Feb 9,1966	Previously an independent post office in Summit county. Summer post office only, 5/15 to 10/15
	RB	Feb 10,1966		
Radium	IRS	Dec 7,1963	Feb 9,1966	Previously an independent post office
	IRB	Feb 10,1966		
LA JUNTA				
Air Base	CLBR	Aug 15,1942	Oct 31,1943	
	BR	Nov 1,1943	Nov 15,1949	Closed 4/27/46
Village	RS	Nov 1,1943	Mar 31,1956	
C.O.D.	STA	1924	1951	
LA PORTE				
Virginia Dale	RB	Feb 11,1967		
LA VETA				
Cuchara	RS	Jul 1,1959	Feb 9,1966	Previously independent post office. Summer post office only, 5/15 to 9/30
	RB	Feb 10,1966		
LAMAR				
Amache	BR	Sep 15,1942	Nov 30,1945	Evacuee Camp
C.O.D.	STA	Oct 1,1946	1951	
LAS ANIMAS				
Fort Lyon	BR	Jun 12,1918	Jun 14,1920	Changed to U.S.Fort Lyon. The first rural station in Colorado.
	RS	Nov 1,1921	Before 1924	

OFFICE	TYPE	ESTABLISHED	DISCONTINUED	REMARKS
U. S. Fort Lyon	BR	Jun 15,1920	Oct 31,1921	Changed to Fort Lyon RS
LITTLETON				
Brookridge	BR	Oct 1,1960	Jan 31,1962	5180 S. Broadway
		Apr 16,1962	Jan 21,1966	5130 S. Broadway, changed to CNSTA of Englewood
Centennial	BR	May 16,1960	Jun 30,1962	5050 S. Federal Blvd. Changed to CNBR of Englewood
Orchard Plaza	CNBR	Mar 1,1965		5910 S. University Blvd.
C.O.D.	STA	Jan 15,1949	1951	
No. 1	CNSTA	Jan 1,1965	Mar 31,1969	100 Woodlawn Center, closed 7/1/66
No. 2	CNSTA	Jan 1,1966		112 W. Littleton Blvd.
LOWRY **(LOWRY AIR FORCE BASE)**				
M.O.U. No. 1	STA	Feb 15,1943	1965	
MINTURN				
Vail	IRS	Oct 1,1962	Jan 28,1966	Changed to a second class post office
MONTE VISTA				
Homelake	RB	Dec 4,1965		Previously an independent post office
NEDERLAND				
Eldora	IRB	May 19,1967		Previously an independent post office. Summer post office only, 6/1 to 9/30
PAGOSA SPRINGS				
Chimney Rock	RB	Apr 8,1967		Previously an independent post office
PANDO				
M.O.U. No. 1	STA	Jan 1,1943	Oct 25,1945	During this period, Pando in Eagle County, was a branch of Denver serving nearby Camp Hale, Colorado. Previously Pando was an independent post office.
M.O.U. No. 2	STA	Apr 3,1944	Oct 25,1945	
M.O.U. No. 3	STA	Apr 3,1944	Oct 25,1945	
M.O.U. No. 4	STA	Apr 3,1944	Oct 25,1945	

OFFICE	TYPE	ESTABLISHED	DISCONTINUED	REMARKS
PANDO				
M.O.U. No. 1	STA	Jan 1,1943	Oct 25,1945	During this period Pando, in Eagle County, was a
M.O.U. No. 2	STA	Apr 3,1944	Oct 25,1945	branch of Denver serving nearby Camp Hale, Colorado.
M.O.U. No. 3	STA	Apr 3,1944	Oct 25,1945	Previously Pando was an independent post office.
M.O.U. No. 4	STA	Apr 3,1944	Oct 25,1945	
M.O.U. No. 5	STA	Apr 3,1944	Oct 25,1945	
PINE				
Buffalo Creek	RS	Sep 14,1963	Feb 9,1966	Previously an independent
	RB	Feb 10,1966		post office
PUEBLO				
Air Base	BR	Sep 21,1942	Jan 29,1948	Closed 1/5/46
Airport	RS	Dec 1,1953	Aug 31,1955	Became CNBR No. 6
Belmont	CLSTA	May 10,1969		Bonforte Blvd. (Belmont Shopping Center)
Bessemer	STA	1895	1929	Also known as Sta. A Not listed as Bessemer in the Postal Guides after 1929.
Colorado City	RS	Sep 1,1964	Feb 9,1966	Do not confuse with Colorado City indepen-
	RB	Feb 10,1966		dent post office in El Paso County.
Mesa	STA	Apr 1,1945		In Mesa Junction area
North Avondale	RS	Aug 1,1964	Feb 9,1966	Previously an independent
	RB	Feb 10,1966		post office
Pueblo Army Depot	BR	Apr 1,1964	Jul 31,1964	Became M.O.U. No. 1
Pueblo West	RB	Oct 20,1969		Pueblo West Inn
C.O.D.	STA	Apr 1,1922	1951	

OFFICE	TYPE	ESTABLISHED	DISCONTINUED	REMARKS
M.O.U. No. 1	STA	Aug 1,1964	1965	Previously Pueblo Army Depot branch
Sta. A	STA	Feb 1,1904	1965	Also Called Bessemer until 1929
No. 1	STA	Oct 1,1904	Feb 28,1931	701 South Union Ave.
		Mar 1,1931	Oct 30,1943	1445 E. 8th St.
		Nov 1,1947	Sep 27,1948	717 Glendale
		Sep 28,1948	Sep 6,1952	1225 E. 8th St.
		Oct 13,1952	Feb 15,1953	1401 E. 8th St.
		Jun 23,1954	Jun 30,1957	
	CNSTA	Jul 8,1957	Oct 5,1968	1349 E. 8th St.
		Oct 28,1968		
No. 2	STA	Oct 1,1904	Jun 30,1911	24th St. and Grand Ave.
		Jul 1,1911	Jun 30,1927	2333 Grand Ave.
		Dec 1,1928	Jun 30,1935	
No. 2	CNSTA	?	Feb 20,1959	2333 Grand Ave.
		Feb 24,1959		
No. 3	STA	Oct 1,1904	Apr 8,1909	1230 E. 8th St.
		Apr 9,1909	Jun 30,1911	1228 E. 8th St.
		Jul 1,1911	Dec 4,1922	1230 E. 8th St.
		Feb 16,1923	Sep 30,1936	1230 E. 8th St.
		Oct 22,1926	May 31,1954	Closed 10/30/43
No. 3	CNSTA	Jun 1,1955	May 31,1966	1941 Lake Ave.
		Jun 1,1966	Aug 15,1970	1904 Lake Ave.
		Aug 16,1970		1207 Highland
No. 4	STA	Jul 1,1906	Jul 1,1929	204 S. Union Ave.
		Jul 1,1933	Jun 29,1934	201 N. Union Ave.
		Sep 14,1934	Dec 4,1939	
		Feb 1,1940	Sep 5,1944	
		Jul 1,1946	May 31,1954	Closed 12/11/46
No. 4	CNSTA	Jan 1,1956	Aug 31,1963	1721 Prairie Ave.
		Sep 1,1963	Jun 30,1966	Eakers (King Soopers Shopping Center)
		Jul 1,1966	Jul 31,1969	1221 S. Prairie (Republic National Bank Building)

OFFICE	TYPE	ESTABLISHED	DISCONTINUED	REMARKS
				Closed 5/30/69
No. 5	STA	Jul 16,1906	Apr 30,1907	2044 E. Evans Ave.
		May 1,1907	Jun 30,1919	2113 E. Evans Ave.
		Apr 1,1922	May 19,1954	2044 E. Evans Ave.
	CNSTA	Jul 1,1955		2226 E. Evans Ave.
No. 6	STA	Jun 16,1908	Mar 20,1911	17th and Hooper
		Mar 21,1911	Jul 31,1911	1710 Hooper
		Oct 1,1911	Mar 31,1931	314 Park St., closed 6/30/29
		Sep 16,1938	Jul 24,1961	314 Clark St.
		Jul 25,1961	Sep 30,1964	312 Clark St., closed 6/30/64
	CNBR	Dec 4,1967		Pueblo Memorial Airport, previously Airport RS
No. 7	STA CNSTA	May 1,1909		1247 Berkeley Ave.
No. 8	STA	Jul 1,1916	Jun 30,1919	703 Jackson St.
		May 16,1926	Feb 28,1936	1200 S. Santa Fe Ave.
		Mar 20,1936	Oct 28,1938	
		Nov 18,1938	May 31,1954	Closed 8/7/42
No. 8	CNBR	Aug 1,1960		1401 Santa Fe Ave.
No. 9	STA	Jul 16,1941	May 31,1954	1519 West 4th St., closed 11/8/43
No. 9	CNSTA	Feb 16,1962	Jul 31,1969	1020 Constitution Rd., closed 6/30/69
No. 10	CNBR	Mar 3,1969		Highway 50 East and 25 Lane
RANGELY				
C.O.D.	STA	1949	1951	
RIFLE				
Rio Blanco	IRS	Oct 9,1964	Feb 9,1966	Previously an independent post office
	IRB	Feb 10,1966		
SALIDA				
Garfield	RS	Dec 30,1963	Feb 9,1966	Previously an independent post office
	RB	Feb 10,1966		

OFFICE	TYPE	ESTABLISHED	DISCONTINUED	REMARKS
Hillside	RB	Jul 25,1970		Previously a rural branch of Canon City
SAN LUIS				
Garcia	RS	Jul 4,1964	Feb 9,1966	Previously an independent
	RB	Feb 10,1966		post office
STEAMBOAT SPRINGS				
Milner	RB	Feb 26,1966		Previously an independent post office
STERLING				
Fair	CNSTA	Feb 16,1963	Dec 24,1966	116 Jackson St.
		Jan 1,1967	May 31,1967	112 Jackson St. (House of Art) closed 2/10/67
TRINIDAD				
Internment Camp	BR	Apr 15,1943	Jan 31,1946	
C.O.D.	STA	Jul 1,1928	1951	
No. 1	STA	Feb 1,1906	Jan 1,1908	825 Arizona
		Jan 8,1908	May 31,1909	
		Jun 1,1909	Aug 31,1917	300 Pine St.
No. 2	STA	Dec 16,1914	Jan 31,1915	131 Main St.
		Mar 16,1915	Jun 30,1916	200 Pine St.
		Jul 5,1916	Aug 31,1918	200 Pine St. (this location until 7/9/16)
		Nov 16,1918	May 21,1919	
UNITED STATES AIR FORCE ACADEMY				
M.O.U. No. 1	STA	1959	Oct 31,1970	Became Cadet CLSTA
Cadet	CLSTA	Nov 1,1970		Previously M.O.U. No. 1
WALDEN				
Glendevey	IRS	Jun 22,1963	Apr 23,1965*	Previously an independent post office. * RS of Jelm, Wyoming during this period.
	IRS	Apr 24,1965	Feb 9,1966	Summer post office only
	IRB	Feb 10,1966		5/1 to 9/30
WALSENBURG				
Red Wing	RS	Sep 25,1965	Feb 9,1966	Previously an independent
	RB	Feb 10,1966		post office

OFFICE	TYPE	ESTABLISHED	DISCONTINUED	REMARKS
WESTMINSTER Shaw Heights	CNSTA	Jul 1,1964	Apr 16,1965	3795 W. 88th Ave. (Ben Franklin Store), closed 1/15/65
WHEATRIDGE No. 1	CNBR	Apr 16,1966		3300 Youngfield

Mary A. Watters

Mound Valley

Kansas

Miss Lucy N. Dadmun

Marlborough

Mass.

Boulder N 3,
Sept 3rd 1860

Paid

Mr Frederic P. Low Esq

Belvidere

Illinois

Answered
Jan 18th 1861.

If not called for in ten days, return to

O. G. STANLEY,

Attorney at Law.

CANON CITY, - - COLORADO.

CANON CITY
JAN
13
COL.

PAID
JAN. 16 1877
HINSDALE COUNTY BANK
Lake City, Col.

~sdale Co Bank

Lake City

Colorado

HOWLAND,
NOV
5
1879
COLO.

Henry Carey Baird & Co
810 Walnut St
Philadelphia
Pa

S E C T I O N   C

THE ZIP CODE IN COLORADO

On June 20, 1963 in change #3 of U. S. Postal Bulletin #20367, the Post Office Department implemented a system of five-digit numerical codes, called ZIP Codes, designed to improve mail sorting and delivery by assigning a number to every place reached by mail in the United States. Use of this system paves the way for eventual automatic mail handling in which the sorting could be done by machines capable of reading the five-digit number rather than the complicated letter combinations of a city and state name. The United States ZIP Code System is capable of 100,000 numbers, ranging from 00000 to 99999.

Reading the Code

The United States is divided into ten geographic areas. The first digit of the ZIP Code indicates one of the ten areas. The second digit designates a state, a geographic portion of a heavily populated state, or two or more less populated states within a geographic area. The third digit identifies a major destination area within the state. The last two digits define either a postal delivery station of a large city post office, or a post office served from a Sectional Center. The country is divided into 533 Sectional Center areas as a basis for the ZIP code.

Colorado ZIP Codes

Colorado is divided into 13 Sectional Center areas. ZIP Codes are numerically arranged in the alphabetical order of the towns within a Sectional Center, with the Sectional Center town having the lowest number in that section. For some reason the Colorado Springs Sectional Center is an exception and has the highest ZIP Code for that section. The Sectional Centers in Colorado, with their ZIP Code prefixes follow:

ALAMOSA	811
BRIGHTON	806
COLORADO SPRINGS	808-809
DENVER	800-803
DURANGO	813
FORT MORGAN	807

185

GLENWOOD SPRINGS	816
GOLDEN	804
GRAND JUNCTION	815
LONGMONT	805
MONTROSE	814
PUEBLO	810
SALIDA	812

In 1965 the Denver Sectional Center was split into Denver North (800) and Denver South (801-803) making fourteen Sectional Centers in the state. However, these two were later recombined reducing the number back to thirteen.

Under the reorganization by the new Postal Service the country is to be divided for management purposes into Metropolitan Centers, Metropolitan Areas, and Districts. The Denver Metro Area will include ZIP areas 800-803. The Colorado Springs District will be responsible for ZIP areas 804-812 and 814-816. The Sectional Centers remain as previous. The Durango Sectional Center (ZIP area 813) will be under the jurisdiction of the Albuquerque District.

Colorado was assigned ZIP Code numbers from 80000 to 81999 providing a capability for 2000 numbers, although initially only numbers to 81657 have ben assigned. Not all of the numbers within this range have been used, and there have been some changes since the initiation of the ZIP Code system. Anthony, Texas was first assigned, in error, the number 80021 instead of 88021. The highest ZIP number in Texas is 79999 (El Paso) and no other out of state town appears within the framework of the Colorado numbering limits. Later, about 1965, Anthony, Texas was removed from the Colorado ZIP Code number list and changed to its correct number 88021, which is also not within the limits of the Texas ZIP Code numbers. Being on the border of Texas and New Mexico, Anthony is no longer listed in the Texas post office list and is now shown as Anthony, New Mexico, ZIP 88021.

About 25 Colorado post offices have been discontinued since the instigation of the ZIP Code system and at present their numbers have not been reassigned. In addition, Boulder, with original ZIP Code 80301 was divided into ZIP Codes 80301, 80302, and later 80303; and Littleton, with original ZIP Code 80120 was divided into codes 80120, 80121, 80122, and 80123. A further change was made when the Fountain Valley School Rural Branch ZIP Code was changed from 80907 to 80911 in August 1968. When Glendevey was made a rural branch, its ZIP Code was changed from 80531 to 80485. When Adams City became a branch, its ZIP Code was changed from 80001 to 80022. In 1969, a new area in the Denver Sectional Center was assigned the ZIP number 80301.

In this section the ZIP Codes of Colorado are listed in numerical order, with the ZIP Codes also listed for the named branches and stations to which ZIP numbers have been assigned. Where a post office or branch has been discontinued, and its number is now unassigned, it is designated "disc." It is expected that in the future some additional ZIP Code areas will be subdivided into separate numbers as the population of the area expands. Already area 80222 has been split into 80222 and 80231. Currently, towns such as Boulder, Colorado Springs, Denver, Fort Collins, and Golden are experiencing rapid growth and most other large towns in the state are continuing to grow in size and population.

As soon after the inception of the ZIP Codes as was practical, new cancelling devices, incorporating the ZIP Code number in the cancelling dial, were sent to the post offices not having more than one ZIP Code number. Some of the post offices that were discontinued shortly after June 1963 never recieved the new cancelling devices. However, some of the offices discontinued later did, for brief periods, process mail with the new style cancelling equipment.

Boulder and Littleton at one time used machine cancelling dials showing the ZIP Code number in the date stamp. After more than one ZIP Code number was assigned to those cities, the ZIP Code number was removed from the cancel.

To date, the observed cancelling devices incorporating ZIP Code numbers are: two types of machine cancels; two types of 4-bar rubber hand stamps; one parcel post roller type; and one parcel post box hand cancel type.

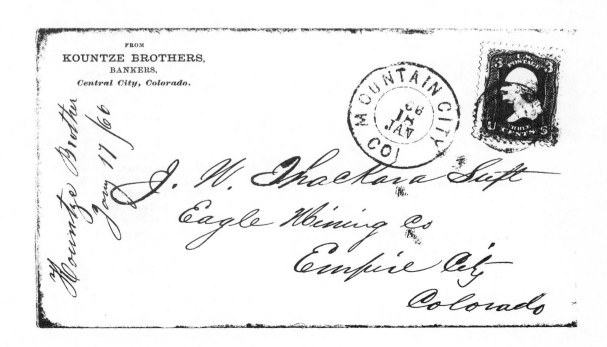

ZIP CODE ASSIGNMENTS FOR COLORADO

DENVER 800-803

800	Denver North (1964)

80001	Adams City (now 80022)
80002	Arvada
80010	Aurora
80010	Altura BR
	Dayton STA
	Hoffman Heights STA
	Peoples STA
	Fan Fair STA (disc)
80020	Broomfield
80021	Anthony, TX (error)
80022	Commerce City
80023	Adams City STA
80024	Dupont
80025	Eldorado Springs
80026	Lafayette
80027	Louisville
80028	Spivak
80030	Westminster
80033	Wheat Ridge

801-803 Denver South (1964)

80101	Agate
80102	Bennett
80103	Byers
80104	Castle Rock
80105	Deer Trail
80106	Elbert
80107	Elizabeth
80110	Englewood
	Brookridge STA
	Centennial STA
	Downtown STA
80115	Fort Logan
80116	Franktown
80117	Kiowa
80118	Larkspur
80120	Littleton
	Orchard Plaza BR
	Rural Routes
80121	Main Office Boxes
80121	(New areas split from
80122	the original area
80123	80120)
80131	Louviers
80132	Monument

80133	Palmer Lake
80134	Parker
80135	Sedalia
80136	Strasburg
80137	Watkins
80138	Westcreek (disc)
80200	Denver
80201	Denver (Main Office)
	Postmaster (new #)
80202	Station No. 1
80202	Station No. 2
	General Delivery (old #)
	Postmaster (old #)
80203	Denver residential area
80204	Santa Fe Drive STA
80205	Residential area
80206	Cherry Creek STA
80207	Park Hill STA
80208	Residential area
80209	South Denver STA
80210	University Park STA
80211	Highlands STA
80212	Alcott STA
80213	Residential Area
80214	Edgewater STA
	Spivak
80215	Lakewood BR
	West Colfax BR
	Applewood BR (disc)
80216	Stockyards STA
80217	Terminal Annex STA
80218	Capitol Hill STA
	East Colfax STA
80219	Westwood STA
80220	Montclair STA
80221	North Pecos STA
	Chaffee STA
80222	Wellshire STA
	Rural Route No. 2
	Windsor Gardens STA
80223	Residential area
80224	Residential area
80225	Residential area
80226	Alameda BR
	Belmar BR
80227	Residential area
80228	Residential area

80229	Thornton BR	80433	Conifer
	Rural Route No. 1	80434	Cowdrey
80230	Lowry Air Force Base	80435	Dillon
80231	Split from the East		Silverthorne RB
	half of area 80222	80436	Dumont
80232	Residential area	80437	Eldora
80233	Residential area	80438	Empire
80234	Residential area	80439	Evergreen
80235	Residential area	80440	Fairplay
80236	Residential area		South Park City STA
80237	Residential area	80441	Foxton
80238	Residential area	80442	Fraser
80239	Residential area	80443	Frisco
80240	Fitzsimons BR	80444	Georgetown
		80445	Gould
80301	New area assigned in 1971	80446	Granby
	Boulder Postmaster	80447	Grand Lake
	Rural Route No. 2 (new #)	80448	Grant
	Rural Route No. 4 (new #)	80449	Hartsel
	Rural Route No. 5	80450	Hideway Park
80302	Boulder Main Office	80451	Hot Sulphur Springs
	High Mar STA (old #)	80452	Idaho Springs
	Rural Route No. 2 (old #)	80453	Idledale
	Rural Route No. 4 (old #)	80454	Indian Hills
	General Delivery	80455	Jamestown
	Flagstaff Star Route	80456	Jefferson
	Jamestown Star Route	80457	Kittredge
	Salina Star Route	80458	Kokomo (disc)
80303	Rural Route No. 1	80459	Kremmling
	Rural Route No. 3		Heeney RB
	High Mar STA (new #)	80460	Lawson (disc)
		80461	Leadville
GOLDEN	804	80463	McCoy
		80464	Montezuma
80401	Golden	80465	Morrison
	Colorado Sierra RB (disc)	80466	Nederland
	Crescent RB	80467	Oak Creek
	Edgemont BR	80468	Parshall
	El Rancho RB	80469	Phippsburg
	Mountain Park RB	80470	Pine
80420	Alma	80471	Pinecliffe
80421	Bailey	80472	Radium RB
80422	Black Hawk	80473	Rand
80423	Bond	80474	Rollinsville
80424	Breckenridge	80475	Shawnee
80425	Buffalo Creek	80476	Silver Plume
80426	Burns	80477	Steamboat Springs
80427	Central City		Milner RB
80428	Clark	80478	Tabernash
80429	Climax	80479	Toponas
80430	Coalmont	80480	Walden
80431	Columbine (disc)	80481	Ward
80432	Como	80482	Winter Park

80483	Yampa	80632	Main Office Boxes
80485	Glendevey (new #)	80640	Henderson
		80641	Hoyt
		80642	Hudson
LONGMONT 805		80643	Keensburg
		80644	Kersey
80501	Longmont	80645	La Salle
80510	Allenspark	80646	Lucerne
80511	Association Camp RB	80647	Masters (disc)
80512	Bellvue	80648	Nunn
80513	Berthoud	80649	Orchard
80514	Dacono	80650	Pierce
80515	Drake	80651	Platteville
80516	Erie	80652	Roggen
80517	Estes Park	80653	Weldona
80520	Firestone	80654	Wiggins
80521	Fort Collins		
80530	Frederick	**FORT MORGAN 807**	
80531	Glendevey (now 80485)		
80532	Glen Haven	80701	Fort Morgan
80533	Hygiene	80720	Akron
80534	Johnstown	80721	Amherst
80535	Laporte	80722	Atwood
80536	Livermore	80723	Brush
80537	Loveland	80725	Buckingham (disc)
80540	Lyons	80726	Crook
80541	Masonville	80727	Eckley
80542	Mead	80728	Fleming
80543	Milliken	80729	Grover
80544	Niwot	80730	Hale
80545	Red Feather Lakes	80731	Haxtun
80546	Severance	80732	Hereford
80547	Timnath	80733	Hillrose
80548	Virginia Dale RB	80734	Holyoke
80549	Wellington	80735	Idalia
80550	Windsor	80736	Iliff
		80737	Julesburg
BRIGHTON 806		80738	Keota
		80739	Laird
80601	Brighton	80740	Lindon
80610	Ault	80741	Merino
80611	Briggsdale	80742	New Raymer
80612	Carr	80743	Otis
80613	Cornish (disc)	80744	Ovid
80614	Eastlake	80745	Padroni
80615	Eaton	80746	Paoli
80620	Evans	80747	Peetz
80621	Fort Lupton	80748	Proctor (disc)
80622	Galeton	80749	Sedgwick
80623	Gilcrest	80750	Snyder
80624	Gill	80751	Sterling
80625	Goodrich		Fair STA (disc)
80631	Greeley	80754	Stoneham
	Rural Routes		

80755	Vernon
80756	Willard (disc)
80757	Woodrow
80758	Wray
80759	Yuma

COLORADO SPRINGS 808-809

80801	Anton
80802	Arapahoe
80803	Aroya (disc)
80804	Arriba
80805	Bethune
80806	Boyero
80807	Burlington
80808	Calhan
80809	Cascade
80810	Cheyenne Wells
80811	Chipita Park RB
80812	Cope
80813	Cripple Creek
80814	Divide
80815	Flagler
80816	Florissant
80817	Fountain
80818	Genoa
80819	Green Mountain Falls
80820	Guffey
80821	Hugo
80822	Joes
80823	Karval
80824	Kirk
80825	Kit Carson
80826	Kutch (disc)
80827	Lake George
80828	Limon
80829	Manitou Springs
80830	Matheson
80831	Peyton
80832	Ramah
80833	Rush
80834	Seibert
80835	Simla
80836	Stratton
80840	U. S. Air Force Academy
	Main Office Carriers
80841	Main Office Boxes
80860	Victor
80861	Vona
80862	Wild Horse
80863	Woodland Park
80864	Yoder

80901	Colorado Springs
	North Pole RB
	General Delivery
	Postmaster
80902	Residential area
80903	Parcel Post Annex
80904	West End STA
80905	Annex STA (disc)
80906	Ivywild STA (disc)
80907	Fountain Valley School RB
	Rural Route No. 1
	Rural Route No. 7
	North End STA
80908	Black Forest RB
	Rural Route No. 3
	Rural Route No. 4
80809	Rural Route No. 2
	Rural Route No. 6
80909	Knob Hill STA
	Station A
80910	Residential area
80911	Fountain Valley School RB
	(new #)
	Security BR
80912	Ent Air Force Base
80913	Fort Carson BR
80914	Peterson Field BR
80915	Residential area
80916	Residential area
80917	Residential area

PUEBLO 810

81001	Pueblo
	Postmaster (old #)
	Belmont BR
81002	General Delivery
81003	Postmaster (new # 1970)
	Parcel Post Annex
81004	Station A
	Rural Route No. 1
	Rural Route No. 2
	Rural Route No. 3
	Rural Route No. 4
	Colorado City RB
81005	Mesa STA
81006	Pueblo (new area 1970)
81007	Pueblo West RB
80120	Aguilar
81021	Arlington
81022	Avondale
81023	Beulah

81024	Bon Carbo	81079	Timpas
81025	Boone	81080	Towner
81026	Brandon RB	81081	Trinchera
81027	Branson	81082	Trinidad
81028	Bristol	81084	Two Buttes
81029	Campo	81085	Tyrone (disc)
81030	Cheraw	81086	Utleyville
81031	Chivington	81087	Vilas
81032	Cokedale	81088	Villegreen
81033	Crowley	81090	Walsh
81034	Delhi	81091	Weston
81035	Deora	81092	Wiley
81036	Eads		
81037	Farisita	ALAMOSA	811
81038	Fort Lyon		
81039	Fowler	81101	Alamosa
81040	Gardner	81120	Antonito
81041	Granada	81121	Arboles
81042	Gulnare	81122	Bayfield
81043	Hartman	81123	Blanca
81044	Hasty	81124	Capulin
81045	Haswell	81125	Center
81046	Hoehne	81126	Chama
81047	Holly	81127	Chimney Rock RB
81048	Jansen	81128	Chromo
81049	Kim	81129	Conejos
81050	La Junta	81130	Creede
81052	Lamar	81131	Crestone
81054	Las Animas	81132	Del Norte
81055	La Veta	81133	Fort Garland
	Cuchara RB	81134	Garcia
81056	Lycan	81135	Homelake RB
81057	McClave	81136	Hooper
81058	Manzanola	81137	Ignacio
81059	Model	81138	Jaroso
81060	Ninaview (disc)	81139	La Garita
81061	North Avondale RB	81140	La Jara
81062	Olney Springs	81141	Manassa
81063	Ordway	81142	Mesita
81064	Pritchett	81143	Moffat
81065	Pryor	81144	Monte Vista
81066	Red Wing RB	81146	Mosca
81067	Rocky Ford	81147	Pagosa Springs
81069	Rye	81148	Romeo
81070	Segundo	81149	Saguache
81071	Sheridan Lake	81150	San Acacio
81072	Sopris (disc)	81151	Sanford
81073	Springfield	81152	San Luis
81074	Starkville	81153	San Pablo
81075	Stonington	81154	South Fork
81076	Sugar City	81155	Villa Grove
81077	Swink		
81078	Thatcher		

SALIDA 812

81201	Salida
81210	Almont
81211	Buena Vista
81212	Canon City
	Buckskin Joe RS (disc)
81220	Cimarron
81221	Coal Creek
81222	Coaldale
81223	Cotopaxi
81224	Crested Butte
81225	Doyleville (disc)
81226	Florence
81227	Garfield
81228	Granite
81230	Gunnison
81232	Hillside RB
81233	Howard
81234	Iola (disc)
81235	Lake City
81236	Nathrop
81237	Ohio
81238	Parkdale
81239	Parlin
81240	Penrose
81241	Pitkin
81242	Poncha Springs
81243	Powderhorn
81244	Rockvale
81245	Rosita (disc)
81246	Royal Gorge RB
81247	Sapinero RB
81248	Sargents
81249	Silver Cliff
81250	Texas Creek
81251	Twin Lakes
81252	Westcliffe
81253	Wetmore

DURANGO 813

81301	Durango
	Rural Routes
	College Heights STA
81302	Main Office Boxes
81303	Fort Lewis College
81320	Cahone
81321	Cortez
81323	Dolores
81324	Dove Creek
81325	Egnar
81326	Hesperus
81327	Lewis
81328	Mancos
81329	Marvel
81330	Mesa Verde National Park
81331	Pleasant View
81332	Rico
81333	Slick Rock
81334	Towaoc
81335	Yellow Jacket

MONTROSE 814

81410	Austin
81411	Bedrock
81412	Bowie (disc)
81413	Cedaredge
81414	Cory
81415	Crawford
81416	Delta
81418	Eckert
81419	Hotchkiss
81420	Lazear
81421	Maher
81422	Naturita
81423	Norwood
81424	Nucla
81425	Olathe
81426	Ophir
81427	Ouray
81428	Paonia
81429	Paradox
81430	Placerville
81431	Redvale
81432	Ridgway
81433	Silverton
81434	Somerset
81435	Telluride
81436	Uravan

GRAND JUNCTION 815

81501	Grand Junction
81520	Clifton
81521	Fruita
	Gilsonite RB
81522	Gateway
81523	Glade Park
81524	Loma
81525	Mack
81526	Palisade
81527	Whitewater

194

GLENWOOD SPRINGS   816

81601	Glenwood Springs
81610	Artesia (now Dinosaur)
81610	Dinosaur
81611	Aspen
	Aspen-Gerbaz RB
	West Village BR
81620	Avon
81621	Basalt
81622	Cameo (disc)
81623	Carbondale
81624	Collbran
81625	Craig
	Lay RB
81630	DeBeque
81631	Eagle
81632	Edwards
81633	Elk Springs RB
81634	Gilman
81635	Grand Valley
81636	Greystone
81637	Gypsum
81638	Hamilton
81639	Hayden
81640	Maybell
81641	Meeker
81642	Meredith
81643	Mesa
81645	Minturn
81646	Molina
81647	Newcastle
81648	Rangely
81649	Redcliff
81650	Rifle
81651	Rio Blanco RB
81652	Silt
81653	Slater
81654	Snowmass
81655	Wolcott
81656	Woody Creek
81657	Vail

S E C T I O N D

THE POST OFFICES OF COLORADO BY COUNTY

On November 1, 1861 the Territorial Legislature of Colorado sub-divided the Territory into 17 counties. The number has since increased to 63, with Alamosa, established March 8, 1913, the last to be authorized.

During the history of Colorado only one county has achieved legal status and then been re-distributed in its entirety to other political jurisdicitions. Greenwood county was authorized on February 11, 1870 and on February 6, 1874 was divided between Bent and Elbert counties.

Some counties have been known by other names, however, only one such name lasted for more than a few days. The present county of Arapahoe was named "South Arapahoe" by the legislative acts that resulted in its current boundaries and the establishment of Adams and Denver counties. Two years later, April 11, 1903, the name was officially changed to Arapa-hoe, which had been the name preceding the sub-division.

When the first boundaries of Conejos County were established, it was given the name "Guadalupe". Six days later, on November 7, 1861, the legislature changed the name to Conejos.

There were two occasions where a division of a county occurred in which the "original" county name was not to be retained by the present holder of that name. In 1879 Lake County was divided to create Carbonate and Lake Counties. Two days later the legislature changed its mind, and what it has first called Carbonate became the Lake County of today, and the remainder was named Chaffee County.

In 1883 the same sequence of events occurred when Ouray County was divided to create what is now partly San Miguel County. The area now named Ouray was to be called Uncompaghre County, with the southwestern portion retaining the name Ouray. This time it took three days to re-verse the decision and introduce the name San Miguel, with "Uncompaghre County" fading into history.

One county, "Platte" was authorized pending a referendum of the residents. The referendum either failed to pass or was not held, and the county, which would have included most of Northeastern Colorado, never came into existence.

195

Another possible area of confusion concerns Adams County. When Adams County was created out of Arapahoe County in 1901, its boundaries were to extend as far east as the state line. However, the portion that lies eastward of the present eastern boundaries of Adams and Arapahoe Counties was to hold a referendum to decide whether they would remain a part of Adams County or be split between Washington and Yuma Counties. The latter choice prevailed, but the postal records show that towns in that area were once a part of Adams County.

In connection with county jurisdictions, knowledge of the towns that served as county seats is important. Where changes have occurred, the succession and the dates of change are difficult to establish from the sources used for this book. The legislative acts that created new counties almost always named a county seat. In many cases, the site se-lected was temporary pending a referendum within the new county. In the act creating Las Animas County no county seat was named. Later changes in county seats were at the pleasure of the residents (by refer-endum) and although the legal procedures for change were specified by the legislature, the actual change required no legislative act.

The alphabetical, by county listings in the Postal Guides in-dicate which town was the county seat. In some early situations, it is possible that the reference is to the nearest post office rather than the actual county seat. This is true for Gilpin County, where the county seat, Central City, did not have its own post office until 1869.

Included in this section is a list, by county, of those towns which we know to have been county seats. This list should be complete for the statehood period. The lack of the Postal Directories for the territorial period means that we have undoubtedly missed some changes prior to 1876. For each county (except Las Animas) the first town listed is the one named in the act that formed the county. The dates given for subsequent changes are the years of the Postal Guides in which the change first appears. Because of the dates of publication, the actual change could have occurred the previous calendar year.

Once again, the authors request additional information from those who can assist.

As a portion of this Section we have included a series of maps that show the approximate county boundary changes as the sub-division progressed. On each map, only the new counties or the ones that "lost" territory are named. The dates of establishment of the new counties are also given.

The balance of Section D consists of a listing by county of the post offices that have exixted within the original or subsequent boun-daries of that county. Post offices are listed under each county of which they were at one time a part. No attempt has been made to list the sites of discontinued post offices within their present county, if the discontinuance occurred prior to the creation of that county.   Also post office names are not repeated for a county, even though two physically different offices of the same name may have existed in that county.   These problems remain to be resolved prior to the publication of Part II of this work.

The list by county is preceded by a list of the Colorado post offices that were established in Kansas, Nebraska, and Utah Territories prior to January 31, 1861.   During that time, no post office is known to have existed in the portion of Colorado that was then New Mexico Territory. The main tabulation is also followed by a listing of the post offices transferred to Colorado from neighboring states.

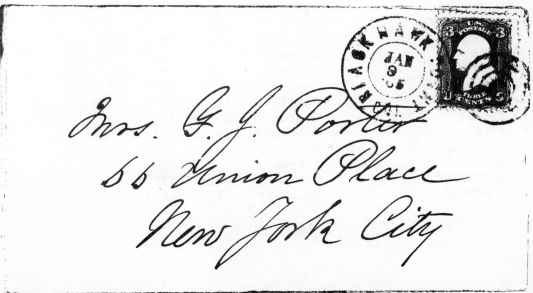

THE COUNTIES OF COLORADO

DATES OF AUTHORIZATION

	County	Month	Day	Year	Note
	ADAMS	April	15,	1901	
	ALAMOSA	March	8,	1913	
*	ARAPAHOE	November	1,	1861	(1)
	ARCHULETA	April	14,	1885	
	BACA	April	16,	1889	
	BENT	February	11,	1870	
*	BOULDER	November	1,	1861	
+	CARBONATE	February	8,	1879	(2)
	CHAFFEE	February	10,	1879	(3)
	CHEYENNE	March	25,	1889	
*	CLEAR CREEK	November	1,	1861	
*	CONEJOS	November	7,	1861	(4)
*	COSTILLA	November	1,	1861	
	CROWLEY	May	29,	1911	
	CUSTER	March	9,	1877	
	DELTA	February	11,	1883	
	DENVER	March	18,	1901	(5)
	DOLORES	February	19,	1881	
*	DOUGLAS	November	1,	1861	
	EAGLE	February	11,	1883	
*	EL PASO	November	1,	1861	
	ELBERT	February	2,	1874	
*	FREMONT	November	1,	1861	
	GARFIELD	February	10,	1883	
*	GILPIN	November	1,	1861	
	GRAND	February	2,	1874	
%	GREENWOOD	February	11,	1870	(6)
+	GRADALUPE	November	1,	1861	(4)
	GUNNISON	March	9,	1877	
	HINSDALE	February	10,	1874	
*	HUERFANO	November	1,	1861	
	JACKSON	May	5,	1909	
*	JEFFERSON	November	1,	1861	
	KIOWA	April	11,	1889	
	KIT CARSON	April	11,	1889	
	LA PLATA	February	10,	1874	
*	LAKE	November	1,	1861	(2)
*	LARIMER	November	1,	1861	
	LAS ANIMAS	February	9,	1866	
	LINCOLN	April	11,	1889	
	LOGAN	February	25,	1887	
	MESA	February	14,	1883	
	MINERAL	March	27,	1893	
	MOFFAT	February	27,	1911	
	MONTEZUMA	April	16,	1889	
	MONTROSE	February	11,	1883	

	MORGAN	February	19,	1889	
	OTERO	March	25,	1889	
	OURAY	January	18,	1877	(7)
*	PARK	November	1,	1861	
	PHILLIPS	March	27,	1889	
+	PLATTE	February	9,	1872	(8)
	PITKIN	February	23,	1881	
	PROWERS	April	11,	1889	
*	PUEBLO	November	1,	1861	
	RIO BLANCO	March	25,	1889	
	RIO GRANDE	February	10,	1874	
	ROUTT	January	29,	1877	
	SAGUACHE	December	29,	1866	
	SAN JUAN	January	31,	1876	
	SAN MIGUEL	March	2,	1883	(7)
	SEDGWICK	April	9,	1889	
+	SOUTH ARAPAHOE	April	15,	1901	
*	SUMMIT	November	1,	1861	
	TELLER	March	23,	1899	
+	UNCOMPAGHRE	February	27,	1883	
	WASHINGTON	February	9,	1887	
*	WELD	November	1,	1861	
	YUMA	March	15,	1889	

SYMBOLS

* One of the original 17 counties
+ County name no longer used
% County no longer in existence

NOTES

(1) When further sub-divided in 1901 to create Adams and Denver counties, the remainder was to become South Arapahoe County. On April 11, 1903 the word 'South' was dropped from the name.

(2) The area that now comprises Lake County was first given the name "Carbonate" in the sub-division of February 8, 1879. On February 10, 1879 the name was re-established as "Lake".

(3) When the first boundaries of Chaffee County were established on February 8, 1879, the area was to be called "Lake" County. On February 10, 1879 the name was changed to "Chaffee".

(4) On November 1, 1861 Guadalupe County was created by the first Territorial Legislature. On November 7, 1861, the county name was changed to Conejos.

(5) The establishment of the "City and County of Denver" required a constitutional amendment, passed by the Legislature on March 18, 1901. The county boundaries were set by a legislative act of April 16, 1901.

200

(6) Greenwood County was dissolved by legislative act on February 6, 1874 and the territory divided between Bent and Elbert Counties.

(7) A subdivision of Ouray County was authorized on February 27, 1883 to create Uncompaghre and Ouray Counties. The portion now named Ouray was to become Uncompaghre, with the name Ouray retained by what is now San Miguel and Dolores counties. On March 2, 1883, the names were changed: Uncompaghre to Ouray, and Ouray to San Miguel.

(8) The creation, from eastern Weld County of Platte County was authorized on February 9, 1872. It required approval by referendum of the residents and apparently failed. The act of creation was repealed by the legislature on February 9, 1874.

COLORADO COUNTY SEATS

ADAMS
* Brighton

ALAMOSA
* Alamosa

ARAPAHOE
* Denver
* Littleton (1901)

ARCHULETA
* Pagosa Springs

BACA
* Springfield

BENT
* Las Animas
  Fort Lyon (1870)
* Boggsville (1872)
  ?
  West Las Animas (prior to 1876)
  Las Animas (4)

BOULDER
* Boulder

CHAFFEE
* Granite
  Buena Vista (1883)
  Salida (1932)

CHEYENNE
* Cheyenne Wells

CLEAR CREEK
* Idaho
  Georgetown (prior to 1876)

CONEJOS
* Guadalupe
  Conejos (prior to 1876)

COSTILLA
* San Miguel
  San Luis (prior to 1868)

CROWLEY
* Ordway

CUSTER
* Rosita
  Silver Cliff (1891)
  Westcliffe (1931)

DELTA
* Delta

DENVER
* Denver

DOLORES
* Rico
  Dove Creek (1953)

DOUGLAS
* Franktown
  Castle Rock (prior to 1876)

EAGLE
* Red Cliff
  Eagle (1923)

EL PASO
* Colorado (sic.)
  Colorado City
  Colorado Springs (prior
    to 1876)

ELBERT
* Middle Kiowa
  Kiowa (prior to 1876)

FREMONT
* Canon City

GARFIELD
* Carbonate
  Glenwood Springs (1885)

GILPIN
* Central City
  Mountain City (2)

GRAND
* Hot Sulphur Springs
  Grand Lake (1885)
  Hot Sulphur Springs (1890)
  Sulphur Springs (1895) (3)
  Hot Sulphur Springs (1912) (3)

GREENWOOD
* Kit Carson

GUNNISON
* Gunnison

HINSDALE
* San Juan
  Lake City (prior to 1876)

HUERFANO
* Autubes
  Hermosilla (prior to 1868)
  Badito (1870)
  Walsenburg (prior to 1876)

JACKSON
* Walden

JEFFERSON
* Golden City
  Golden (1877) (3)

KIOWA
* Sheridan Lake
  Eads (1906)

KIT CARSON
* Burlington

LAKE
* Oro City
  Dayton (prior to 1868)
  Granite (1870)
  Leadville (1879)

LA PLATA
* Howardsville
  Parrott (prior to 1876)
  Durango (1885)

LARIMER
* La Porte
  Fort Collins (prior to 1876)

LAS ANIMAS
* None authorized by act
  Trinidad (prior to 1868)

LINCOLN
* Hugo

LOGAN
* Sterling

MESA
* Grand Junction

MINERAL
* Wason
  Creede (1895)

MOFFATT
* Craig

MONTEZUMA
* Cortez

MONTROSE
* Montrose

MORGAN
* Fort Morgan

OTERO
* La Junta

OURAY
* Ouray

PARK
* Tarryall City
  Buckskin (prior to 1868)
  Fair Play (1870)

PHILLIPS
* Holyoke

PITKIN
* Aspen

PROWERS
* Lamar

PUEBLO
* Pueblo

RIO BLANCO
* Meeker

RIO GRANDE
* Del Norte

ROUTT
* Hayden
Hahns Peak (1882)
Steamboat Springs (1916)

SAGUACHE
* Saguache

SAN JUAN
* Silverton

SAN MIGUEL
* Telluride

SEDGWICK
* Julesburgh

SUMMIT
* Parkville
Breckinridge (prior to
1868)

TELLER
* Cripple Creek

WASHINGTON
* Akron

WELD
* St. Vrain
Evans (1870)
Greeley (1881)

YUMA
* Yuma
Wray (1890)   (5)
Yuma (1891)
Wray (1904)

NOTES:

* The county seat as named in the legislative act of establishment.
"prior to ----" Indicates that the change could have occurred before that
date, but no reference (Postal Guide) was available for
earlier years.
? There could have been another county seat during this time. Although not
indicated, this applies to all counties that were in existence before 1876.

(1)   Colorado is most likely the same as Colorado City.

(2)   Until 1869 there was no "Central City" Post Office, and the Postal Guides
list Mountain City as serving the Gilpin County Court House.

(3)   There was a change in the name of the county seat, but no movement to
another location.

204

(4) From 1887 to 1892 the Post Guides do not indicate the post office
     serving the Bent County Court House.

(5) This could be an error on the part of the Post Office Department.

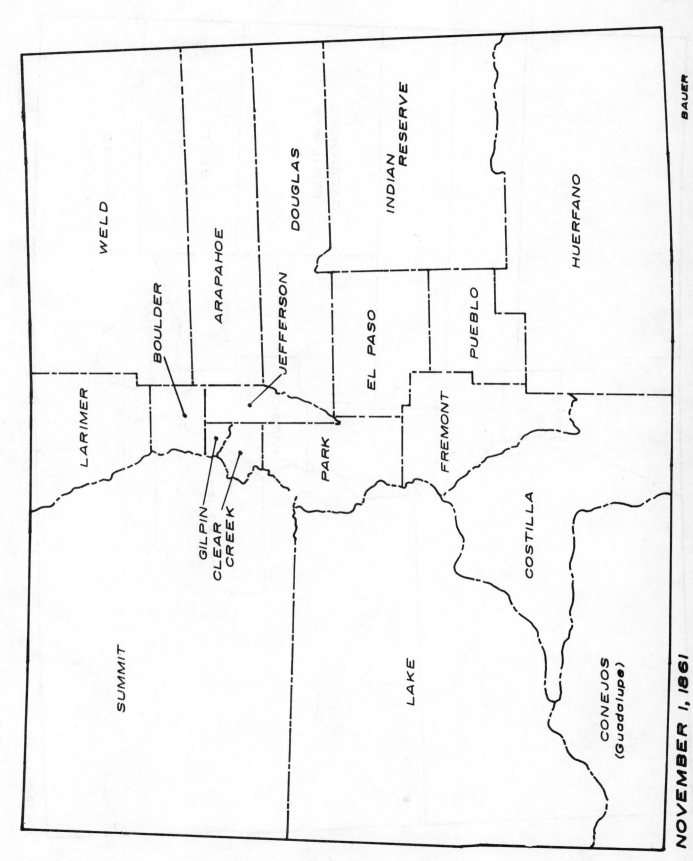

NOVEMBER 1, 1861

BAUER

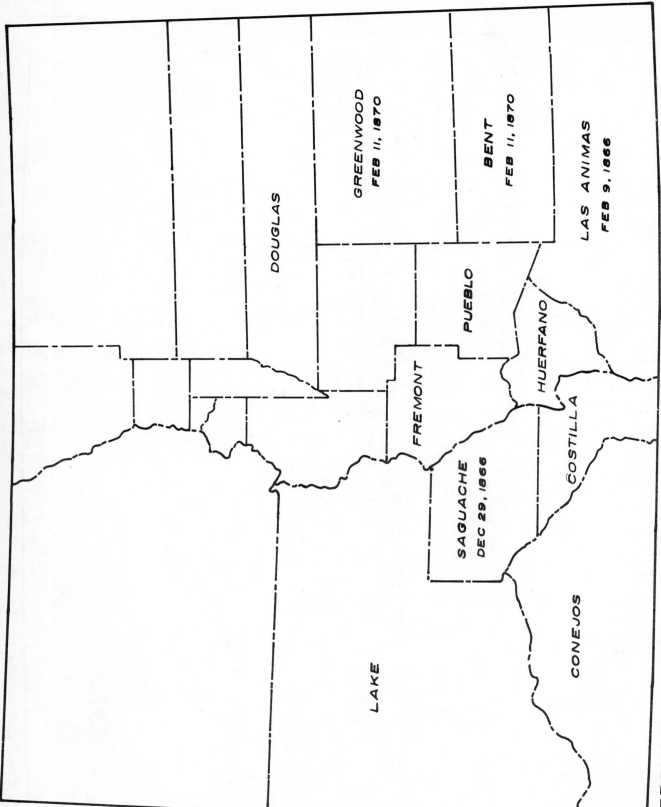

FEBRUARY 11, 1870

BAUER

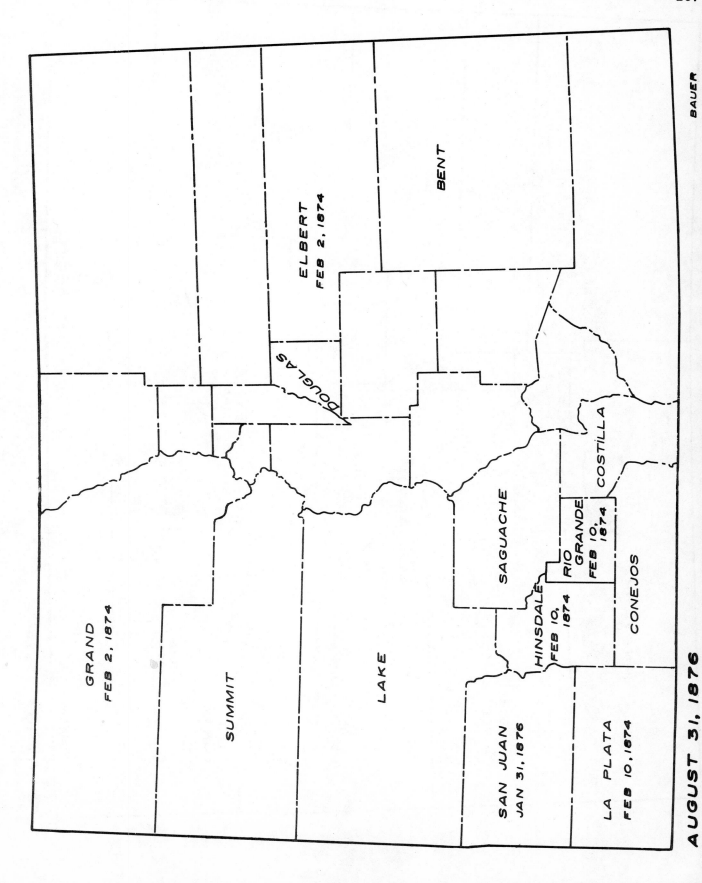

BAUER

AUGUST 31, 1876

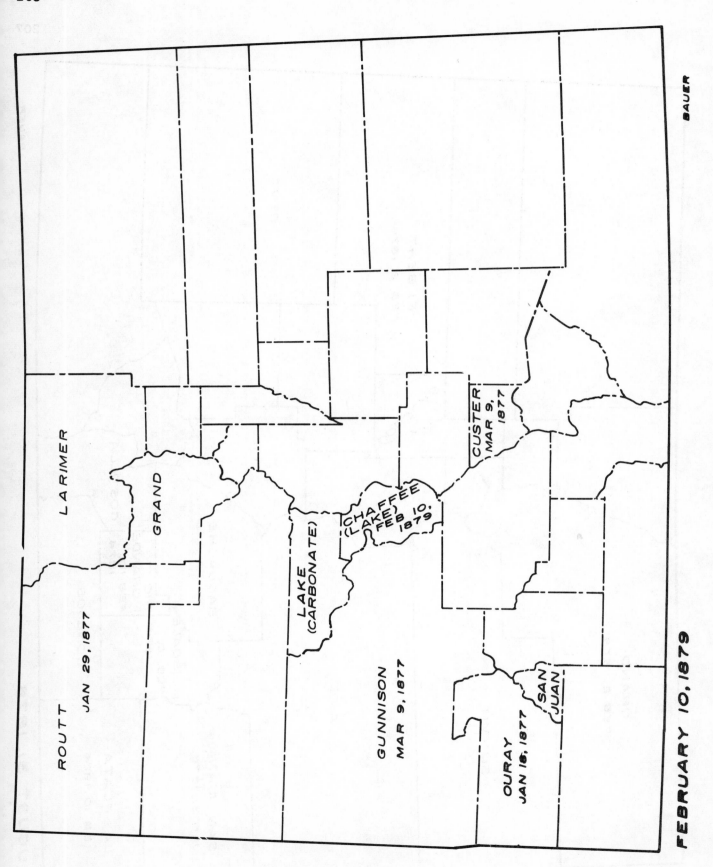

ROUTT
JAN 29, 1877

LARIMER

GRAND

LAKE
(CARBONATE)

CHAFFEE
(LAKE)
FEB 10,
1879

CUSTER
MAR 9,
1877

GUNNISON
MAR 9, 1877

OURAY
JAN 18, 1877

SAN
JUAN

FEBRUARY 10, 1879

BAUER

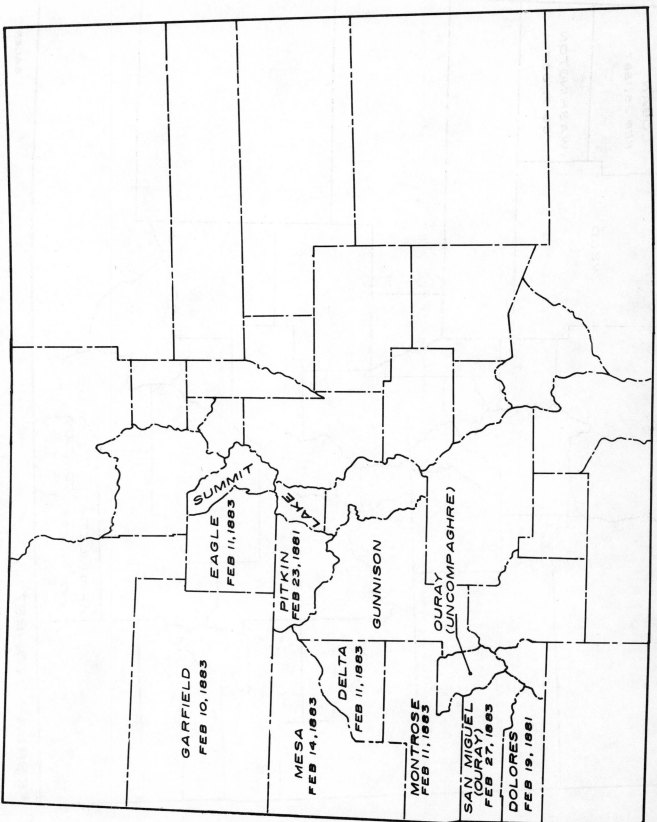

BAUER

FEBRUARY 27, 1883

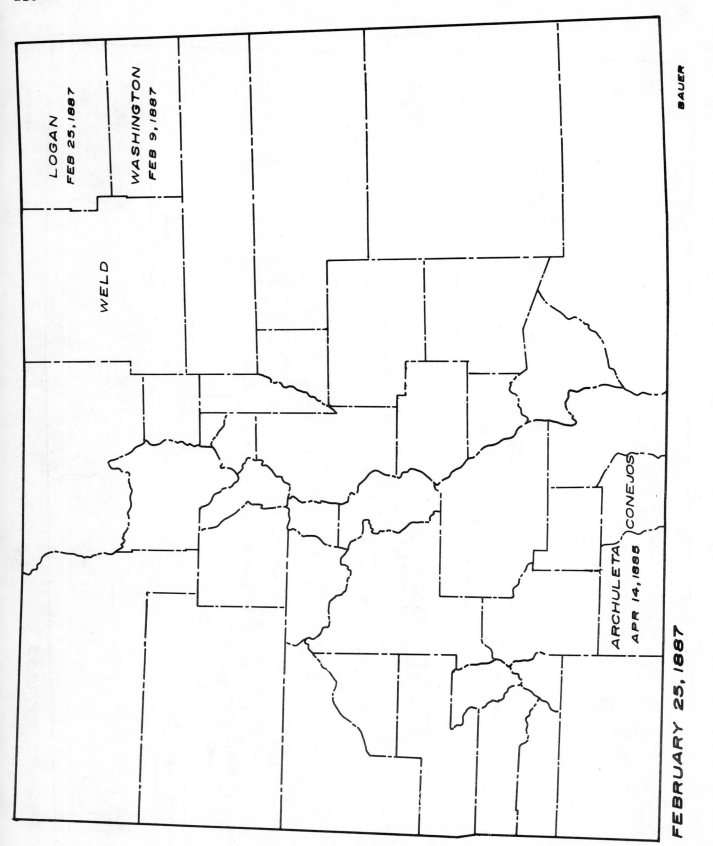

LOGAN
FEB 25, 1887

WASHINGTON
FEB 9, 1887

WELD

ARCHULETA
APR 14, 1885

CONEJOS

BAUER

FEBRUARY 25, 1887

SEDG-
WICK
APR 9,
1889

PHILLIPS
MAR 27,
1889

LOGAN

YUMA
MAR 15,
1889

WASH-
INGTON

MORGAN
FEB 19,
1889

WELD

KIT CARSON
APR 11, 1889

CHEYENNE
MAR 25, 1889

KIOWA
APR 11, 1889

PROWERS
APR 11,
1889

BENT

BACA
APR 16, 1889

ELBERT

LINCOLN
APR 11, 1889

OTERO
MAR 25,
1889

LAS ANIMAS

RIO BLANCO
MAR 25, 1889

GARFIELD

MONTEZUMA
APR 16, 1889

LA PLATA

APRIL 16, 1889

212

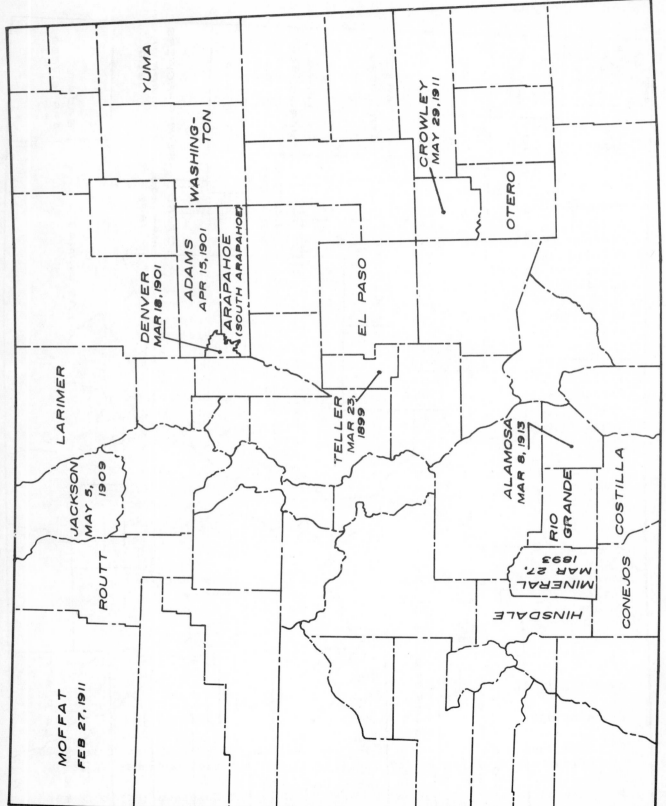

MOFFAT
FEB 27, 1911

LARIMER

JACKSON
MAY 5,
1909

ROUTT

YUMA

WASHING-
TON

DENVER
MAR 18, 1901

ADAMS
APR 15, 1901

ARAPAHOE
(SOUTH ARAPAHOE)

EL PASO

TELLER
MAR 23,
1899

CROWLEY
MAY 29, 1911

OTERO

ALAMOSA
MAR 8, 1913

RIO GRANDE

MINERAL
MAR 27,
1893

HINSDALE

CONEJOS

COSTILLA

BAUER

MARCH 8, 1913

"COLORADO" POST OFFICES
DECEMBER 1858 - JANUARY 1861

KANSAS TERRITORY

	Date Authorized			County **
Arapahoe	January	17,	1860	Arapahoe
Auraria	January	18,	1859	Arapahoe
Canon City	December	8,	1860	Fremont
Colorado City	March	24,	1860	El Paso
Coraville	March	22,	1859	Arapahoe
Denver City	February	11,	1860	Arapahoe
Fort Wise	March	5,	1860	Huerfano
Golden City	April	6,	1860	Jefferson
Golden Gate	September	6,	1860	Jefferson
Hamilton	July	26,	1860	Park
Huntsville	March	24,	1860	Douglas
Jefferson	January	18,	1860	Arapahoe
Missouri City	March	24,	1860	Gilpin
Montana	January	18,	1859	Arapahoe
Mount Vernon	May	9,	1860	Jefferson
Mountain City	January	17,	1860	Gilpin
Nevada	January	12,	1861	Gilpin
Oro City	February	16,	1861	Lake ***
Pueblo	December	13,	1860	Pueblo
Spanish Bar	December	13,	1860	Clear Creek
Tarryall	January	4,	1860	Park

NEBRASKA TERRITORY

	Date Authorized			County
Auroria	December	11,	1858	Larimer (?)
Boulder	April	22,	1859	Boulder
Colona	April	27,	1860	Larimer (?)
Fort Lupton	January	14,	1861	Weld
Julesburgh	May	29,	1860	Weld
St. Vrain	January	18,	1859	Weld

UTAH TERRITORY

	Date Authorized			County
Breckinridge	January	18,	1860	Summit

** The county is the one in which the site was located at the time of the first sub-division by the Territorial Legislature, November 1, 1861.

*** Kansas became a State on January 31, 1861, but Colorado Territory was not authorized until February 28, 1861.

POST OFFICES OF COLORADO
ALPHABETICAL BY COUNTY

ADAMS COUNTY

Abbott
Adams City
Arickaree
Aurora
Barr
Barr Lake
Bashor
Beecher
Bennet
Bennett
Brighton
Bunell
Camp Speer
Comanche
Commerce City
Cope
Derby
Dupont
Eastlake
Eskdale
Fitzsimons
Fox
Hale
Harris
Harrisburg
Hazeltine
Henderson
Idalia
Kirk
Landsman
Lansing
Leader
Lindon
Newton
Oleson
Sigman
Simpson
Strasburg
Swinford
Thedalund
Thurman
Vernon
Watkins
Welby
Westminister

ALAMOSA COUNTY

Alamosa
Garnett
Hooper
Mosca

ARAPAHOE COUNTY

Abbott
Alcott
Alva
Arapahoe
Arickaree
Argo
Athens
Auraria
Aurora
Avoca
Badger
Barnum
Barr
Beecher
Bennet
Beaver Creek
Berkeley
Bird
Bolton
Brighton
Byers
Cary
Cherrelyn
Cherry Creek
College View
Condon
Cope
Corcoran
Deer Trail
Deertrail
Denver
Denver City
Denver Mills
Derblay
Duff
Elyria
Englewood
Fort Logan

ARAPAHOE (CONT)

Fox
Friend
Frost
Fulton
Globeville
Gray
Hale
Harman
Harris
Harrisburg
Hazeltine
Henderson
Highlands
Highlandtown
Hughes
Idalia
Inche
Irondale
Island Station
Jefferson
Kirk
Landsman
Lansing
Lena
Linden
Littleton
Living Springs
Logan
Loretto
Lyman
Montana
Melvin
Montclair
Newton
Oakes
Overland
Peoria
Petersburgh
Quimby
Rogers
Salem
Scranton
Sheffield
Shields
South Denver

ARAPAHOE COUNTY (CONT)

Strasburg
Tabor
Thurman
Townsend
University Park
Valverde
Vernon
Villa Park
Villapark
Wales
Washburn
Watkins
Winnview

ARCHULETA COUNTY

Arboles
Carracas
Chimney Rock
Chromo
Dyke
Edith
Gladwyn
Juanita
Kearns
Pagosa Junction
Pagosa Springs
Piedra
Squaretop
Trujillo

BACA COUNTY

Atlanta
Baker
Blaine
Bartlett
Boston
Brookfield
Buster
Campo
Carriso
Carriso Springs
Carrizo
Clyde
Corrizo
Decatur
Deora
Edler

BACA COUNTY (CONT)

Estelene
Graft
Joycoy
Kirkwell
Konantz
Lamport
Lycan
Maxey
Minneapolis
Monon
Nowlinsville
Oklarado
Onine
Pride
Pritchett
Progress
Regnier
Richards
Rodley
Ruff
Sand Arroyo
Seton
Setonburg
Springfield
Stonington
Townsite
Tuck
Two Buttes
Utleyville
Vilas
Walsh
Westworth
Westola

BENT COUNTY

Albany
Alkali
Arden
Arlington
Ayr
Bee
Bents Fort
Blackwell
Brandon
Caddoa
Catlin
Cheyenne Wells
Chivington

BENT COUNTY (CONT)

Dayton
Eads
Ella
Fergus
Fort Lyon
Fredonia
Galatea
Gem
Granada
Harbourdale
Hasty
Higbee
Holly
Kit Carson
La Junta
Lamar
Las Animas
Lavender
Maine Ranch
Medford Springs
McClave
McMillin
Mud Creek
Mulvane
New Fort Lyon
Ninaview
Opal
Oxford
Prowers
Rawlings
Rocky Ford
Rule
Sanborn
Sheridan Lake
South Side
Stewart
Stockade
Texas Ranch
The Meadows
Toledo
Towner
Water Valley
West Las Animas
Wild Horse
Wilde

BOULDER COUNTY

Allenspark

BOULDER COUNTY (CONT)

Altona
Balarat
Belle Monte
Big Elk
Boulder
Broomfield
Bunce
Burlington
Canfield
Cardinal
Caribou
Coal Creek
Coal Park
Coalpark
Copper Rock
Coraville
Crags
Crescent
Crisman
Davidson
Delphi
Downer
Eagle Creek
Eagle Rock (?)
Eldora
Eldorado Springs
Eversman
Feberite
Frances
Glacier Lake
Gold Dirt
Gold Hill
Goldhill
Gorham
Gresham
Gulch
Hawthorne
Hessie
Hygiene
Ironsides
Jamestown
Lafayette
Lakewood
Langford
Left Hand
Louisville
Longmont
Lyons
Marshall

BOULDER COUNTY (CONT)

Magnolia
Middle Boulder
Modoc
Nederland
Ni Wot
Niwot
Noland
Orodelfan
Osborn
Peaceful Valley
Pella
Penn
Pinecliffe
Primos
Puzzler
Rockville
Rowena
Salina
Shelton
Springdale
Sugar Loaf
Sunset
Sunshine
Superior
Tungsten
Valmont
Vesuvius
Ward
Ward District
Wallstreet
Wheelman
Whitney

CHAFFEE COUNTY

Alpine
Antero
Arbourville
Arkansas
Bath
Brown Canon
Browns Canon
Buena Vista
Calumet
Carmel
Centreville
Chaffee
Chalk Creek
Cleora

CHAFFEE COUNTY (CONT)

Cochem
Columbus
Conrow
Cottonwood Springs
Divide
Dolomite
Dora
Fisher
Free Gold
Garfield
Granite
Helena
Heywood
Higgins
Hortense
Kraft
Krain
Mahonville
Maysville
Mears
Meily
Monarch
Mount Princeton
Mount Princeton
   Hot Springs
Nathrop
Neva
Newett
Poncha Springs
Poncho Springs
Riverside
Romley
Saint Elmo
Salida
Shavano
Silverdale
Skinner
Sylvanite
Turret
Vicksburg
Whitehorn
Winfield

CHEYENNE COUNTY

Arapahoe
Arena
Aroya
Chemung

CHEYENNE COUNTY (CONT)

Cheyenne Wells
Firstview
Kit Carson
Medill
Mount Pearl
Pilot
Sorrento
Wild Horse

CLEAR CREEK COUNTY

Alice
Belford
Brookvale
Brownsville
Dumont
East Argentine
Elephant
Empire
Empire City
Floyd Hill
Freeland
Georgetown
Graymont
Hukill
Idaho (Idahoe)
Idaho Springs
Lamartine
Lawson
Lombard
Marshallpark
Mill City
Red Elephant
Silver Plume
Silverplume
Spanish Bar
Waldorf
Yankee
Yates

CONEJOS COUNTY

Alamosa
Antonito
Arboles
Broyles
Capulin
Catherin
Cenicero
Cockrell

CONEJOS COUNTY (CONT)

Conejos
Cumbres
Del Norte
Del Rio
Ephraim
Espinoza
Freedom
Henry
Joya
La Jara
La Sauses
Lado
Lajara
Lasauses
Lobatos
Loma
Los Cerritos
Los Sauses
Loyton
Manassa
Mogote
Morgan
Navajoe
Newcomb
Ortiz
Osier
Pagosa Springs
Paisaje
Piedra
Platoro
Price
Romeo
San Antonio
San Rafael
Sanford
Stunner
Sunflower
Terrace
Vadner

COSTILLA COUNTY

Bernice
Blanca
Chama
Coryell
Costilla
Eastdale
Fort Garland
Garcia

COSTILLA COUNTY (CONT)

Garland
Garnett
Garrison
Hirst
Hooper
Jaroso
La Veta Pass
Lavalley
Manzanares
Margaret
Medano Springs
Mesita
Meyer
Montville
Mosca
Mosco
Norman
Orean
Rio Grande
Russell
San Acacio
San Luis
San Pablo
Stanley
Streator
Underhill
Veta Pass
Wayside
Zapato

CROWLEY COUNTY

Crowley
Hester
Olney Springs
Ordway
Sugar City

CUSTER COUNTY

Augusta
Bassick
Blackburn
Blumenau
Camargo
Cleveland
Clinton
Colfax
Dora
Fairview

CUSTER COUNTY (CONT)

Focus
Forestdale
Gove
Greenwood
Ilse
Keating
Millbrook
Neeley
Querida
Rosita
San Isabel
Silver Cliff
Silver Park
Ula
Westcliffe
Wetmore

DELTA COUNTY

Alda
Austin
Bowie
Cedaredge
Chipeta
Coalby
Cory
Crawford
Delta
Dominquez
Eckert
Grand Junction
Grand Mesa
Hotchkiss
Lazear
Maher
Marion
Paonia
Read
Roubideau
Verne
Welcome

DENVER COUNTY

Alcott
Argo
Denver
Denver Mills
Elyria
Harman

DENVER COUNTY (CONT)

Montclair
Overland
Stockyards
University Park
Valverde

DOLORES COUNTY

Alkali
Beaty
Bowen
Cahone
Disappointment
Dove Creek
Dunton
Egnar
Hermitage
Jual
Lavendar
Lizard Head
Northdale
Molding
Rico
Squaw Point
Willow Gulch

DOUGLAS COUNTY

Acequia
Bear Canon
Bear Canyon
Bennet Springs
Bethesda
Bijou Basin
Case
Castle Rock
Cherry
Cheyenne Wells
Colfax
Daffodil
Dakan
Deane
Deansbury
Deckers
Douglas
Franktown
Frost's Ranch
Glen Grove
Golddale
Gomer's Mills

DOUGLAS COUNTY (CONT)

Greenland
Hill Top
Hilltop
Hugo
Huntsville
Irving
Keystone
Keystone Park
Kiowa
Larkspur
Louviers
New Memphis
Parker
Pemberton
Perry
Perry Park
Pine Grove
Platte Canon
Rock Butte
Rock Ridge
Running Creek
Russellville
Sedalia
Spring Valley
Strontia
Strontia Springs
Tyler
Virginia
Westcreek

EAGLE COUNTY

Aspen Junction
Avon
Basalt
Blaine
Bond
Burns
Castle
Cleveland
Copper Spur
Copperton
Coppertown
Derby
Dotsero
Eagle
Edwards
Emma
Fulford
Gilman

EAGLE COUNTY (CONT)

Gold Park
Gypsum
Holy Cross
McCoy
Minturn
Mitchell
Pando
Peach Blow
Red Cliff
Redcliff
Riland
Robinson
Rondebush
Ruedi
Seven Castles
Sheephorn
Sherman
Sloss
Squaw Creek
State Bridge
Taylor
Tennessee Pass
Tigiwon
Troutville
Vail
Wolcott
Yarmony

EL PASO COUNTY

Albano
Alnwick
Altman
Amo
Anaconda
Arequa
Bardeen
Barry
Bassetts Mills
Big Sandy
Bijou Basin
Black Forest
Boaz
Burt
Buttes
Calhan
Cascade
Chipita Park
Colorado City
Colorado Springs

EL PASO COUNTY (CONT)

Cragmor
Cripple Creek
Crows Roost
Curtis
Divide
Dragoo
Drennan
Easton
Eastonville
Edgerton
Edlowe
Elkton
Ellicott
El Paso
Elsmore
Falcon
Florissant
Fountain
Fountain Valley School
Franceville
Franceville Junction
Freemont
Gillett
Gleneath
Glenn
Goldfield
Goldrock
Granger
Green
Green Mountain Falls
Gwillimsville
Halfway
Hanover
Highpark
Holtwold
Horace
Husted
Ivywild
Jimmy Camp
Kelker
Keysor
Lawrence
Love
Lowland
Lytle
Macon
Majors
Manitou
Manitou Park
Manitou Springs

EL PASO COUNTY (CONT)

McFerren
Midland
Monument
Morland
Mosby
Mound
Myers
Newfield
North Pole
O. Z.
Pacific
Palmer
Palmer Lake
Peyton
Pikeview
Preston
Ramah
Rosa
Roswell
Rush
Saint Peters
Seward
Signal
Southwater
Squirrel Creek
Sublime
Suffolk
Summit Park
Sun View
Surbur
Table Rock
Tacony
Torrington
Turkey Creek
U. S. Air Force
    Academy
Victor
Waverly
Wayne
Weissport
Wheatland
Wigwam
Woodland Park
Woodmen
Yoder

ELBERT COUNTY

Agate
Arriba

220

ELBERT COUNTY (CONT)

Arroya
Avendale
Beloit
Benko
Bethune
Beuck
Bijou Basin
Bland
Bovina
Bowser
Buick
Burlington
Carlisle
Chenoweth
Claremont
Claud
Clemmons
Clermont
Elbert
Elizabeth
Flagler
Fondis
Gebhard
Godfrey
Goff
Gomer's Mills
Graceland
Hargisville
Holtwold
Hoyt
Hugo
Kanza
Keysor
Kiowa
Kuhn's Crossing
Kutch
Laketon
Landsman
Matheson
Mattison
Melville
Norton
Oranola
Orsburn
Resolis
River Bend
Running Creek
Saint Peters
Schley
Seibert

ELBERT COUNTY (CONT)

Simla
Tuttle
Vona
Wolfcreek
Yoman

FREMONT COUNTY

Adelaide
Anita
Barehills
Beaver
Beaver Creek
Boaz
Brewster
Brookside
Buckskin Joe
Calcite
Canon City
Canyon City
Chandler
Clonmell
Coal Creek
Coalcreek
Coaldale
Colfax
Concrete
Copperfield
Crocker
Cotopaxi
Cramer
Cyanide
Currant
Currant Creek
Driscoll
Eldred
Fairy
Fidler
Florence
Ford
Galena
Glendale
Grape
Greenwood
Hatton
Hayden Creek
Heathton
Hendricks
Hickman
Hillsdale

FREMONT COUNTY (CONT)

Hillside
Howard
Juniper
Kalbaugh
Kenwood
Littell
Manoa
Marigold
Micanite
Palmer
Parkdale
Penrose
Pleasant Valley
Portland
Pyrolite
Radiant
Rockdale
Rockvale
Rosita
Royal Gorge
Sunol
Taclamur
Texas
Texas Creek
Titusville
Toof
Ula
Wellsville
Whitehorn
Wilbur
Williamsburgh
Wulstenville
Yorkville

GARFIELD COUNTY

Antlers
Atchee
Austin
Axial
Balzac
Barlow
Carbonate
Carbondale
Cardiff
Catherin
Chapman
Coalridge
Dailey
Early Springs

221

GARFIELD COUNTY (CONT)

Emma
Farwell
Ferguson
Glenwood Springs
Grand Valley
Gresham
Hecla
Highmore
Marion
Meeker
Morris
New Castle
Parachute
Rangely
Rangley
Raven
Rifle
Riland
Satank
Shoshone
Silt
South Canon
Trapers Lake
Sunlight
Vulcan
Waterman
White River

GILPIN COUNTY

Apex
Bald Mountain
Baltimore
Black Hawk
Black Hawk Point
Blackhawk
Central City
Colorado Sierra
East Portal
Fort Junction
Gilpin
Gold Dirt
Missouri City
Mountain City
Nevada
Nugget
Pactolus
Perigo
Rollinsville
Russell Gulch

GILPIN COUNTY (CONT)

South Boulder
Tip Top
Tolland

GRAND COUNTY

Arrow
Canadian
Clarkson
Colorow
Coulter
Crescent
Dexter
Elkdale
Fairfax
Fraser
Gaskill
Granby
Grand Lake
Grandlake
Haworth
Hayden
Hebron
Hermitage
Hideaway Park
Hot Sulphur Springs
Kinsey
Kremmling
Leal
Lehman
Lulu
Martin
Monarch
Parshall
Pearmont
Pinkhamton
Radium
Rand
Red Mountain
Scholl
Selak
Spicer
Stillwater
Sulphur Springs
Tabernash
Teller
Tiptop
Troublesome
Twelve Mile
Walden

GRAND COUNTY (CONT)

West Portal
Winter Park

GREENWOOD COUNTY

Kit Carson
Lake Station

GUNNISON COUNTY

Abbeville
Aberdeen
Allen
Almont
Anthracite
Argenta
Ashcroft
Aspen
Baldwin
Bardine
Barnum
Bittner
Bowerman
Bowman
Cameville
Camp Genter
Castleton
Cebolla
Chance
Chaney
Chipeta
Chloride
Clarence
Cosden
Cox
Crested Butte
Crookstown
Crooksville
Crystal
Curran
Dayton
Delta
Dorchester
Doyleville
Drake
Drew
Dubois
Elgin
Elko
Elkton

GUNNISON COUNTY (CONT)

Emma
Floresta
Gateview
Gilman
Glacier
Gothic
Grand Junction
Gunnison
Haverly
Hawxhurst
Hillerton
Hotchkiss
Howeville
Iola
Irwin
Jacks Cabin
Jackson
Kannah
Kezar
Lawrence
Lodge
Los Pinos
Marble
Minaret
Montrose
Mount Carbon
Naturita
North Star
Northstar
Ohio
Orson
Oversteg
Paonia
Paradox
Parlin
Pieplant
Pitkin
Pittsburgh
Powderhorn
Prospect
Providence
Quartz
Quartzville
Ragged Mountain
Red Mountain
Roaring Fork
Ruby
Sage
Sapinero
Scofield

GUNNISON COUNTY (CONT)

Sherrod
Sidney
Sillsville
Snowmass
Somerset
Spencer
Spring
Standish
Stevens
Suttle
Tin Cup
Tincup
Tolifaro
Tomichi
Tucker
Tunuchi
Turner
Uncompaghre
Ute
Virginia
Vulcan
Waunita
Waunita Hot Springs
White Pine
Whitepine
Woodstock

HINSDALE COUNTY

Antelope Springs
Belford
Burrows Park
Capitol City
Carson
Cathedral
Childs Park
Debs
Henson
Hermit
Jennison
Lake City
Lakeshore
Lost Trail
Roses Cabin
San Juan
Sherman
Spar
Sunnyside
Teller
Tellurium

HINSDALE COUNTY
(CONT)
Timber Hill
White Cross

HUERFANO COUNTY

Alamo
Apache
Badito
Bents Fort
Birmingham
Bradford
Butte Valley
Cacharas
Camp Shumway
Capps
Carson
Clover
Consolidated
Cuchara
Cuchara Camps
Cucharas
Del Carbon
Dickson
Farisita
Farr
Fort Lyon
Fort Wise
Gardener
Gordon
Grays Ranch
Greenhorn
Hermosilla
Hezron
Houck
Huerfano
Huerfano Canon
Huerfano Canyon
Ideal
Larimer
Lascar
La Veta
Lester
Little Orphan
Maitland
Malachite
Mayne
McGuire
McMillan
Mooney
Muriel

HUERFANO COUNTY (CONT)

Mustang
Niggherhead
North Veta
Nunda
Oakview
Ojo
Pauley
Pictou
Point of Rocks
Pryor
Quebec
Rattlesnake Buttes
Ravenwood
Redwing
Rockland
Round Oak
Rouse
Saint Marys
Santa Clara
Scissors
Seguro
Sharpsdale
Solar
Spanish Peak
Spanish Peaks
Strong
Tabeguache
Talpa
Tioga
Toltec
Tourist
Trinidad
Ute
Veta Pass
Walsen
Walsenburg
Walsenburgh
Warrantsville
Yellowstone Creek

JACKSON COUNTY

Butler
Chedsey
Cowdrey
Dryer
Gould
Hebron
Higho
Kings Canyon

JACKSON COUNTY (CONT)

Larand
Lindland
Northgate
Owl
Paulus
Pearl
Peneold
Rand
Spicer
Walden
Zirkel

JEFFERSON COUNTY

Archers
Arvada
Beaver Brook
Belleville
Brightside
Brook Forest
Brownsville
Buffalo Creek
Cheesman
Cliff
Cliffdale
Cloudcrest
Conifer
Copperdale
Creswell
Critchell
Crosson
Crossons
Crystal Lake
Daffodil
Daniels
Dawson
Deercreek
Dome Rock
East Tincup
Edgemont
Edgewater
El Rancho
Elk Creek
Enterprise
Evergreen
Forks Creek
Forkscreek
Foxton
Gillespie
Gilman

JEFFERSON COUNTY (CONT

Glen Robbins
Golden
Golden City
Golden Gate
Grotto
Herndon
Hutchinson
Idledale
Indian Hills
Jefferson
Joylan
Junction
Kittredge
Lakeview
Lakewood
Lamb
Longview
Magic Mountain
Medlen
Michigan House
Morrison
Mount Morrison
Mount Vernon
Mountain Park
Olio
Park Siding
Phillipsburg
Pine
Plainview
Platte Canon
Ralston
Ralstons
Resort
Ridge
Sanatorium
Semper
Spivak
South Platte
Starbuck
Symes
Tindale
Turkey Creek
Urmston
Vermilion
Wheat Ridge
Willowsville

KIOWA COUNTY

Arlington

KIOWA COUNTY (CONT)

Brandon
Chivington
Diston
Eads
Fergus
Galatea
Haswell
Kilburn
Queen Beach
Segreganset
Sheridan Lake
Stewart
Stuart
Sweetwater
Towner
Water Valley

KIT CARSON COUNTY

Ashland
Avendale
Baltzer
Beavertown
Beloit
Berry
Bethune
Bonny
Burlington
Carlisle
Carey
Chapin
Claremont
Cole
Dodgeville
Elphis
Farley
Flagler
Goff
Hanover
Hermes
Hukkuk
Landsman
Loco
Morris
Oriska
Seibert
Stratton
Tuttle
Valley
Vansville
Vona

KIT CARSON COUNTY (CONT)

Wallet
Yale

LA PLATA COUNTY

Allison
Animas
Animas City
Animas Forks
Bayfield
Breen
Cascade
Castelar
Columbus
Content
Cortez
Dix
Dolores
Durango
Elco
Emery
Eureka
Falfa
Florida
Fort Lewis
Griffith
Grommet
Hermosa
Hesperus
Hewit
Howardsville
Hynes
Ignacio
Kline
La Boca
La Plata
Laboca
Laplata
Lone Dome
Los Pinos
Mancos
Marvel
Mayday
McQuiety
Meserole
Mineral Point
Morgan
Murnane
Needleton
Ouray
Oxford

LOS PLATA COUNTY (CONT)

Pargin
Parrott
Perin
Perins
Pine River
Pineriver
Porter
Redmesa
Rockwood
Silverton
Tacoma
Tiffany
Toltec
Trimble
Uncapahgre
Uncompahgre
Vallecito
Viceto
Walls
Young

LAKE COUNTY

Adelaide
Alexander
Alicante
Alpine
Arkansas Junction
Bond
Busk
Cash Creek
Centreville
Cleora
Climax
Dayton
Divide
Everett
Gunnison
Helena
Henry
Hobergs
Hope
Hortense
Howland
Ibex
Interlaken
Ironhill
Leadville
Mahonville
Malta
Oro City

LAKE COUNTY (CONT)

Poncho Springs
Riverside
Saint Kevin
Snowden
Soda Springs
South Arkansas
Tabor
Tacoma
Tennessee Pass
Twin Lakes
Wortman

LARIMER COUNTY

Adams
Alford
Arkins
Association Camp
Bellvue
Berthoud
Big Thompson
Bighorn
Boiler
Box Elder
Boxelder
Bristol
Buckhorn
Bulger
Bush
Butler
Canadian
Chambers Lake
Cherokee Park
Cowdrey
Chambers
Crescent
Drake
Eggers
Elkhorn
Estes Park
Forks
Fort Collins
Glen Haven
Glendevey
Gleneyre
Haworth
Hebron
Higho
Home

LARIMER COUNTY (CONT)

Kelim
Killburn
La Porte
Laporte
Little Thompson
Livermore
Log Cabin
Longs Peak
Loveland
Manhattan
Mason
Masonville
Michigan
Miner
Mountearl
Moraine
Moraine Park
Namaqua
Otis
Owl
Pearl
Petra
Pinewood
Pinkhamton
Pullen
Rand
Red Feather Lake
Roach
Ruction
Rustic
Saint Cloud
Spicer
Stout
Teller
Timnath
Trail Ridge
Tyner
Valdai
Virginia Dale
Walden
Waverly
Wellington
Westlake
Wheatland
Wilds
Winona
Zirkel

LAS ANIMAS COUNTY

Abeyta
Abeyton
Aguilar
Alcreek
Alfalfa
Andrix
Apishapa
Atlanta
Atwell
Augusta
Aylmer
Badito
Barela
Beacon
Bent Canyon
Bents Fort
Berwind
Beshoar
Boncarbo
Boston
Bowen
Branson
Brazil
Brodhead
Brookfield
Buster
Carriso
Carriso Springs
Carsonhart
Cedarhurst
Chapel
Chicosa
Clanda
Clyde
Coloflats
Coledale
Cordova
Corinth
Cuartro
Dalerose
Davis
Dean
Decatur
Delagua
Delhi
Dicks
Dodsonville
Downing
Druce

226

LAS ANIMAS COUNTY (CONT)

Duncan
Earl
Edenview
Edwest
El Moro
Elmoro
Engle
Engleburg
Flues
Forbes
Forbes Junction
Fort Lyon
Fouret
Gillette
Glenham
Gotera
Graycreek
Green Canon
Grinnell
Gulnare
Hastings
Hicks
Higgins
Hoehne
Hoopup
Humbar
Indianapolis
Irwin Canyon
Jansen
Jaroso
Kant
Katrina
Kazan
Kilroy
Kim
Laub
Link
Linwood
Lone Oak
Ludlow
Madrid
Majestic
Maldonado
Martinsen
Maxey
Menger
Mesaview
Minneapolis
Model
Moore
Morley

LAS ANIMAS COUNTY (CONT)

Ninaview
Officer
Onine
Patches
Patt
Plum Valley
Powell
Primero
Progress
Pulaski
Rapson
Raton
Roby
Rugby
San Antonia
San Jose
San Pedro
Segundo
Sopris
Springfield
Springvale
Springville (?)
Stage Canyon
Stamford
Starkville
Stevenson
Stockville
Stonewall
Stonington
Strange
Tabasco
Tercio
Thatcher
Tobe
Tollerburg
Torres
Trinchera
Trinidad
Troy
Tyrone
Valdez
Vallorso
Varros
Vega Ranch
Vigil
Vilas
Villegren
Watervale
Wenger
Weston
Wootton

LAS ANIMAS COUNTY (CONT)

Wormington
Yachita
Yeiser
Yetta

LINCOLN COUNTY

Amy
Arriba
Bovina
Boyero
Cable
Carr Crossing
Clifford
Cowans
Damascus
Forder
Genoa
Girard
Green Knoll
Hugo
Karval
Kendrick
Kutch
Limon
Limon Station
Luslo
McCollin
Owen
Sanborn
Saugus
Shaw
Swift
Wellons
Wezel
White

LOGAN COUNTY

Amherst
Armstrong
Arnold
Atwood
Bryant
Calvert
Chenoa
Crook
Dailey
Emerson
Fleming
Graylin

LOGAN COUNTY (CONT)

Haxtum
Holyoke
Iliff
Julesburg
Kelly
Laura
Le Roy
Leroy
Merino
New Haven
Padroni
Paoli
Peetz
Proctor
Red Lion
Rockland
Sedgwick
Sterling
Wakeman
Westplains
Willard
Winston

MESA COUNTY

Arlington
Bernard
Cameo
Carpenter
Clifton
Clover
Collbran
Copper
De Beque
Debeque
Eaglite
Escalante
Escalante Forks
Excelsior
Fruita
Fruitvale
Gateway
Gavin
Gilsonite
Glade Park
Grand Junction
Harlow
Hawxhurst
Heiberger
Hope
Ionia

MESA COUNTY (CONT)

Jones
Leon
Loma
Mack
Mainard
Mesa
Molina
Mountainvale
Orson
Palisade
Palisades
Pine Bluff
Plateau
Plateau City
Ravens
Ravensbeque
Rhone
Roan
Rocky
Sinbad
Skyway
Snipes
Tunnel
Unaweep
Vega
Whitewater

MINERAL COUNTY

Amethyst
Antelope Springs
Creede
North Creede
San Juan
Spar
Teller
Thornton
Wagon Wheel Gap
Wason

MOFFAT COUNTY

Artesia
Axial
Blue Mountain
Caisson
Craig
Cross Mountain
Deep Channel
Dinosaur
Elk Springs

MOFFAT COUNTY (CONT)

Elkhead
Fortification
Great Divide
Greystone
Hamilton
Jack Rabbit
Juniper
Juniper Springs
Ladore
Lay
Lily
Lodore
Loyd
Massadona
Maybell
Morapos
Mount Streeter
Price Creek
Rivas
Slater
Skull Creek
Sparks
Sunbeam
Youghal

MONTEZUMA COUNTY

Ackmen
Arloa
Arriola
Bearcreek
Cortez
Dolores
Formby
Gradens
Golconda
Hogg
Lakevista
Lebanon
Lewis
Lone Dome
Lonedome
McElmo
McPhee
Mancos
Mesa Verde National
  Park
Mildred
Millard
Moqui
Morgan

MONTEZUMA COUNTY (CONT)

Navaho Springs
Paymaster
Pleasant View
Point Lookout
Quarry
Renaraye
Ruin Canyon
Sago
Spargo
Stoner
Towaoc
Westfork
Yellowjacket

MONTROSE COUNTY

Barnes
Bedrock
Brown
Cameville
Cashin
Cedar Brook
Cimarron
Coventry
Eva
Horsefly
Hydraulic
Jojunior
Lujane
Maher
Menoken
Micheols
Montrose
Naturita
Nucla
Olathe
Paradox
Paxton
Pinon
Redvale
River Portal
Rudolph
Sams
Sapinero
Shenandoah
Sherman (?)
Sinbad
Uncompahgre
Uranium
Uravan
Ute

MORGAN COUNTY

Adena
Antelope Springs
Bijou Springs
Bijouview
Brush
Corona
Deuel
Dodd
Dublin Bay
Fort Morgan
Gary
Goodrich
Hillrose
Hoyt
Orchard
Pawnee
Snyder
Vallery
Weldona
Wiggins
Woodrow

OTERO COUNTY

Alexander
Angora
Ayer
Bloom
Catlin
Cheraw
Fairmount
Fowler
Hester
Higbee
Holbrook
La Junta
Manzanola
Meredith
Mindeman
Olney
Olney Springs
Omer
Ordway
Oxford
Pultney
Rene
Rocky Ford
Sugar City
Swink
Timpas
Village

OTERO COUNTY (CONT)

Vroman
Wait
Weitzer

OURAY COUNTY

Alder Creek
Ames
Ash
Aurora
Campbird
Colona
Dallas
Dallas Divide
Dallasville
Folsom
Gabbert
Guston
Hot Springs
Ironton
Lawrence
Mount Sneffells
Ophir (old)
Ouray
Pandora
Placerville
Plumer
Portland
Red Mountain
Rico
Ridgeway
Rogersville
Ruby City
San Miguel
Sneffels
Telluride
Trout
Trout Lake
Virginius
Wareville
Windham

PARK COUNTY

Alma
Bailey
Balfour
Black Mountain
Bordenville
Buckskin
Buffalo Springs

PARK COUNTY (CONT)

Cassells
Chase
Como
Conrad
Cortrite
Dake
Deer Valley
Devine
Doran
Dudley
Estabrook
Fair Play
Fairplay
Fairville
Florissant
Garo
Glentivar
Granite Vale
Grant
Grousemont
Guffey
Hall Valley
Hallvale
Hamilton
Hammond
Hartsel
Hayman
Holland
Horse Shoe
Horseshoe
Howbert
Idaville
Insmont
Jefferson
Kaiserheim
Kenosha
Kester
King
Lake George
Laurette
Leavick
London
Montgomery
Montgomery City
Mountaindale
Mullenville
Olava
Park
Platte
Platte Station

PARK COUNTY (CONT)

Rocky
Shawnee
Slaghts
Spinney
Springer
South Park
Sterling
Sulphur Springs
Tarryall
Timberton
Trump
Truro
Wadleigh
Webster
Weston
Amherst
Bryant
Emerson
Haxtun
Haxtun
Holyoke
Paoli
Starr
Wakeman

PITKIN COUNTY

Ashcroft
Aspen
Aspen-Gerbaz
Calcium
Carey
Chipeta
Chloride
Coalbasin
Davies
Emma
Farwell
Gerbazdale
Gulch
Ivanhoe
Janeway
Lenado
Meredith
Nast
Norrie
Placita
Redstone
Satank
Sellar

PITKIN COUNTY (CONT)

Sidney
Snowmass
Sparkill
Spring Gulch
Thomasville
Tourtelotte
Watson
Woody Creek

PROWERS COUNTY

Albany
Amity
Ayr
Barton
Bristol
Carlton
Cheney Genter
Duer
Granada
Hartman
Holly
Lamar
Martynia
Mulvane
Northway
Plains
Rowe
Toledo
Verdun
Webb
Wilde
Wiley
Zuck

PUEBLO COUNTY

Abbey
Agate
Airport
Andersonville
Arland
Armour
Artman
Avondale
Beaver
Beaver Creek
  (to Fremont) (?)
Bents Fort
Bessemer

PUEBLO COUNTY (CONT)

Beulah
Boone
Booneville
Bronquist
Burnt Mill
Cedarwood
Chilcott
Colorado City
Cousin Springs
Crow
Dawkins
Duke
Eden
Excelsior
Fisher
Foothills
Fort Lyon
Fort Reynolds
Goodpasture
Graneros
Greenhorn
Grimaldi
Haynes Ranch
Hermosilla
Holden
Huerfano
Jackson (?)
Juniata
Keble
Kinkel
Lamar
Lebanon
Lees
Lime
Maces Hole
Marnel
Mercier
Muddy Creek
Myrtle
Nepesta
North Avondale
Nyburg
Osage
Osage Avenue
Overton
Pinon
Pueblo
Rock Creek
Rye
Saint Charles
Salt Creek

PUEBLO COUNTY (CONT)

Siloam
Sitton
South Pueblo
South Side
Sparrow
Sperryvale
Stone City
Swallows
Table Mountain
Tacony
Taylorville
Undercliffe
Verde
Waremont
White Rock
Wilson
Wood Valley

RIO BLANCO COUNTY

Angora
Buford
Farwell
Little Beaver
Marvine
Meeker
Morapos
Piceance
Pyramid
Rangely
Rio Blanco
Rioblanco
Sulphur
Thornburg
White River

RIO GRANDE COUNTY

Blainvale
Bowen
Bowenton
Cornwall
Del Norte
Elwood
Granger
Henry
Home Lake
Jasper
Lariat
Liberty
Loyton

RIO GRANDE COUNTY (CONT)

Monte Vista
Nichols
Norma
Parma
Perry
Piedra
South Fork
Summit
Summitville
Wagon Wheel Gap
Wason

ROUTT COUNTY

Anthracite
Axial
Barbee
Battle Creek
Bear River
Bison
Brookston
Cary Ranch
Clark
Coalview
Columbine
Conger
Craig
Dawson
Deepcreek
Drygulch
Dunkley
Eddy
Edith
Egeria
Elkhead
Escalante
Eula
Fortification
Fourmile
Hahns Peak
Hamilton
Hardscrabble
Harrison
Haybro
Hayden
Honnold
Huggins
Hydrate
Junction City
Juniper
Ladore

ROUTT COUNTY (CONT)

Lay
Lily
Maybell
McGregor
Milner
Mobley
Mount Harris
Mystic
Oak Creek
Oneco
Pagoda
Pallas
Pershing
Phippsburg
Pinnacle
Pool
Puma
Pyramid
Routt
Sidney
Slater
Steamboat Springs
Theisen
Toponas
Tosh
Trout Creek
Trull
Wallrock
Willow Creek
Windsor
Yampa
Yarmony

SAGUACHE COUNTY

Alder
Amethyst
Barnum
Biedell
Bismark
Bonanza
Bonito
Carnero
Center
Centerview
Claytonia
Cochetopa
Cotton Creek
Creede
Crestone

SAGUACHE COUNTY (CONT)

Cristonie
Crookstown
Cuenin
Duncan
Dune
Embargo
Exchequer
Garibaldi
Gibsom
Green
Haumann
Herard
Iris
Kimbrell
LaGarita
Lanark
Liberty
Lockett
Loma
Los Mogotes
Los Pinos
Marshall Pass
Marshalltown
Mineral Hot Springs
Mirage
Moffat
Orient
Oriental
Parkville
Perry
Pruden
Pyke
Rito Alto
Rock Cliff
Saguache
San Isabel
Sangre De Christo
Sargents
Schistos
Sedgwick
Shirley
Spanish
Tetons
Veteran
Villa Grove
Villagrove
Wabash
Wagon Wheel Gap
Watonga
White Earth

SAGUACHE COUNTY (CONT)

Willow

SAN JUAN COUNTY

Animas Forks
Arastra
Chattanooga
Congress
Del Mine
Eureka
Gladstone
Grassy Hill
Highland Mary
Howardsville
Jennison
Los Pinos
Mineral Point
Needleton
Niccora
Niegoldstown
Ouray
Poughkeepsie
Silver Ledge
Silverton
Sylvanite
Uncompaghre

SAN MIGUEL COUNTY

Ames
Bulkley
Cedar
Cornell
Dallas Divide
Dinan
Egnar
Fall Creek
Gladel
Haskill
Illium
Leonard
Leopard
Lizard Head
Newmire
Noel
Norwood
Ophir
Pandora
Placerville
Red Mountain (?)

232

SAN MIGUEL COUNTY (CONT)

San Bernardo
San Miguel
Sawpit
Seymour
Slick Rock
Smuggler
Sultana
Telluride
Trout Lake
Vanadium
Vance
Wilson

SEDGWICK COUNTY

Flora
Julesburg
Ovid
Sedgwick
Weir

SUMMIT COUNTY

Adrian
Argentine
Boreas
Braddock
Breckenridge
Buffer
Carbonateville
Chihuahua
Cleveland
Climax
Conger
Cooper
Crocker
Delaware City
Decatur
Dickey
Dillon
Eagle
Emma
Farnham
Frawley
Frisco
Gold Park
Haywood
Heeney
Holy Cross
Josie

SUMMIT COUNTY (CONT)

Kokomo
Lakeside
Langdon
Laurium
Lincoln City
Meeker
Montezuma
Naomi
Paige City
Parkville
Plain
Preston
Rathbone
Red Cliff
Rexford
Robinson
Rondebush
Saints John
Silver Lake
Silverthorne
Swan
Swandyke
Taylor
Ten Mile
Tiger
Wapiti
Wheeler
White River

TELLER COUNTY

Altman
Anaconda
Cameron
Clyde
Cripple Creek
Crystola
Divide
Edlowe
Elkton
Florissant
Gillett
Goldfield
Highpark
Hobart
Independence
Langdon
Love
Macon
Marigold

TELLER COUNTY (CONT)

Midland
Rosemont
Seward
Torrington
Touraine
Victor
Woodland Park

WASHINGTON COUNTY

Abbott
Akron
Anton
Arickaree
Brunker
Burdett
Cope
Curtis
De Nova
Dillingham
Eckley
Elba
Flat Top
Fremont
Glen
Harrisburg
Henry
Hyde
Laird
Leslie
Lindon
Meekton
Messex
Millett
Otis
Pinneo
Platner
Plum Bush
Prairie
Rago
Schlueter
Simpson
Spence
Thurman
Waitley
Woodrow
Wray
Yuma

WELD COUNTY

Akron
Alfalfa
American Ranch
Atwood
Ault
Avalo
Barnesville
Blackwolf
Briggsdale
Brush
Buckingham
Buffalo
Camfield
Carr
Chapelton
Chenoa
Cherokee City
Clearwater
Coleman
Cornish
Corona
Cotsworth
Crest
Crook
Dacona
Denver Junction
Deuel
Dover
Eaton
Eatonton
Eckley
Erie
Evans
Firestone
Flemmings Ranch
Fort Junction
Fort Lupton
Fort Moore
Fort Morgan
Fort Sedgwick
Fosston
Frederick
Fremonts Orchard
Galeton
Gault
Geary
Gilcrest
Gill
Gowanda
Graham

WELD COUNTY (CONT)

Greeley
Green City
Grover
Hardin
Henderson
Hereford
Highland Lake
Hillsboro
Hillsborough
Hiltonville
Hudson
Hyde
Iliff
Ione
Johnstown
Julesburgh
Junction House
Kalous
Kauffman
Keenesburg
Keota
Kersey
Koenig
Kuner
La Salle
Latham
Levinson
Lillian Springs
Lucerne
Mamre
Masters
Mead
Merino
Milliken
Morgan
Nantes
New Liberty
New Raymer
New Wattenburg
New Windsor
Nunn
Omar
Orchard
Orr
Osgood
Otis
Peckam
Pierce
Pinneo
Platte Valley

WELD COUNTY (CONT)

Platteville
Purcell
Raymer
Red Lion
Rinn
Roggen
Saint Vrains
Sarinda
Sedgwick
Serene
Severance
Sligo
Snyder
South Platte
Spurgin
St Vrain
Sterling
Stoneham
Tipperary
Vim
Vollmar
Wachtel
Weld
Weldon Valley
Wentz
Wheatland
Whitman
Windsor
Wray
Yuma
Zilar
Zita

YUMA COUNTY

Abarr
Alvin
Arlene
Armel
Arnold
Beecher
Beecher Island
Bryant
Clarkville
Eckley
Ford
Fox
Glory
Gurney
Hale

234

YUMA COUNTY (CONT)

Happyville
Hartstrong
Hermes
Hughes
Hyde
Idalia
Joes
Kirk
Laird
Landsman
Lansing
Ludlum
Mildred
Newton
Robb
Schramm
Seebarsee
Steffens
Vernon
Wages
Witherbee
Wray
Yuma

COUNTY UNKNOWN

Delaware Flats
Springville

FORMERLY IN KANSAS

Gurney
Konnantz
Monon
Westola

FORMERLY IN NEBRASKA

Kauffman

FORMERLY IN NEW MEXICO

La Boca

S E C T I O N   E

SELECTED COLORADO CANCELLATIONS

To illustrate the variety of postal markings that have been used
in Colorado, approximately 115 cancellations from 1859 (Coraville) to 1968
(Tyrone) have been chosen for reproduction. This is not an attempt to
show every type of cancel, but rather to illustrate the broad areas that
are open in collecting the handstamps, machine cancels, county and postmaster cancels, and fancy cancels from Colorado. The final page of
cancellations are representative of those used in the branches, stations,
and rural establishments of Colorado.

Again, the authors would welcome correspondence with anyone
having Colorado cancellations in their collections.

236

CORAVILLE,K.T.
JUN 22

Boulder N.J.
Oct 3rd 1860

Paid

CANCELLATIONS   PLATE 1

BAUER

Antelope Springs, Colo
11~7

CANCELLATIONS PLATE 2

BAUER

MANASSA
FEB 1 1881
COLORADO

CRESTED BUTTE
DEC
6
1881
COLO.

CANCELLATIONS PLATE 3

BAUER

CANCELLATIONS PLATE 4

BAUER

240

CANCELLATIONS PLATE 5

BAUER

ASPEN
AUG
20
7 PM
1894
COLO.

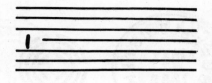
DENVER, COLO
APR 9
12 - M
1895

GREELEY
DEC
17
6 PM
1895
COLO.

REGISTERED
JUL
8
1896
SILVERTON, COLO.

DENVER. COLO
DEC 26 1- PM '96

DENVER
COL.
DEC 9 230 M 97

DENVER, COLO.
APR 15
5 PM
STA. A
98

DENVER
JUL 7
9-30P
18   98
COLO.

DENVER. COLO.
OCT 16
9 - PM
1898

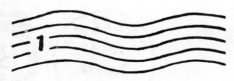

DENVER.
MAR 10
7- PM
18 COLO 99

CANCELLATIONS PLATE 6

BAUER

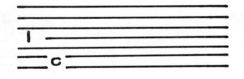

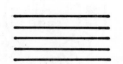

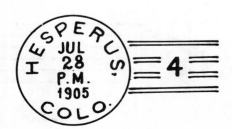

CANCELLATIONS PLATE 7

BAUER

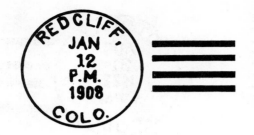

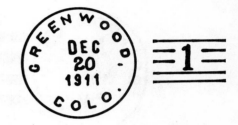

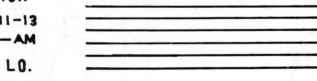

VICTOR

NOV 11-13

7 —— AM

C O LO.

DURANGO, COLO
SEP 10
7-PM
1920

MESA VERDE
NATIONAL
PARK

COTOPAXI.
AUG
31
1927
1 PM
COLO.

BRANDON, COLO.
MAY
26
1938
P.M.

DENVER, COLO.
DEC
10
130 PM
1941
HIGHLANDS STA.

CAMPO
FEB 12
8 AM
1942
COLO

1

DENVER
MAR 7
2 30 PM
1947
COLO

1847 ★ CENTENARY ★ 1947
INTERNATIONAL
PHILATELIC
EXHIBITION
NEW YORK
N. Y.
MAY 17-23
POSTAGE STAMPS

MOUNT HARRIS
JAN 16
5 PM
1954
COLO.

1

TABERNASH
SEP
3
1964
COLO

U.S. AIR FORCE ACADEMY. CO
AUG 12
PM
1968
80840

TYRONE, CO
DEC
6
A.M.
1968
81085

CANCELLATIONS PLATE 9

BAUER